PRAISE FOR *FUNDAMENTALS OF OPERATIONAL RISK MANAGEMENT*

T0295920

'Simon Ashby is very well placed, through his long association with the Institute of Operational Risk, to write what will prove to be the definitive book on operational risk. He challenges us to expand our understanding of operational risk to encompass "unpredictable outcomes of the efficiency and effectiveness of operations.". Using a series of compelling case studies, he brings the subject alive. It is sobering to see how many of the selected case studies had underlying cultural drivers. I found the section on risk culture particularly practical in its insights on monitoring and taking action. The approach to operational risk event data establishes the benefits of learning from past events and ensuring recurrence is prevented, which surely is the essence of any robust approach to operational risk.'
Alex Hindson, Chief Risk & Sustainability Officer, Argo Group

'This is an excellent book, serving as an effective, pragmatic tool for risk practitioners working in all three lines across the world, as well as a good guide for academics in operational risk.'
Dominic Wu, Director, Risk Management, BCT Group

'Simon Ashby presents a very well structured, research-based and informative guide to operational risk management. This excellent book covers every key topic, from embedding risk culture to conducting scenario analysis. A remarkably rewarding resource for practitioners.'
Elena Pykhova, Director and Founder, The OpRisk Company

'It is becoming more and more clear that operational risk models are of limited use, while taking behavioural elements into account in risk culture, governance etc is of tremendous importance. This book sets absolutely the right focus – and numerous case studies confirm that Simon Ashby is not just a seasoned academic, but very familiar with the important details of practical implementation as well. Really worthwhile reading!'
Thomas Kaiser, Founder, Professor Kaiser Risk Management Consulting and Honorary Professor, Goethe University

Fundamentals of Operational Risk Management

Understanding and implementing
effective tools, policies and frameworks

Simon Ashby

KoganPage

First published in Great Britain and the United States in 2022 by Kogan Page Limited

2nd Floor, 45 Gee Street	8 W 38th Street, Suite 902	4737/23 Ansari Road
London	New York, NY 10018	Daryaganj
EC1V 3RS	USA	New Delhi 110002
United Kingdom		India

www.koganpage.com

Kogan Page books are printed on paper from sustainable forests.

© The Institute of Risk Management, 2022

The right of Simon Ashby to be identified as the author of this work has been asserted by him in accordance with the Copyright, Designs and Patents Act 1988.

ISBNs

Hardback	978 1 3986 0504 6
Paperback	978 1 3986 0502 2
Ebook	978 1 3986 0503 9

British Library Cataloguing-in-Publication Data
A CIP record for this book is available from the British Library.

Library of Congress Cataloging-in-Publication Data
Names: Ashby, Simon, author.
Title: Fundamentals of operational risk management: : understanding and implementing effective tools, policies and frameworks / Simon Ashby.
Description: 1 Edition. | New York, NY : Kogan Page Inc, 2022. | Includes bibliographical references and index.
Identifiers: LCCN 2021062513 (print) | LCCN 2021062514 (ebook) | ISBN 9781398605022 (paperback) | ISBN 9781398605046 (hardback) | ISBN 9781398605039 (ebook)
Subjects: LCSH: Risk management. | Industrial management.
Classification: LCC HD61 .A864 2022 (print) | LCC HD61 (ebook) | DDC 338.5–dc23/eng/20220216
LC record available at https://lccn.loc.gov/2021062513
LC ebook record available at https://lccn.loc.gov/2021062514

Typeset by Integra Software Services, Pondicherry
Print production managed by Jellyfish
Printed and bound by CPI Group (UK) Ltd, Croydon, CR0 4YY

CONTENTS

ABOUT THE AUTHOR

Dr Simon Ashby is Professor of Risk Management at Vlerick Business School in Belgium, where he teaches and researches risk management, banking and financial markets. Simon has published many academic papers, practitioner reports and book chapters on operational risk management and corporate risk management more widely. Simon also provides training and consultancy services on risk management and is a director of Plymouth Community Homes.

Simon has worked as an academic, regulator and an operational risk practitioner. He is a Fellow of the Institute of Operational Risk and a past Chair of the Governing Council.

Simon lives in Cornwall, UK with his wife Alison. They like to spend as much time as possible in their garden growing food and looking after their chickens. When not at home they enjoy long walks and even longer lunches.

FOREWORD

This book demonstrates that operational risk management has reached maturity and shines a light on how organizations will operate in the future.

In the chapters that follow you will find not only closely argued statements about what operational risk management is, supported by relevant and topical case studies, but above all you will also find a sensible handbook of how operational risk management should be practised today – in our new post-Covid era.

As a direct product of the Institute of Operational Risk (IOR) joining forces with the Institute of Risk Management (IRM) in 2019, this book illustrates the value of our combined approach. As Chair of the IRM I am proud that we could play our part in bringing together the various strands that make up *Fundamentals of Operational Risk Management* into the coherent and robust study that you have before you.

We are privileged to have Simon Ashby provide the fruit of his many years of study and practice in the field. He was there at the first meeting of what became the IOR at the Bank of England in 1999 and has been both a regulator and a practitioner as well as the leading academic in the field. As you read it will become clear that you are acquiring true value from his years of experience.

Importantly, this book will help you to bring a firm conceptual foundation to your inquiries. It will show you how operational risk management is about adding value rather than adding cost, how it contributes directly to an organization's objectives and how it can encompass opportunities and not just 'downside' risks.

I was particularly pleased to see the frequent use of case studies taken not only from the field of financial services but also organizations that operate in the 'real' economy. These real-life examples range from the original failures that formed the catalyst for operational risk management to those arising from the recent changes in the way we work as a result of the Covid-19 pandemic. They vividly illustrate the concepts Simon has so cogently highlighted here.

As we move into the 2020s, the techniques, rules and guidelines of operational risk management are all becoming increasingly recognized as ways for professionals to raise their skills and performance to the next level, all while preparing for an even more digital future. The time is now, so enjoy Simon's book!

Stephen Sidebottom
Chair, Institute of Risk Management

PREFACE

I started learning about risk management in 1991, as an undergraduate student at the University of Nottingham, one of only two universities in the UK to teach risk management at the time. The other was the equally excellent Glasgow Caledonian University. During my time at the University of Nottingham I was fortunate enough to receive a funded place at the annual Association of Insurance and Risk Managers in Industry and Commerce (AIRMIC) conference, a conference I then attended annually when I commenced my PhD studies in 1992. Never did I hear the term 'operational risk' mentioned, though almost all of the risks under discussion fell within the accepted scope of the term (fraud, health and safety, business continuity, asset damage, etc).

It was not until 1999 that I first heard the term 'operational risk'. I was then a lecturer in Risk and Insurance at the University of Nottingham's Centre for Risk and Insurance Studies and, in that capacity, had been invited to the inaugural meeting of the Operational Risk Research Forum (ORRF), chaired by the irrepressible Professor Brendon Young. ORRF had been created by Brendon in response to the work of the Bank of International Settlements on the regulation of operational risk, as part of the second Basel Accord for the supervision of internationally active banks. Representatives from the banking and operational risk management consultancy sectors were invited, along with a few academics and regulators from the UK Financial Services Authority. As a young academic I was in auspicious company. Still, as I always had something to say at that time I became a regular attendee. Subsequently I worked with Brendon on a number of research projects, including an influential report on the use of insurance as a mitigant for operational risk (https://www.bis.org/bcbs/ca/oprirefo.pdf).

Thanks to Brendon and the other learned members of the ORRF my fate was sealed. I first shifted my research focus to the discipline of operational risk and then became a practitioner. Working first on drafting operational risk policy at the UK Financial Services Authority and then becoming an operational risk manager and head of operational risk in various financial institutions. I was later honoured to be one of the founding Fellows of the Institute of Operational Risk (IOR) in 2004 and subsequently Chair of the Institute's governing council. I even terminated my membership of the Institute of Risk Management (IRM) to focus on the IOR, sorry about that IRM!

It has been an unexpected but rewarding journey for a precocious student of risk management, who had no idea that operational risk even existed. I have witnessed first-hand the development of the discipline – one in great need today as we battle unprecedented operational risk events, such as the effects of climate change and the Covid-19 pandemic.

In the early days, research and practice in the field of operational risk was like the Wild West. Lots of tools and techniques existed, each coming from a different category of operational risk (e.g. health and safety, fraud, IT security, etc), as well as from different professional disciplines such as insurance, finance and accounting. It seemed that everyone had a different view on how best to manage operational risk. This made for an exciting and creative time, but one where practices differed extensively.

Since then, the practice of operational risk has matured and there is significantly less difference in approach between organizations. In part, lessons have been learnt from major loss events such as the global financial crisis of 2007–08, the roots of which were operational risk in nature. In addition, practitioners have learnt from each other what works and what does not. Institutes like the IOR and IRM played an important part in this sharing of good practice. Without them it would have been much more difficult for practitioners to share their insights and develop the field.

Though the term 'operational risk' emerged from the banking sector, many other industry sectors have since embraced the term and adopted the tools and techniques developed by banks, though it is fair to say that some of these tools and techniques were originally borrowed and adapted from practices that originated outside the banking sector. What goes around, comes around, though through this iteration much of this practice is vastly improved from before.

Is operational risk fully mature as a field of professional practice? Probably not. That said, all professions benefit from continuous improvement. Perhaps full maturity is an impossible goal. Nevertheless, the practice of operational risk is sufficiently grown-up to merit the development and dissemination of sound practice – practice developed by practitioners for their peers and rooted in what has been shown to work, time and time again.

The purpose of this book is to share the sound practice for operational risk management that has evolved over the last 20 or more years, practice that I have both implemented during my time as an operational risk professional and observed through my research, consultancy and training work. In this regard my aim is to act as the conduit through which the fundamentals of effective operational risk management can be communicated, both to existing professionals looking to improve their practice and to those looking to pursue a career in operational risk. In this regard the content that follows builds on the Sound Practice Guidance Papers for operational risk, published by the IOR and IRM (https://www.ior-institute.org/sound-practice-guidance), papers that have been refined and updated over the last decade to reflect improvements in professional practice. Though I have further developed this work, adding numerous cases, examples and insights based on my own experience, the content of this book very much relies on the progress made by numerous professional giants in the field of operational risk, professionals who have contributed to the various Sound Practice Guidance Papers and taught me much about the management of operational risk. My thanks to you all!

ACKNOWLEDGEMENTS

I would like to thank Ian Livsey, CEO of the Institute of Risk Management, for giving me the opportunity to write this book and for the support of Tony Chidwick and the wider Advisory Committee of the Institute of Operational Risk (IOR). Tony, your insights were much appreciated, as were those of other Advisory Committee members.

To the many giants of operational risk management practice that I have had the privilege of working with and learning from over the decades thank you for your support. Special thanks go to Professor Brendon Young for inviting me onto the Operational Risk Research Forum (ORRF) back in 1999 and for creating the IOR, which I hold very dear to my heart. Thanks also to Helmut Bauer and Jeremy Quick for hiring an opinionated, young upstart with little practical knowledge. Without your faith in me I would never have become an operational risk professional. The many others that I have had the privilege to learn from and work with are too numerous to mention in full. However, I would like to express my sincere thanks to Dick Baker, Arianne Chapelle of Chapelle Consulting, Mike Finlay of Risk Business, Philip Martin and Brian Rowlands – each of whom played a major role in the development of the IOR's Sound Practice Guidance Papers, on which this book is based.

Last and by no means least, my love and thanks to my amazing wife Alison. My professional career in operational risk has at times been a stressful one, especially my tenure as Chair of the IOR. Her love, patience and support has been unwavering. And from a professional perspective her experience in factory operations and supply chains has taught me much about the management of operations outside the financial services sector.

Boost your career with the IRM

IRM is the leading professional body for risk management. We drive excellence in managing risk to ensure organisations are ready for the opportunities and threats of the future.

We do this by providing internationally recognised qualifications and training, publishing research and guidance, and setting professional standards. We are a not-for-profit educational institute, with members working in all industries, in all risk disciplines and in all sectors around the world.

What IRM offers Risk Professionals

Training courses
Our risk management training gives you the knowledge, tools and techniques you need to protect your organisation.

Free webinars
You can access free webinars that cover a wide range of presentations, helpful for professionals at every level.

Blended Learning
Increase your chances of exam success and learn directly from module coaches in our face-to-face Blended Learning workshops.

Qualifications
Our risk management qualifications give you the broad knowledge and the practical skills you need to manage risks.

Building a community
We help people connect with our sector-specific Special Interest Groups, Regional Groups and social media platforms.

> ❝
> IRM qualifications provide a practical framework and a structured way of thinking.
> This is vital to success in a risk role. ❞

The Institute of
Risk Management

Find out more at **www.theirm.org** »

Understanding operational risk: key concepts and management objectives

01

LEARNING OUTCOMES

- Define key concepts such as risk, operational risk and uncertainty.
- Describe how operational risk fits within a wider enterprise risk management context.
- Explain how real-world operational risk events have impacted on the ability of organizations to create value through the achievement of their strategic objectives.

1. Introduction

The purpose of this chapter is to explain what operational risk is and how the management of operational risk fits within a wider 'enterprise' risk management context. Experienced operational risk practitioners may decide to skim through this chapter. Those with less experience of operational risk will find that a careful review of the material contained here will support their understanding of subsequent chapters.

In the course of this chapter, a number of myths that relate to operational risk management will be dispelled. Such as the myths that operational risks are exclusively downside risks, and that operational risk management is predominantly a cost centre that does not contribute directly to the achievement of an organization's strategic objectives. On the contrary, operational risk management is as important, and value adding, as any other type of risk management, potentially more so. In addition, different perspectives on some established ideas will be provided, such as the definition of operational risk. It will be argued that, as the discipline of operational risk management matures, there is a need to rethink these ideas, to help cement the discipline on firmer conceptual foundations.

The chapter starts with a brief history of operational risk, explaining how the term emerged and how the discipline of operational risk management was formed. We will then move to discussing some important foundation concepts such as risk, uncertainty and, of course, operational risk. We will then explore the links between operational risk and the wider context of enterprise risk management. Here it will be argued that effective operational risk management should protect *and* create value for organizations, helping them to improve their efficiency and effectiveness while reducing the potential for financial, reputational, physical or any other form of damage. Finally, case studies of some real-world operational risk events will be used to help illustrate the value of effective operational risk management in a range of organizations.

2. A brief history of operational risk

In 1999, the inaugural meeting of the Operational Risk Research Forum (ORRF), the forerunner of the Institute of Operational Risk (IOR), was held at the Bank of England in London. For some participants, the author included, this was their first exposure to the term 'operational risk'. It was also the first time that practitioners, academics and regulators had assembled for a serious discussion about the practice of operational risk management. Interest in operational risk management had been stimulated by the Basel II reforms of banking regulation and supervision. The Basel Committee on Banking Supervision (BCBS) was the first international institution to officially use the term and to provide a definition of operational risk – one that remains in widespread use.

High-profile banking failures, such as the failure of Barings Bank (see the case study later in this chapter) and the Bank of Credit and Commerce International, stimulated the interest of banking regulators in so-called 'non-financial risks' (risks other than market, credit or liquidity risk – risks that the BCBS labelled operational risk. Regulatory interest in operational risk spread quickly to the insurance sector, as part of the Solvency II reforms for European insurers. Here research by insurance supervisors revealed that the roots of almost all insurance company failures since 2000 across Europe were non-financial in nature (Ashby, Sharma and McDonnell, 2003).

Outside of the financial sector the US corporate governance committee, the Committee of Sponsoring Organizations of the Treadway Commission (COSO), used the term 'operations risk', as early as 1991 when consulting on its new internal control guidance (COSO, 1991), but the term 'operational risk' did not enter widespread use in non-financial organizations until much later. Notably, the UK Government's revised Orange Book (HM Treasury, 2020) guidance on risk management for organizations includes operational risk in its taxonomy of major risks (more on this taxonomy in Chapter 3, on risk categorization). The International Organization for Standardization (ISO) stops short of providing such a taxonomy but does suggest that risk management should be applied at the 'strategic, *operational*, programme or project levels' (ISO 31000:2018, section 6.1, author's emphasis). In contrast, the updated COSO guidance on enterprise risk management makes no mention of operations or operational risk, though it does say that risks are present in 'day-to-day operational decisions' (COSO, 2017, p1).

From a financial services perspective the term 'operational risk' has been labelled an invention (Power, 2005) – a negotiating device used by regulators and financial services executives to reorganize and reposition their respective viewpoints on a variety of well-established risks (fraud, system and process failures, damage to physical assets, etc). Regulators use the term to increase the capital requirements of banks, bank executives to reduce these requirements. This may well have been the base in the late 1990s; however, the discipline of operational risk management has matured much since. The creation of the IOR in 2004, by the irrepressible Professor Brendon Young, the instigator of the ORRF, did much to further the cause and help cement operational risk management as a profession – a cause strengthened when the IOR merged with the Institute of Risk Management (IRM). Practice in areas such as risk culture, risk and control self-assessments and risk indicators, have benefited much from the discipline and the hard work of its practitioners to develop new risk management tools and techniques – work reflected in the IOR's Sound Practice Guidance Papers for Operational Risk, on which this book is based, as well as the IOR's Certificate in Operational Risk (www.ior-institute.org/education/certificate-in-operational-risk-management).

As the 21st century progresses there remains much to do. Consider the standard definition of operational risk, for example – the definition remains a dumping ground for a wide variety of seemingly disconnected non-financial risks. In addition, the definition remains shackled to the myths that operational risk events can only result in losses, and that operational risk management is an administrative activity and a cost centre that does little to enhance the revenue of organizations. It is to these definitional issues and associated myths that we now turn.

3. Defining risk: key concepts

Risk is a difficult concept to define, let alone partition into categories such as operational risk. However, it is human nature to simplify complex and ambiguous concepts to make them more amenable as management disciplines. A book on the management of operational risk would, therefore, not get very far without addressing the definition of operational risk, and risk more generally.

That said, such definitions should not be created and used lightly. A poorly worded, imprecise or misleading definition can disrupt the focus of management attention. At best this will result in an inefficient use of resources; at worst it may cause key risks or management concerns to be overlooked, threatening the survival of the organization or the lives and financial wellbeing of its stakeholders.

Though there are poor definitions for all of the concepts addressed here, there are often several good ones. It is not the intention to cover them all, not least because an entire book could be written on the subject of defining risk and operational risk in particular. Instead, some of the more salient points that operational risk professionals need to consider will be highlighted.

3.1 Risk

The ISO defines risk as: 'the effect of uncertainty on objectives' (ISO 31000:2018, section 3.1). It further notes that an 'effect' reflects any kind of deviation from the expected, and that such deviations may be either positive or negative (i.e. a threat or an opportunity).

A strength of the ISO approach is its recognition that risk arises whenever decisions are made, and activities are performed that result in two or more outcomes – outcomes that are not certain at the time the decision is made or when the activity is performed. In this regard, risk is the antithesis of certainty.

A further strength is the recognition that risk is associated with outcomes that may be positive or negative. Such risks are sometimes termed 'speculative' risks and contrasted with 'pure' risks that only have negative consequences. However, the construction of so-called pure risks often requires risks to be framed in a very specific and limited way. True, the risk of physical injury only has a downside. But an injury outcome is often part of a wider risk context, such as driving a vehicle or operating machinery, activities that can have positive and negative outcomes.

A potential problem with the ISO 31000 definition is the use of the word 'uncertainty'. In 1921, a respected economist, Frank Knight, distinguished risk from uncertainty. For Knight, uncertainty is something that cannot be quantified in terms of probability or impact, while risk can be quantified (Knight, 1921). Hence gambling in a casino is a risk, while the effects of global warming remain uncertain. We know that the Earth is warming, and that this is our fault, but we still cannot quantify, accurately, the positive and negative effects of this on people, businesses, economies or nature.

Taking account of Knight, an alternative definition of risk, used in this book is:

The effect of unpredictable outcomes on objectives.

Even in the case of statistically quantifiable risk, outcomes cannot be predicted in advance, only their probability of occurrence and impact can be estimated. When you roll a dice you know that there are six outcomes and you have a 1 in 6 chance of each, but you can never predict the actual outcome. This outcome is simple random chance.

3.2 Uncertainty

Knight's distinction between risk and uncertainty is a useful one in the context of operational risk. Risk can be quantified in terms of its probability and impact, uncertainty cannot. When dealing with operational risks, an absence of reliable, statistical data is commonplace. This means that organizations must frequently attempt to manage operational uncertainties, opposed to operational risks. Understanding this can help a lot when applying the tools of operational risk management, such as risk and control self-assessments or risk indicators. Never assume that the output from such tools is 100 per cent objective. Instead, experienced operational risk professionals know to adopt a healthy degree of scepticism when reviewing and using these outputs.

Because of its usefulness in an operational risk context this book adopts Knight's perspective on risk and uncertainty. Hence uncertainty is defined as:

The absence of reliable data on the outcomes of risk exposures.

3.3 Risk exposure

Risk exposures arise whenever a risky (or uncertain) decision or activity is undertaken. Most decisions and activities involve multiple operational risk exposures, whether they are undertaken by individuals, groups of people or organizations.

We will return to the concept of operational risk exposure in Chapter 7: Risk and control self-assessments. In Chapter 7 we look at different aspects of operational risk exposure and how exposure can be expressed to support the day-to-day management of operational risks. However, before we get to these managerial practicalities we will explore an important theoretical aspect to the definition of exposure in an operational risk context, to help explain the limitations of these practices. Just because a practice has limitations does not mean that it is not a 'sound' practice. However, competent operational risk professionals need to understand these limitations to ensure that they apply these practices correctly.

There is a growing branch of academic research on risk management that explores organizational responses to operational risk exposures (e.g. Bednarek, Chalkias and Jarzabkowski, 2021; Hardy and Maguire, 2016; Maguire and Hardy, 2013; Palermo, Power and Ashby, 2017). The conclusion of this research is that operational risk exposures (and very probably all other risk exposures) are socially constructed. This means that people, usually groups of people, determine what operational risk exposures are, why they matter and whether an exposure is good or bad.

It is tempting to think of operational risk management as a science. Certainly in the early days of operational risk, this was the focus, as practitioners and academics all proposed different ways to model (quantify) operational risk exposures. However, given the uncertain nature of many operational 'risks', they found that even scientific estimates of exposure are, at best, approximate.

In the absence of scientific data, and sometimes even when it is present (often people do not accept the data as reliable or accurate), most estimates of operational risk exposure are socially constructed. This means that it is the values and beliefs of a social group (e.g. an organization or its respective departments and functions) that determine exposure. These values and beliefs can even influence whether an exposure is viewed in a positive (opportunity) or negative (threat) light, meaning that one organization may perceive an operational risk to be a major threat, whereas another may perceive the same risk to be an opportunity (see Bednarek, Chalkias and Jarzabkowski, 2021).

Given that risks are socially constructed estimates of operational risk, exposure should always be viewed as approximate, never objective or reliable. The point of estimating operational risk exposure is not to arrive at a perfect priority order of exposures. Rather it is to stimulate discussions about operational risk, which risks matter right now and how best to alter these exposures where necessary. Granted, putting operational risk exposures into a priority order can help stimulate discussion, but never assume that this is an accurate reflection of reality, whatever reality might be!

In the light of this discussion risk exposure is defined as:

> *The importance attached to a given operational risk, or group of connected operational risks.*

3.4 *Financial versus non-financial risk*

In the financial services sector, and increasingly elsewhere, it is common to differentiate between financial and non-financial risks. The term financial risk is a catch-all for market, credit and liquidity risks. These are the risks that banks and other financial institutions are supposed to take to make money for their investors, depositors and policyholders. Non-financial risks pretty much relate to all other types of risk, including operational risk, legal risk, regulatory risk, reputation risk and strategic risk.

However, this distinction is misleading. All risks have a financial impact. Moreover, many organizations, whether financial or non-financial in focus, choose to take non-financial risks as a necessary part of achieving their objectives, including their financial objectives (e.g. to generate a profit). So, it is not only market, credit and liquidity risks that are taken to generate financial returns.

A better distinction might be financial market versus non-financial market risks for financial organizations, or financing versus non-financing risks for non-financial organizations. Alternatively, such arbitrary distinctions could be removed, especially when they do little to support effective enterprise risk management (more on this below).

CASE STUDY 1.1   TSB systems failure

In April 2018, the TSB bank in the UK implemented a major core systems migration. The aim of the migration was to improve the TSB's online banking systems (e.g. to speed up mortgage applications, offer digital identity verification on the banking app, improve fraud prevention, etc), making the bank more competitive. Unfortunately, the migration failed, and 1.9 million customers were unable to access their accounts, some for several weeks.

The cost of the failure resulted in an annual loss of £105 million for the bank and resulted in a major regulatory investigation. The cause of the failure was identified as inadequate testing of the new system. The system was only tested offline, never in the live environment before the migration.

Of the £330 million in extra costs reported by the bank in its 2018 annual report, around £125 million was for customer compensation and sorting out their problems, £49 million was due to fraud and other transaction processing errors, £122 million for extra help and advice to sort out the IT problems, and £33 million in lost income from waived fees and charges (TSB, 2018). An independent report into the event concluded that the final costs exceeded £350 million (Slaughter and May, 2019).

The case highlights the financial consequences of non-financial events, the costs of which can far exceed most market, credit or liquidity losses outside of major systemic events such as the 2007 global financial crisis. The case also illustrates that operational risks are often taken to achieve strategic objectives, in this case a core systems migration, designed to improve customer service and attract new customers. Had the TSB managed effectively the non-financial, operational risks associated with the migration, it would have been able to exploit the opportunities offered by the migration sooner, while mitigating the associated threats.

3.5 *Operational risk*

In the early days of the Basel II negotiations, operational risk was defined as any risk other than market, credit or liquidity risk. Hence it was used as a dumping ground for risks that did not fit the idealized parameters of the financial risks thought to be the main focus of banks.

Subsequently the BCBS arrived at a more concrete definition for operational risk, one that remains in widespread use today:

> Operational risk is defined as the risk of loss resulting from inadequate or failed internal processes, people and systems or from external events. This definition includes legal risk, but excludes strategic and reputational risk. (BCBS, 2006, p144)

However, there are several fundamental problems with this definition that arguably means it is no longer fit for purpose. Firstly, it is assumed that operational risk can only result in loss outcomes, a conclusion that is at odds with modern perspectives on risk, as contained within ISO 31000:2018, perspectives that should include operational risk.

Secondly, the causal factors used to demarcate operational risk are equally applicable to other types of risk, including market, credit and liquidity risk. Take for example the Covid-19 pandemic. As an external event, this is very much an operational risk. However, the pandemic also caused turmoil in financial markets, increased credit insolvency and impacted on market liquidity.

Thirdly, why the focus on inadequate or failed processes? What about inefficient processes? Or processes that have variable levels of effectiveness? Such concerns are central in the discipline of operations management, why not the discipline of operational risk?

Finally, the definition does not explain why strategic and reputation risks are excluded, an exclusion that is at odds with the latest research on risk management. The research identifies three types of risk management decision (Aven and Aven, 2015):

1 strategic;

2 tactical;

3 personal (primarily by employees).

Strategic risk management decisions relate to the setting of an organization's strategic objectives (e.g. whether to implement a new core system, launch a new product or engage in research and development). Tactical risk management decisions relate to the achievement of these objectives (the project risk management of a core systems implementation, for example), while personal decisions relate to the financial and physical condition of the decision maker (e.g. their income, return, health, etc). All of these are speculative decisions that can have positive and negative outcomes.

Given the BCBS definition's exclusion of strategic risks, it is tempting to place operational risk under the tactical decision category. However, operational risk management decisions can just as easily be considered strategic or personal. Choosing to launch a new product or to replace a core IT system are strategic management decisions, but they also require consideration of operational risk. After all, strategy and operations are interdependent, not separate constructs. Equally, individual decision makers must manage their own personal operational risks, along with the risks of the organization of which they form a part.

This means that attempting to differentiate operational risk from other categories or types of risk is fraught with difficulty. Better to define operational risk based on what it is, rather than artificial notions of what it is not.

A solution to the definition dilemma of operational risk lies in operations management. This is a discipline not well understood in many financial organizations, because of the intangible nature of their operations. However, it is very much part of the management of most non-financial organizations, especially those in sectors like manufacturing, construction, mineral extraction or agriculture.

This book defines operational risk as:

The effect of unpredictable outcomes on the efficiency and effectiveness of operations.

Hence by extension operational risk management can be defined as:

The management of unpredictable outcomes on the efficiency and effectiveness of operations.

All organizations have operations. These operations require people, processes, systems and equipment (e.g. machinery). Sometimes these operations work well, potentially even exceeding expectations in terms of effectiveness or efficiency. Equally there may be times when things go wrong and the effectiveness and efficiency of these operations decline, potentially disastrously so, threating the survival of the organization.

Efficiency relates to the level of output (e.g. products for sale, return on investment, revenue) that can be gained from a given set of inputs (e.g. labour, materials, information). Effectiveness relates to things like the cost of the raw inputs and the cost associated with processing these inputs into outputs, costs that might include things like legal and compliance costs. Both efficiency and effectiveness will impact on operating margins, such as profit, interest and non-interest margins.

Management disciplines like Total Quality Management (TQM) and Six Sigma also address the efficiency and effectiveness of operations (Oakland, Oakland and Turner, 2020). The difference is that TQM and Six Sigma focus on quality control and the minimization of operational defects, while the above definition of operational risk addresses any type of outcome (whether positive or negative) that could impact on efficiency and effectiveness, including outcomes outside the control of an organization. Another key difference is the emphasis on uncertainty in the above definition of operational risk. TQM and Six Sigma are heavily data driven, however, as highlighted in the above discussion on uncertainty, data is not always available. The effective management of operational risk helps organizations to address this lack of data.

Ultimately, any definition of operational risk will involve an element of overlap with other risk types and management disciplines. Such is the breadth of operational risk. However, it is essential that the discipline of operational risk management moves on from the BCBS definition of operational risk. Defining operational risk based on causes that are equally applicable to other categories of risk does not provide a clear enough demarcation for the discipline. Better to make clear what operational risk is, rather than what it is not.

3.6 Summary of definitions

Table 1.1   Summary of definitions

Risk	'The effect of unpredictable outcomes on objectives.'	Risk is present whenever an action or decision can result in two or more outcomes, and the occurrence of an outcome is not known in advance.
Uncertainty	'The absence of reliable data on the outcomes of risk exposures.'	The terms 'risk' and 'uncertainty' are not interchangeable. Both deal with the potential for multiple outcomes. However, the probability and impact of these outcomes cannot be predicted accurately in a situation of uncertainty.
Risk Exposure	'The importance attached to a given operational risk, or group of connected operational risks.'	Risk exposure is a social construct. People decide what risks matter, based on their attitudes, perceptions and social practices.
Operational Risk (Basel Committee on Banking Supervision)	'Operational risk is defined as the risk of loss resulting from inadequate or failed internal processes, people and systems or from external events. This definition includes legal risk, but excludes strategic and reputational risk.'	The most common, but flawed, definition of operational risk. This definition does not properly differentiate operational risk from other risk types.
Operational Risk (Institute of Risk Management)	'The effect of unpredictable outcomes on the efficiency and effectiveness of operations.'	A definition rooted in the operations of organizations and the twin goals of operations management: efficiency and effectiveness.

4. The role of operational risk management within an enterprise risk context

In this section we explore the role of operational risk management and how it fits within a wider risk management context. In particular we focus on the concept of enterprise risk management, as most risk management standards (e.g. ISO 31000:2018; COSO, 2017) recognize this as good practice.

Risk management is a device for organizing risk. Typically, this occurs through the identification, assessment, monitoring and control of risk exposures. This never-ending, circular process is the same for every type of risk in almost every organization that has formalized its risk management activities.

What does vary are the tools and techniques used to identify, assess, monitor and control risk. Also variable are the management infrastructures (risk governance, risk policies, risk categorizations, etc) that can be used to underpin this process. To a certain extent the selection of these tools and infrastructures depend on the nature, scale and complexity of an organization and its activities. However, increasingly organizations are converging on one overarching approach to the organization of their risk management processes and infrastructures: enterprise risk management (ERM).

4.1 Enterprise risk management

A key driver of the spread of ERM in organizations is the promotion of the concept by the US governance standard setter Committee of Sponsoring Organizations of the Treadway Commission (COSO). COSO has issued various guidance documents on ERM, the latest was issued in 2017. COSO (2017) describes ERM as:

The culture, capabilities and practices integrated with strategy setting and performance, that organizations rely on to manage risk in creating, preserving and realizing value.

From this description ERM is characterized by three essential elements:

- a holistic focus;
- an emphasis on value added risk management;
- the blending of formal and informal risk management tools and activities.

Figure 1.1   The basic risk management process (author's own)

4.1.1 Holistic

ERM embraces all types of risk in every part of an organization, recognizing that different risks, functions, business lines and processes are interconnected and together they influence strategy setting and performance.

When organizations began using organized risk management process in the mid-20th century, they adopted what is now called a silo approach to risk management. This meant that different categories of risk were managed individually, often by different people or functions across the organization. The problem with such an approach is that gaps and overlaps between risk categories may be ignored. In terms of gaps, important risks may go undetected and unmanaged because they do not fall within the responsibilities of the different individuals or functions tasked with managing specific categories of risk. New risks, as in the case of technology risk during the latter part of the 20th century and climate risks in the early part of the 21st century, may be ignored because no individual or function has been assigned responsibility for their management. In terms of overlaps, correlations between risk types may be ignored. For example, in order to help manage business risk the sales and marketing function may decide to launch a new product. However, this could create new operational risks, which the sales and marketing function might ignore as they do not fall within its area of responsibility.

CASE STUDY 1.2   Benzene in Perrier

A classic case study of the problems of a silo approach to risk management is the Perrier benzene scandal. In 1990, high levels of the toxic substance benzene were discovered in bottles of Perrier. The company took steps to recall the product and within a week Perrier withdrew 160 million bottles worldwide.

When the media first found out about the problem, Perrier did not know how to respond. For a brand whose whole identity was based around the idea of 'natural purity' the benzene incident was a major disaster. Perrier's failure to recognize and manage the growing reputation risk, as well as how it had managed the recall, led to an information vacuum that provoked much more consumer anxiety than there should have been.

The Perrier brand survived the scandal. However, Groupe Perrier was taken over by Nestlé in 1992, and the brand has never regained its pre-1990 sales volume.

One way in which the holistic characteristic of ERM can be implemented is through the creation of an integrated risk function, often under the control of a chief risk officer (CRO). The role of the integrated risk function is to look at all risks across all levels of the organization in order to build a comprehensive picture of where risk lies within the organization – particularly risks that may affect the strategic objectives and value of an organization. Risks that can affect the strategic objectives and value of an organization may come from anywhere, not just from top-level decision making and activities. One operational risk example is IT-related risks: although IT risks may be viewed as the responsibility of IT professionals they can have far-reaching implications, particularly if systems are disrupted for a prolonged period or sensitive data is lost.

4.1.2 Value added

Historically, before the rise of ERM, risk management was sometimes viewed as an activity inconsistent with objectives like profit or shareholder value maximization. The rationale was that risk management should focus on the prevention of downside threats, such as health and safety incidents, and that the prevention of such threats could hinder strategic success via the implementation of bureaucratic processes and procedures.

From an ERM perspective risk management should, if applied correctly, create and protect value for an organization. This value is created through effective strategic-level risk management decision making and operations that function effectively and efficiently.

Strategic-level decisions – such as business expansion decisions, the creation of a major new project, cost cutting or process and product innovations – come with a variety of risks that may affect the success or failure of these decisions. To make effective strategic decisions, an organization's management must understand what these risks are and their potential significance. Never should strategic decisions be made without first considering the associated risks.

4.1.3 Formal and informal factors

This element relates to the management of the formal and informal factors within organizations that can influence exposure to risk.

Formal factors relate to the tangible systems, processes, procedures, policies, committees and forums that exist within organizations, as well as organization structures, hierarchies and such like. The design and implementation of these formal factors will affect many aspects of an organization, including how risks are perceived and managed.

Informal factors relate to things like organizational culture, social networks and how risk and risk management are perceived. For example, whether risk is viewed as a threat or an opportunity, or whether risk management is perceived to be costly red tape or value adding. Within an ERM context, using these informal factors to help manage risk is just as important as using the formal ones.

In this book we will be looking at both. Risk culture is an example of an informal factor, risk and control self-assessments (RCSAs) and risk indicators are formal factors.

4.2 Where does operational risk management fit in?

Given the all-encompassing nature of ERM, it is tempting to conclude that the concept subsumes operational risk management. Operational risk management is thus replaced by ERM or at best subservient to its ERM master.

This assumption reflects a myth linked to the holistic nature of ERM. The application of a holistic ERM framework does not mean that all risks should be identified, assessed, monitored or controlled using the same tools or the exact same infrastructure. Operational risks often require very different assessment tools than credit or market risk – for example, ones that are less quantitative and statistical. Equally the application of infrastructure mechanisms like risk appetite can look very different when applied to operational risks.

In addition, the discipline of operational risk management has led the way in the management of informal factors like risk culture. Often it is the operational risk function that takes the lead in assessing risk culture and in finding mechanisms to help influence risk culture where appropriate. In this respect, operational risk management has done much to further the practice of ERM and is a vital part of a well-functioning ERM framework.

In short, operational risk management is a vital and distinct component of ERM, as important as any other type of risk management. Never should ERM be seen as a replacement for operational risk management. Nor should the tools and infrastructure of operational risk management be replaced by some generic approach designed to address all risks.

5. The value of operational risk: case studies of real-world events

As a vital component of ERM, operational risk management must add value to an organization. There is no point managing an operational risk if this does not help to protect or create value.

Unfortunately, operational risk management is sometimes perceived as a 'business prevention' activity that is bureaucratic and compliance focused, and whose costs exceed the benefits. Occasionally, pedantic operational risk managers, and internal auditors or regulators, can be the source of this perception. But this is the exception, rather than the rule. More often the reason for this perception is that people fail to connect the dots between operational risk, corporate strategy and financial performance. In this section three case studies are provided to illustrate the connection between operational risk management, strategic success and strong financial performance.

CASE STUDY 1.3   The collapse of Barings Bank

Barings Bank had a long and distinguished history as a British merchant bank, with many important clients, including the British monarchy. However, the bank threw all of this away in 1995, when rogue trader Nick Leeson lost £827 million in unauthorized derivatives trading.

Research into the failure of the bank (Stein, 2000) revealed a complex array of related causal factors, all of which fall within the realms of operational risk. For example, weaknesses in the bank's recruitment processes meant that Leeson's county court judgements were not identified. Nor was his competency to trade derivatives assessed. Then when Leeson was employed his work was not sufficiently scrutinized, allowing him to maintain a false set of accounts and to make large derivative trades that exposed the bank to a high risk of insolvency.

The collapse of Barings illustrates that weaknesses in operational risk management can result in the failure of an organization, destroying all of the franchise value it had created over the years (e.g. brand value). Many of the errors made by the bank were relatively minor, taken in isolation, but combined they helped to cause a major event, one that shook the banking sector and banking regulators internationally. The BCBS used the case, among several other high-profile banking failures, to help justify the inclusion of operational risk in the Basel II rules. So, while the case was a disaster for Barings and its stakeholders, it helped to create the discipline of operational risk management that is in practice today.

CASE STUDY 1.4   The VW emissions scandal

The VW emissions scandal is an example of how ineffective operational risk management can seriously damage the financial performance and reputation of an organization and affect its ability to create value for a long time in the future.

In September 2015, the US Environmental Protection Agency (EPA) found that a software device (known as the defeat device) had been installed on certain models of diesel car to provide false readings in emissions tests. VW had repeatedly denied that it had tampered with emissions testing and only admitted wrongdoing when presented with evidence that the device existed.

Subsequent investigations revealed that there were problems with the emissions testing of millions of vehicles worldwide. The scandal forced VW to recall millions of its vehicles and led to it reporting its first quarterly loss in 15 years in October 2015 (of US $2.5 billion). During the height of the scandal (September to November 2015) the value of VW's shares also dropped by 38 per cent (Sharman and Brunsden, 2015).

The scandal did not end in 2015. Subsequent investigations by regulators in several countries resulted in multibillion euros of fines for breaches of environmental regulations. This was accompanied by a number of class action lawsuits, which again cost several billion to settle and kept the scandal in the headlines until 2020.

The scandal was a painful lesson in the long-term strategic implications of operational risk events, especially where deliberate wrongdoing has been identified. Managing such a large and prolonged scandal diverts resources from developing new products and process improvements. Plus, sales were impacted in some countries because VW was unable to certify the emissions of new diesel engines launched in 2016. More generally, sales of diesel cars fell across Europe in the wake of the scandal (Campbell, 2016).

CASE STUDY 1.5   Peloton product recall

In May 2021, the fitness technology group Peloton voluntarily recalled its treadmills after reports of injuries and one death associated with use of the machines. The announcement sent the value of the company's shares to a seven-month low (Rocco and McGee, 2021).

The decision came two weeks after the US Consumer Safety Commission asked people with young children or pets to stop using the treadmills, following an investigation into the death of a child. Initially Peloton criticized the recommendation, but subsequently admitted that this had been a mistake and apologized.

Peloton faced criticisms on two sides. Criticism from politicians for delaying the recall and social media anger from customers who did not want to send their product back for a full refund, despite the potential faults.

Peloton was a company that grew fast during the height of the Covid-19 pandemic, with people forced to stay home and gyms closed. This put pressure on the company's operations to meet the high level of demand for its products. The recall is a great example of how strategic success can create operational risks – risks that must be considered at the strategy-setting phase, not after. When production processes are overloaded errors can occur. In turn, the financial and reputational consequences of these errors can impact on the future strategic success of the organization.

Whenever organizations make strategic decisions it is essential that they consider the operational opportunities and threats associated with these decisions. Many textbooks state that organizations should consider the operational risks associated with the achievement of their strategic objectives. But they forget that operational risk should be considered when selecting these objectives in the first place. Only by integrating discussions about operational risk into strategy-setting decisions can organizations like Peloton avoid becoming victims of their own success. In so doing they can plan how to meet the operational challenges associated with higher-than-expected demand, while mitigating the threats associated with these challenges, such as increased levels of product defects.

6. Conclusion

In this chapter we have explored the conceptual foundations of the discipline of operational risk management, a discipline that has matured much in the last 20 years, but which has not quite come of age.

One of the barriers to the maturity of operational risk management is the definition of operational risk. In this chapter the flaws inherent in the commonly accepted definition have been shown, and a new one more aligned to the field of operations management was proposed. Practitioners of operational risk management and the academics that study their work would do well to pay more attention to this field. It provides a more coherent basis for the discipline of operational risk management than is currently in place.

Another barrier is a lack of clear alignment between operational risk management and ERM. Though they are not the same, the practice of operational risk management must not be divorced from the tenets of ERM. Notably operational risk management activity must be value adding, helping to protect and create value. In addition, we must distance ourselves from the notion that operational risks can only have a downside. Exposure to operational risk can confer both opportunities and threats for an organization. Effective operational risk management must consider both.

Reflective practice questions

At the end of each chapter, a number of points for reflection, drawing on the themes presented within, will be available. Practitioners and students of this practice are encouraged to reflect on these questions based on their own experiences and research.

1 Why does your organization need an operational risk management function? What value do operational risk managers add?

2 Is there such a thing as a risk-free decision? Are operational risk managers in your organization involved in supporting all decisions that have an element of operational risk? Are these decisions they are not involved in? If not, why?

3 Are you a risk manager or an uncertainty manager? How does this affect your use of tools like RCSAs and risk indicators?

4 Can you provide examples of how you, as an operational risk practitioner, have helped your organization to exploit upside opportunities?

5 How do your organization's operational risk management activities fit within a wider ERM perspective? Are operational risks managed in the same way as other risks or are their differences reflected in the tools and infrastructure that you use to manage operational risk?

References

Ashby, S, Sharma, P and McDonnell, W (2003) Lessons about risk: Analysing the causal chain of insurance company failure, *Insurance Research and Practice*, 18 (2), 4–15

Aven, E and Aven, T (2015) On the need for rethinking current practice that highlights goal achievement risk in an enterprise context, *Risk Analysis*, 35 (9), 1706–16

BCBS (2006) International Convergence of Capital Measurement and Capital Standards: A revised framework comprehensive version, Bank for International Settlements, Basel

Bednarek, R, Chalkias, K and Jarzabkowski, P (2021) Managing risk as a duality of harm and benefit: A study of organizational risk objects in the global insurance industry, *British Journal of Management*, 32 (1), 235–54

Campbell, P (2016) Diesel sales fall to lowest in seven years after VW scandal, Financial Times, 24 October, www.ft.com/content/f3e59748-978f-11e6-a80e-bcd69f323a8b = (archived at https://perma.cc/7KMY-X4H9)

COSO (1991) Internal Control: Integrated framework, Committee of Sponsoring Organizations of the Treadway Commission

COSO, 2017, Enterprise risk management: Integrating with strategy and performance, Committee of Sponsoring Organizations of the Treadway Commission

Hardy, C and Maguire, S (2016) Organizing risk: Discourse, power, and 'riskification', *Academy of Management Review*, 41 (1), 80–108

HM Treasury (2020) *Orange Book*, HM Government, London

ISO 31000:2018 (2018) Risk management: guidelines, International Organization for Standardization, https://www.iso.org/obp/ui/#iso:std:iso:31000:ed-2:v1:en (archived at https://perma.cc/KM2M-3WYZ)

Knight, F H (1921) *Risk, Uncertainty and Profit*, Houghton Mifflin, Boston, MA

Maguire, S and Hardy, C (2013) Organizing processes and the construction of risk: A discursive approach, *Academy of Management Journal*, 56 (1), 231–55

Oakland, J S, Oakland, R J and Turner, M A (2020) Total Quality Management and Operational Excellence: Text with cases, Routledge, London

Palermo, T, Power, M and Ashby, S (2017) Navigating institutional complexity: The production of risk culture in the financial sector, *Journal of Management Studies*, 54 (2), 154–81

Power, M (2005) The invention of operational risk, *Review of International Political Economy*, 12 (4), 577–99

Rocco, M and McGee, P (2021) Peloton recalls treadmills after injuries and a child's death, *Financial Times*, 5 May

Sharman, A and Brunsden, J (2015) Volkswagen scandal spills beyond diesel, Financial Times, 4 November, www.ft.com/content/15cb2940-8305-11e5-8095-ed1a37d1e096 (archived at https://perma.cc/MZ8A-PGL5)

Slaughter and May (2019) An independent review following TSB's migration onto a new IT platform in April 2018, www.tsb.co.uk/news-releases/slaughter-and-may (archived at https://perma.cc/TPA4-C9KP)

Stein, M (2000) The risk taker as shadow: A psychoanalytic view of the collapse of Barings Bank, *Journal of Management Studies*, 37 (8), 1215–30

TSB (2018) Annual Report, TSB Banking Group, https://www.tsb.co.uk/investors/tsb-banking-group-annual-report-and-account.pdf (archived at https://perma.cc/6RQS-Z5YD)

Embedding operational risk management

02

LEARNING OUTCOMES

- Describe the components of an effective operational risk framework.
- Explain the formal and informal factors that influence the embeddedness of an operational risk management framework.
- Understand how real-world organizations have embedded operational risk management frameworks. Learn from their successes and failures.

1. Introduction

In this chapter we explore how to embed an operational risk management framework (ORMF) in an organization. Though the design can vary, most organizations have in place some form of framework for the management of operational risks. This will typically include formal tools for the identification, assessment, monitoring and control of operational risks. Often these tools will be documented in policies and procedure manuals and supported by a formal governance infrastructure, as well as informal elements like the organization's risk culture.

The presence of an ORMF is a necessary part of effective operational risk management, but it is rarely adequate in isolation. Organizations must ensure that the ORMF is embedded in day-to-day business activities and decisions. The aim is to implement an ORMF that brings benefits to the organization, benefits that the users of the framework recognize as valuable, both to the organization and to themselves in the performance of their duties.

The term 'embedding' is open to interpretation and can mean different things to different people. This chapter also explores what this means from an operational risk management perspective. In addition, we will examine the critical success factors involved in achieving an embedded ORMF; how framework components and activities can be integrated and aligned to businesses' processes to maximize their net benefit; and how 'embeddedness' can be assessed.

Note that below, and throughout the remainder of this book, I use the term 'operational risk function' to refer to the person or people with responsibility for the design and implementation of the ORMF. In some organizations this function may be very small (e.g. a single full- or part-time operational risk manager). It may also be that operational risk is not organized as a discrete function but subsumed within a wider risk or enterprise risk function. Either way there should be a person or persons with responsibility for the ORMF. The same applies for smaller organizations. Though they may be too small for even a general risk function, let alone a specialist operational risk function, someone should be allocated responsibility for the management of operational risks.

2. A sound framework for operational risk management

The specific design and implementation of an ORMF will vary according to the nature, scale and complexity of an organization. However, most combine a number of common elements. In this section we outline these elements. The aim is to provide a sound basis for an effective ORMF, a basis that can be customized depending on the needs of an organization.

An organization's ORMF consists of the infrastructure and tools that it uses to support the identification, assessment, monitoring and control of operational risk. Figure 2.1 illustrates the common components that comprise a sound framework and situates this framework within the wider strategic and operational environments of an organization.

The ORMF exists within an organization's external environment (e.g. the economy, regulation, competitors, etc) and its own internal operating environment (e.g. the activities that it performs). In turn, these environmental factors will drive its strategy and objectives and, through this, influence the design and implementation of its ORMF.

Figure 2.1   A sound framework for operational risk management

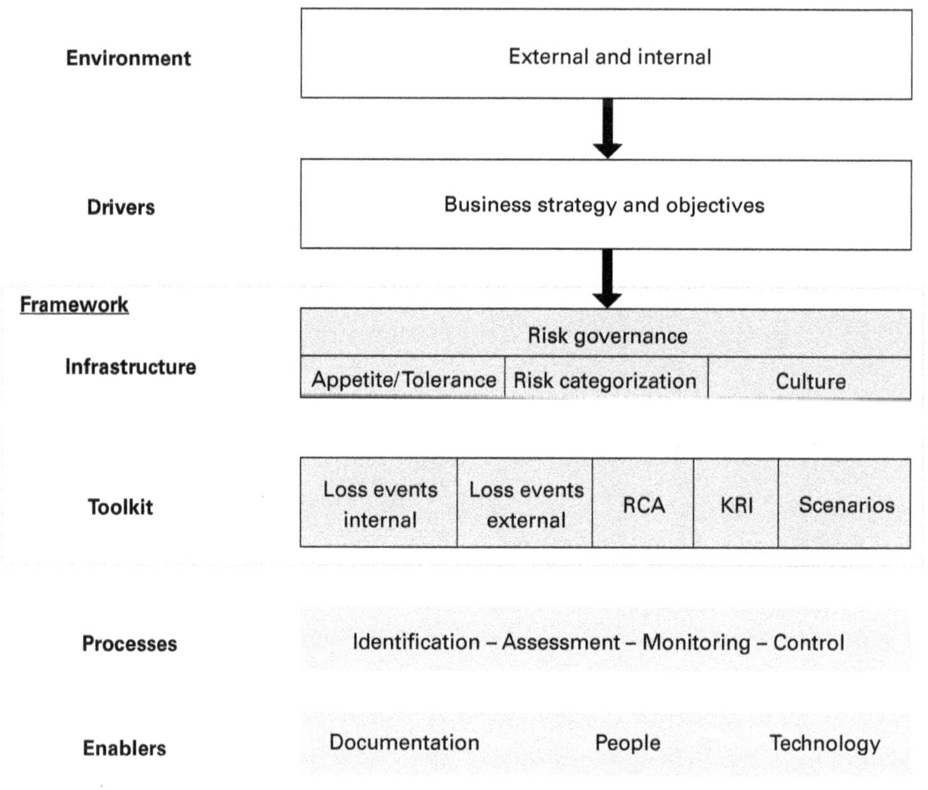

| Environment | External and internal |
| Drivers | Business strategy and objectives |

Framework

Infrastructure

| Risk governance |
| Appetite/Tolerance | Risk categorization | Culture |

| Toolkit | Loss events internal | Loss events external | RCA | KRI | Scenarios |

| Processes | Identification – Assessment – Monitoring – Control |

| Enablers | Documentation | People | Technology |

CASE STUDY 2.1   Contrasting two organizations with different approaches to the design and implementation of their ORMF

As part of a recent research project for the Association of Certified Chartered Accountants (Ashby, Bryce and Ring, 2019) a number of organizations were visited to investigate their ORMFs. This investigation revealed a range of design and implementation approaches, though the basic structure of each organization's ORMF was essentially the same.

Two of these organizations were implementing new operational risk assessment and risk appetite tools. Both organizations were resource constrained and hoped that the new tools would reduce bureaucracy and help management to focus on the most significant operational risks. This included operational risks that were significant at the enterprise-wide and business unit/function level.

A further shared risk management objective was to enhance the control of risk by first-line management. In each case the pressures of the 'day job' were a problem. In the first case study this manifested as a 'non-accountability culture' where managers were reluctant to take responsibility for certain risks or controls. Resource pressures meant that managers did not want to take responsibility for risk and control problems because this might mean more work:

'I have seen the behaviours in the first line that people don't like to be open when things aren't working well. People don't like the colour red; they don't like having events. And they don't like raising events because: a) it acknowledges that something has gone wrong; and b) it means they've got admin work to do. So, there's a real culture of people trying to avoid managing risk or identifying risk' (Risk Manager).

In the second case study, first-line management were willing to take responsibility for managing risks but did not always complete the actions required. Here the culture was described as 'can do' and 'just go and do it'. First-line management were quick to accept potential risk or control problems, but this enthusiasm could soon wane because of the complexity of a problem. Problems were not always addressed in a permanent manner. The risk manager comments:

'We do a lot of things in our organization where, just go and do it and see if it works, and then we kind of say, well, that was really, really good but we don't really know it's really, really good because we didn't actually put the correct infrastructure before we actually try something out. So, we get lots of good ideas and we're in a very dynamic environment, so people say, we've got a really good idea, we're going to go and tackle a problem here and then we're going to have really good outcomes from that, but they don't really think about what they wanted. They don't know how they're really going to measure and capture before they actually go out there and do it. So, it's almost like we're on a bit of a back foot and we have to say, okay, before you go and try something new, you need to capture how you're going to do it, why you're doing it. What's the outcome from that? What will it affect?'

While the cases shared similar objectives, the external and internal environmental factors that drove the changes to their risk management activities were different. The first case study chose to implement a significantly more formal risk assessment/risk appetite approach, with detailed process mapping, evidence-based control testing, risk appetite metrics and a new IT system. In contrast, the second case study was implementing a much less formal risk register/risk appetite matrix approach that relied on management judgement and was recorded on spreadsheets.

Key internal factors that influenced the formal/informal mix of both case studies were the personalities and past experiences of the senior risk management team. In the first case study a new chief risk officer (CRO) was a key driver. The CRO had come from an organization that worked within a heavily regulated jurisdiction where rigorous and formal control testing was perceived as important. The other members of the senior team also came from organizations that had emphasized formal risk management. In contrast, the senior risk team in the second case study placed much more weight on informal mechanisms.

In terms of external factors, though both cases were subject to significant external scrutiny, only the first case study talked about regulators driving a relatively formal risk management approach: 'we're regulated, and we have got to do things right. So, you've got to have governance in place, and it's got to be strict' (Risk Manager).

Both cases used a range of informal mechanisms to help reinforce the risk assessment and appetite approaches that they had designed. However, the second case study gave much more emphasis to these mechanisms and was more involved in the work of the first line. Its risk function acted as a risk facilitator and helped the first line to identify, assess and control significant risks. This included help implementing action plans and acting as a 'critical friend' where necessary. It also required a lot of 'hand holding'. In contrast, the first case study was not as close to the first line and gave more emphasis to a formal second-line risk oversight role.

The ORMF is underpinned by the essential risk management process of identification, assessment, monitoring and control, along with a number of enablers, including documented policies and procedures, IT systems and the capacity and capability of its people. This process and the various enablers are not necessarily specific to operational risk management. Often they will form part of the wider ERM activities conducted by an organization. See Chapter 1 for a discussion on the relationship between operational risk and ERM.

3. Operational risk management infrastructure

The operational risk management infrastructure exists to coordinate and control operational risk management activity. The elements of this infrastructure combine formal, tangible structures like hierarchies, with informal and often less tangible human elements, such as risk culture.

3.1 Operational risk governance

Operational risk governance is the organizational architecture within which operational risk management operates (e.g. reporting lines, roles and responsibilities, etc). Since operational risk management is fundamental to running any organization, its governance is an essential part of effective corporate governance.

An effective governance structure for operational risk management should involve everyone in the organization. This means that it can only operate successfully if there are clear and effective lines of communication both up and down the organization and a culture in which good and bad news is allowed to travel freely. Please refer to Chapter 6 for a detailed discussion of how to implement effective governance from an operational risk perspective.

3.2 Operational risk appetite

Operational risk appetite involves deciding on and monitoring the level and types of operational risk exposure that an organization will take in pursuit of its objectives. It is common practice when monitoring the operational risk profile against appetite to determine criticality and the urgency of mitigating action by assigning a 'red–amber–green' (RAG) status.

This approach can be applied across a range of ORMF components, including risk and control self-assessment, loss event reporting and scenario analysis, and indicates the proportional response to specific types or levels of operational risk exposure. Chapter 5 provides a detailed discussion of how to implement an effective risk appetite approach from an operational risk perspective.

3.3 Categorization

Categorization helps to determine the scope of operational risk management and to demarcate exposures by cause, event and effect. The categorization of operational risks provides a common frame of reference to help organize operational risk assessments, monitor reports and control responses. Please refer to Chapter 3 for further information on how to categorize operational risks.

3.4 Culture

An organization's risk culture is a sub-component of its overall culture, which in turn is influenced by the macro-cultures that an organization operates within. In this context the term 'culture' refers to the social processes and structures that affect how people perceive the world around them and make decisions. A culture is reflected in the customs, beliefs, common experiences and behaviours of the people within it. Please refer to Chapter 4 for a discussion of how to assess and influence the risk culture of an organization.

4. The operational risk management toolkit

The components of an organization's operational risk management toolkit are concerned with recording, estimating and monitoring operational risk exposures. These tools provide information to support the identification, assessment, monitoring and control of risk, while the operational risk management infrastructure provides the mechanisms through which this information is organized and decisions are taken.

4.1 Loss events internal and external

While other components of the ORMF (i.e. risk and control self-assessment (RCSA), key risk indicators and scenario analysis) involve varying degrees of subjectivity, loss event data provides an objective source of historical information regarding the probability and impact of operational risk events.

Internal losses arise from actual events, i.e. the materialization of operational risks, and reflect the organization's own experience. Therefore, this has the potential to be the most relevant basis for analysis and management response. External losses provide valuable content for the construction of scenarios and risk assessments. Chapter 8 explains how to collect and use data on operational loss events.

4.2 Risk and control self-assessment (RCSA)

RCSA provides a systematic means for identifying and assessing operational risk events and potential control gaps that may threaten the achievement of defined business or process objectives, and for monitoring what management does to close these gaps. Chapter 7 explains how to design and use RCSAs to support the management of operational risks.

4.3 Key risk indicators

Risk indicators facilitate the monitoring and control of operational risks. They support a range of operational risk management activities and processes, including risk identification; risk and control assessments; and the implementation of effective risk appetite, risk management and governance frameworks. The role of risk, control and performance indicators in an operational risk context is explored in Chapter 9.

4.4 *Scenario analysis and stress testing*

Scenario analysis and stress testing are used to assess the impact of hypothetical, yet foreseeable, extreme operational loss events. They focus on defining realistic situations that could have a sizeable impact on the organization but occur very rarely: the so-called 'tail risks', sitting at the tail of the loss distribution. They differ from the typical expected losses observed by the organization on an annual basis. Please refer to Chapter 10 for further information on the use of scenario analysis and stress testing to support the management of operational risks.

5. What 'embedding' means

Organizational activity of any kind requires resources, both physical and financial, along with time and effort from its employees. Most organizations will only expend their limited resources on activities that derive value, that is, the benefits in terms of resource gains must exceed the costs in resources expended. The same is true of the employees that work for an organization.

An embedded ORMF is one that adds value. This value may be actual or perceived, but it is essential that employees at all levels believe that value is being generated. In practical terms this means they must be confident that the ORMF is not only beneficial for the organization as a whole or its regulators, but that it can help them in their work.

It is important to emphasize that added value may be both tangible, in terms of cost savings (e.g. a reduction in operational losses or fines), better decision making or efficiency improvements, and intangible, in terms of employee perceptions regarding the usefulness of operational risk management. This distinction is important for two reasons:

- The costs of operational risk management activity must typically be incurred *before* any benefits are realized.
- The costs associated with operational risk management are usually tangible (e.g. purchasing a risk assessment system or time spent populating a risk register), while the benefits (a potential reduction on operational risk events) are much less so. Proving that a costly operational risk event has been avoided can be hard when it has not actually occurred.

Hence an embedded ORMF from an organizational perspective should not only add tangible value, but also be perceived as adding value by its employees. Typically, both are necessary – an ORMF that adds tangible value, but which employees do not believe in, is not truly embedded. Equally, employees are less likely to believe in the value of an ORMF if it does not yield some form of measurable benefit.

CASE STUDY 2.2   Halifax Bank of Scotland

Halifax Bank of Scotland (HBOS) was a successful retail bank prior to the global financial crisis of 2007–08. It was also recognized as a leader in operational risk management with a best-in-class ORMF. However, an enquiry into the failure of the bank, in October 2008, revealed a range of weaknesses in the management, governance and culture of HBOS (FCA and PRA, 2015). A key problem was that staff, management and the bank's board did not value risk management.

The FCA and PRA report into the failure of HBOS concludes that the bank pursued a high growth strategy without properly considering the operational, credit and liquidity risks involved. Effective risk management is essential when implementing a high-risk strategy, but in HBOS a number of serious weaknesses were identified, many of which related to the management of its operational risks. This included the lack of a clearly defined group risk appetite statement, ineffective internal controls and a risk culture that prioritized business growth. Crucially risk management, especially operational risk management, was perceived as a constraint on business rather than an enabler. Plus, discussions about risk and risk management were not given sufficient time or priority by the board, and internal controls were overridden when it was felt necessary (e.g. to achieve aggressive growth targets).

The failure of HBOS highlights the importance of embedding effective risk management, especially operational risk management. Though HBOS appeared to have an effective risk management framework, including a best-in-class ORMF, it was not embedded effectively. The main problem was the failure on the part of management and the board to understand the value of risk management as a business enabler, especially when pursuing a risky, high-growth strategy.

6. Adding value: critical success factors

To generate actual and perceived value for its ORMF an organization should consider a number of critical success factors. Progress against each of these factors should be reviewed on an ongoing basis, as well as whenever an ORMF is designed, reviewed or modified. See section five in this chapter for guidance on assessing embeddedness.

Though some of these factors are more formal and structured than others, they are equally important. Moreover, they are complementary. Each works with the other factors to ensure that an ORMF is embedded in the day-to-day activities and decisions of an organization.

6.1 *Risk culture*

From an embedding perspective an organization's risk culture will have a significant influence over whether its staff and management believe in the value of operational risk management. Risk culture affects both how people perceive risk and the time and effort they devote to risk management activities.

Every organization and risk culture are different. As a result, it is impossible to provide a single, optimal risk culture for an effectively embedded ORMF. However, it is possible to identify cultural behaviours and beliefs that can help or hinder effective embedding; some examples are identified in Table 2.1.

Table 2.1   Cultural elements that can help or hinder an effectively embedded ORMF

Risk Culture Embedding Inhibitors	Risk Culture Embedding Enablers
Operational risk is not perceived as a risk that is an inherent part of business activities	Operational risks are perceived as risks that are an essential part of achieving an organization's objectives
Operational risk management is seen as the job of the operational risk function	Operational risk management is accepted as a collective responsibility
Operational risk is not considered in routine activities and decisions	Employees are operational risk aware and consider its management as part of their activities and decisions
The ORMF is perceived as bureaucratic red-tape and/or a compliance exercise	The ORMF is perceived as business-focused, helping to save costs or improve efficiency
The operational risk function is segregated or disengaged from the wider organization	The operational risk function plays an active part in the organization's activities and decisions
The organization is underresourced, meaning that employees struggle to fulfil their role in full	The organization has adequate resources, allowing all employees to fulfil every aspect of their role, including their responsibilities for operational risk management
Leadership tone on operational risk management is either absent or hostile	Leadership tone towards operational risk management is positive. Leaders regularly emphasize the benefits of the ORMF

6.2 *Effective risk governance*

From a risk governance perspective, the embeddedness of the ORMF can be impacted by:

- the formal structure of the risk governance arrangements, in terms of the efficiency of its communication network and the ability of senior management/directors to exercise their authority; and

- relations between the various groups that work within the arrangements, especially business management, the operational risk function, and internal audit.

It is important that the formal governance structure for operational risk is not too complicated. A complicated structure can hinder effective reporting. Structures with multiple reporting lines and committees can be slow to pick up potential embedding issues, either because reports take too long to reach the relevant decision makers or because of gaps and overlaps in responsibilities. It is recommended that the governance structure is kept as simple as possible. This means keeping the number of risk committees to a minimum (e.g. avoiding separate committees for different risk types or organizational divisions) as well as allocating clear and unambiguous responsibilities for operational risk management.

In terms of personal relations, the key factor is how the operational risk function balances oversight of the ORMF with providing operational risk insight to both business managers and internal audit. Within the three lines of defence approach to operational risk governance (see Chapter 6) it is common to separate the implementation of the ORMF with its design/oversight and assurance activities. This means that front-line managers are tasked with its implementation, the operational risk function for ensuring that managers implement it correctly, while internal audit provide assurance that the ORMF is operating effectively and compliantly with any relevant laws or regulations.

Problems can arise with embedding when these three roles are kept completely separate. For example, an operational risk function may decide that in order to maintain independent oversight it should not support implementation of the ORMF by business managers and only engage where challenge is required. Equally, internal audit may not work with the risk function at the design stage of the ORMF to maintain 'independence'. The net effect of such strict segregation is mistrust and sometimes hostility. Hence, while business managers, risk functions and internal auditors may have different accountabilities, this does not mean that they should not work together to ensure the ORMF is implemented effectively.

The importance of cooperation between the three lines is reflected in the Institute of Internal Auditors (IIA) 2020 revision of the three lines of defence approach, which they term the 'Three Lines Model' (IIA, 2020). The IIA emphasizes the importance of close cooperation between the first and second lines (business management and the risk function). This is to ensure that good relationships are maintained and that the skills and experience within each line are combined effectively. The IIA's approach still recommends that the third-line audit function must remain independent, but that does not mean this function need be divorced from the wider organization. Close working and cooperation with the first and second lines remains essential.

Various strategies can be used to help build trust and prevent hostility between business management, the operational risk function and auditors. Below are some example strategies:

- The operational risk function provides information and reports on operational risk exposures to business management. This might include information on risk events that have affected peer organizations, good practice implemented internally by managers or changes in regulation.

- The operational risk function should schedule regular informal one-to-one meetings with relevant business managers, to share ideas and concerns. Where there is more than one operational risk manager each individual might be allocated specific relationship management responsibilities.

- When designing or modifying the ORMF the operational risk function should consult with business management, incorporating their feedback where possible or explaining why it is not possible to do so.

- The operational risk function could programme regular communication initiatives to promote specific aspects of the ORMF (e.g. awareness campaigns, consultations, surveys, etc).

- The operational risk function provides online and/or face-to-face training on specific aspects of the ORMF, as well as ongoing support on how to use it effectively.

- The operational risk function should engage with internal audit regularly to share ideas, concerns and advise of changes to the ORMF.

It cannot be emphasized enough that the more the operational risk function works to build good personal relations across the organization the more embedded will be the ORMF. People are much more likely to believe in the value of operational risk management if they know and respect those responsible for its design and oversight.

6.3 Operational risk reporting

Operational risk reports are an important output from the ORMF. These reports should provide information to support a wide range of strategic and tactical (e.g. process management) decisions. The design, scope and audience to which these reports are provided can have a significant impact on the extent to which operational risk management is embedded across an organization. Poor quality or hard-to-use reports will present the ORMF in a poor light and may lead management to question its value. Equally, an exclusive focus on the board or senior management team may leave other managers questioning the value of the ORMF for them.

6.3.1 The intended recipients of reports

In most organizations operational risk reports will be produced for the board and senior management team. However, it is hard to embed an ORMF if these are the only reports that are produced, however good they may be.

Typically, it is an organization's front-line managers that are tasked with the implementation of an ORMF (e.g. managers working in operational departments concerned with things like production, sales, finance, supply chains, etc). Among other tasks, they and their teams will have to devote significant time and effort to providing the data required for operational risk reports. For example, ensuring that risk profiles and control self-assessments are completed, recording loss events, and collating risk and control indicator metrics. Therefore, it is important that they not only understand the benefits of their efforts for the wider organization, but also gain some direct benefits for themselves.

Where possible the ORMF should be used to provide reports for management across an organization. These reports should contain information that managers can use to fulfil their duties and support the activities of their teams. This might include helping them to identify efficiency improvements, improve their performance in internal audits or ensure compliance with laws and regulations (e.g. to fulfil their duty of care in relation to the health and safety of their workplace).

Operational risk management IT systems are one way to partially automate business management reporting, saving time in the risk function. An effective IT system should allow business management to produce their own operational risk reports, to meet their local needs, at the same time as providing consistent data for the risk function to use in board and senior management reporting.

6.3.2 Quality of reporting

Management will perceive more benefit from operational risk reports that are timely, accurate and complete.

Managers will quickly lose confidence in reports that contain inaccuracies, especially if they cause resources to be diverted from more important areas. Equally managers will expect 'complete' reports, which provide the information that they need to make decisions. Note, however, that completeness does not imply that all possible data should be reported, since this may result in an overly long and complex report (see section 6.3.3 below).

Timeliness has two dimensions – the currency of the data, that is, how up to date it is at the point of extraction, and the effectiveness of the reporting process in terms of how long it takes for the most recent data to reach its audience. The more historic the data and the longer the reports take to compile and submit, the less appropriate and effective may be the management responses by way of decisions and actions.

Operational risk managers should spend time ensuring that the reports produced using the ORMF are as timely, accurate and complete as possible. One way to achieve this is by consulting with the intended recipients to understand their business needs. Before a report is designed they should be asked for their requirements, and once a draft report is ready they should be able to suggest changes. Reports should also be regularly reviewed and updated to ensure that management continue to be satisfied with their quality.

Another solution is to use an IT system for reporting. A good-quality system should be able to reduce the time it takes to produce a report and prevent data processing errors. Plus, as indicated previously, it may allow managers to generate their own customized reports.

6.3.3 Report usability

To help embed an ORMF, reports should support the decisions that must be made by business management and the activities of their departments, functions or teams. This will help managers to see the benefits of the ORMF, and in particular how these benefits can improve their own personal effectiveness and the performance of their staff.

Operational risk reports are more likely to support management decision making when they:

- *Are concise.* Managers have many responsibilities and are time limited. This means that they will engage more in shorter, focused reports. Hence, operational risk reports are more likely to help embed an ORMF when they are one to two pages long. Instead of length, the focus should be on providing a mechanism for discussion and debate. Reports should be viewed as the start of an operational risk management conversation (e.g. what are the key current risk and control priorities), not the end point.

- *Focus on the real issues.* Excessive amounts of data can prevent managers from seeing the 'big picture' in terms of their overall operational risk profile and how this is impacting on their objectives. One solution is to adopt the principle of 'exception reporting'. This means that reports focus on the most current or significant operational risk exposures or control issues rather than trying to cover every single risk or issue.

- *Are easy to absorb.* Sometimes diagrammatic representations of data can be helpful, but complex and sophisticated graphics may not be the answer. Clarity and simplicity are key to getting beyond awareness to understanding.

6.4 Allocating responsibilities outside the risk function

The operational risk function cannot, on its own, embed an effective ORMF. Help is needed from the wider organization. Two common solutions are to create the roles of risk owners and risk champions.

Risk owners are typically department or function managers. They may also be senior managers or executives in the case of strategic-level operational risks. The role of a risk owner is to take responsibility for the day-to-day management of an operational risk. This will include ensuring that the ORMF is applied correctly (e.g. that risk and control assessments are performed in a timely manner) and that action is taken to address control weaknesses or a significant increase in exposure. The risk owner should be able to determine the amount of risk exposure that is undertaken.

Some organizations supplement risk owners with control owners and occasionally data owners for specific risk and control indicators. Control owners are responsible for ensuring that a specific control is functioning as intended. Data owners are responsible for providing data for operational risk reports.

Risk champions are individuals tasked with promoting and supporting the function of the ORMF in their area. Their role may include:

- providing locally relevant advice and training on the operation of the ORMF;.
- helping local managers to make operational risk management decisions (e.g. whether or not to implement a new control or remove an old one);
- providing a consistent point of contact for the central risk function;
- explaining the benefits of the ORMF to management in their area.

Operational risk managers can build better relationships with risk owners and champions when they invest time to support them in their role. This might include regular one-to-one meetings, specialist training and the creation of a risk forum, where risk owners and/or champions are invited to share ideas and concerns.

CASE STUDY 2.3   Using risk champions to embed the ORMF

One of the case studies examined by Ashby, Bryce and Ring (2019) had a network of first-line operational risk specialists working as local risk champions. Each operational division and head office function had one or more operational risk specialists. These specialists supported the completion of RCSAs and provided local subject-matter expertise in areas including human resource (HR) risk management, cyber risk, data protection and finance. Building a strong working relationship between the first-line specialists with the second-line operational risk function created synergies for the organization. The second line brought the conceptual operational risk management expertise to complement the first line's local risk knowledge:

> I think sometimes, it's a genuine discovery on both sides, so the (operational) risk team don't necessarily know what they're trying to ask, but we'll apply our expertise and come up with what we think the right answer is. (Risk Champion)

The first-line risk specialists were instrumental to implementing a new process-based operational risk assessment and controls-testing approach, as well as a complementary IT data management and reporting system. The first-line risk specialists did this through informal channels working on a one-to-one basis with local operational risk and control owners to help them complete the assessments and populate the system. In turn, the first-line risk specialists had regular one-to-one contact with the second-line operational risk function that had designed the new approach and system.

During the design and implementation phases of the new approach and system the first-line specialists were consulted regularly on the new approach, system and related documentation. This helped to refine the approach and reduce the time required to complete the new operational risk assessments. It also helped to improve the accuracy of the assessments and embed the new approach across the organization.

'So, that's meant that because we've all had to work together to build those documents out, we all understand much better what we're meant to be doing. And risk management becomes part of how you do your job, rather than it being something that the risk team do or something that somebody else worries about. It's absolutely intrinsic to what we're doing, which is exactly the outcome I think everybody strives for' (Risk Champion).

6.5 Integrating operational risk management within all organizational processes

The final critical success factor is to integrate operational risk management within routine organizational process. The closer these are aligned, the clearer should be the benefits of the ORMF to management. Close integration should also help management to join the dots between operational risk management and other organizational activities, helping to improve decision making and increasing the level of added value.

Effective integration requires close coordination between the operational risk function and the wider management of the organization. It is imperative that the operational risk function is seen to add value, helping management to achieve their objectives in an efficient, cost-effective and sustainable manner. Below, a number of value-adding strategies are outlined.

6.5.1 Integrating the ORMF with strategic decision making

The operational risk function should support strategic planning and objective setting. All strategies and objectives involve an element of operational risk. The operational risk function should advise on the associated risk exposures and propose mechanisms to help assess and control them. It is strongly advised that the operational risk function is involved at the initial planning and objective-setting stages, not after the strategy has been determined. Management will value early input to help prevent unnecessary revisions. Providing the operational risk function maintains a separate reporting line to front-line functions and departments; conflicts of interest should be avoided.

6.5.2 Integrating the ORMF with change management

As with strategic decision making, the operational risk function should play an active role in change management. This might include facilitating change risk assessments and advising on control responses. Providing there are clear risk governance arrangements, it is possible for the operational risk function to support change management initiatives without conflicting their oversight role. The key is to ensure that front-line management are held accountable for all decisions, with the operational risk function acting, primarily, in a facilitation capacity.

6.5.3 Using the ORMF to support management decision making

Actions taken, and decisions made by management, should be supported by information provided through the ORMF. This includes decisions regarding the acceptance versus mitigation of operational risks.

6.5.4 Incentives, performance management and reward

Organizations should avoid incentivizing/rewarding inappropriate risk taking. Plus, where appropriate, they might consider rewarding effective use of the ORMF. It is recommended that the operational risk function should advise on the design and implementation of new performance management initiatives, and where necessary should escalate any concerns they may have about their design. However, such escalation should be a last resort, where management refuse to listen to advice.

6.5.5 Staff training and development

Training and development for operational risk management may, at times, be provided on a stand-alone basis. However, where possible it should be integrated into wider training and development initiatives (e.g. leadership training, personal effectiveness, induction, etc). This will help staff to make links between operational risk management and their day-to-day roles and responsibilities.

6.5.6 Communication

Messages about the management of operational risk should ideally be integrated within routine business communications, rather than issued as separate announcements from the risk function.

6.5.7 Integrating with the three lines of defence

Organizations that apply a strict interpretation of the three lines of defence approach may have concerns about close working between the operational risk function and 'front-line' managers. However, they should remember that there are trade-offs. As explained in section 6.2, a segregated operational risk function that only oversees business decisions and that does not get involved in decision making is likely to experience resentment and mistrust. In turn this will hinder the effective embedding of the ORMF.

To avoid any conflicts of interest the operational risk function should retain an independent reporting line from business management (e.g. via the chief risk officer or equivalent, who reports directly to the chief executive officer, managing director or even directly to the board). They should also be provided training in building and maintaining personal relationships, along with technical risk management training.

7. Assessing the embeddedness of the operational risk management framework

Many corporate governance codes and risk management regulations expect organizations to maintain effective risk management frameworks, and this includes an embedded ORMF. In addition, the governing body (e.g. board of directors) is often required to assure itself that organizationally significant risks are being managed effectively, many of which will be operational in nature. To comply with these requirements, it is important that organizations regularly (i.e. quarterly or annually, as appropriate) assess the embeddedness of their ORMF, and take action to improve embeddedness where necessary. Usually, this responsibility is delegated to the chief risk officer, or equivalent, supported by the operational risk function. It may also be that they are supported by Internal Audit, and external experts where necessary.

7.1 Approaches to assessing effectiveness

There are a number of recognized approaches to assessing how effectively an ORMF is embedded. Table 2.2 outlines some common examples.

Table 2.2   Techniques for assessing the effectiveness of an ORMF

Approach	Description/ Source	What is Assessed
Key Principles approach	Based on the premise that any operational risk management process must satisfy a minimum set of principles. Such as those described in ISO 31000 (the International Standard for Risk Management)	The extent to which implementation of the ORMF satisfies a set of agreed principles for good practice. For example: • The ability of the ORMF to create and protect value • Whether the ORMF is an integral part of organizational processes • The extent to which the ORMF is used to support strategic and operational decision making • Whether the ORMF explicitly addresses the potential for uncertainty (see Chapter 1) • Whether the output from the ORMF is systematic, structured, timely and based on the best available information • The extent to which the ORMF is tailored to the nature, scale and complexity of an organization • Whether the ORMF takes human and cultural factors into account • Whether the ORMF is transparent, inclusive, dynamic, iterative and responsive to change • The extent to which the ORMF facilitates continual improvement across the organization (in terms of the effectiveness and efficiency of operations)
Maturity Model approach	Builds on the assertion that the quality of operational risk management processes should improve over time. A number of models have been developed by the major consultancies.	Assessed components normally include: • A protocol of performance standards based on current practice and requirements • A guide to how the standards and requirements can be satisfied in practice • A means of measuring actual performance • A means of recording and reporting performance and proposing improvements • Periodic independent verification of management assessments

(continued)

Table 2.2   (Continued)

Approach	Description/ Source	What is Assessed
Process Element approach	Look at the effectiveness of the identification, assessment, monitoring and control processes used to underpin the ORMF. For example, ISO 31000:2018 outlines seven 'Process Elements' that could be assessed.	The ISO 31000 Process Elements are as follows: • Communication (effectiveness across the three lines) • Setting the context (an organization's understanding of its internal and external environments) • Identification (are new risks identified in a timely fashion, are risks overlooked?) • Analysis (methods used to assess probability and impact) • Evaluation (mechanisms to support the prioritization of assessed risks) • Treatment (techniques used to avoid, share, manage or accept the risk) • Monitor and review (are processes reviewed regularly and improved where necessary?)

7.2 Key assessment steps

Whichever approach from Table 2.2 is adopted (or indeed an alternative approach) there are some key steps that they will have in common:

1 Establish a target state against which to measure current status. This will illustrate 'what good looks like' and represent the position to which the organization aspires.

2 Measure current status as the baseline starting point. This can be achieved through structured interviews with key stakeholders or a desk-based review of evidence, or both. The former provides informed but subjective opinion, whereas the latter can be more objective and for this reason it may be preferable to deploy both. Depending on which approach is adopted, ratings can be on a scale representing the degree to which framework components are being used effectively and this can be demonstrated, or the level of maturity. In either case the ratings can be converted to a percentage for aggregation and reporting.

3 Identify gaps. Any difference between the target and current positions represents a gap for attention. Each gap will need a recommended action with details of who should own/lead the action and the expected delivery date.

4 Report the findings of the assessment to senior management and, where appropriate, the managing body. Updates on actions taken to close gaps should also be provided (e.g. quarterly).

5 Repeat the review at regular intervals (e.g. annually) to assess progress or, if the desired position has been attained, to maintain this against a background of changes in processes, procedures, key stakeholders etc.

Organizations that have linked improved embedding of the ORMF to performance management scorecards often find that they have a measurable and high-profile methodology that encourages improved use of the ORMF.

CASE STUDY 2.4   Operational risk management at Tesco

In 2007, Margaret Woods, a respected risk management academic, conducted a study into the balanced scorecard approach that Tesco used to assess the effectiveness and embeddedness of its ERM framework (Woods, 2007). Many of the elements assessed were also components of Tesco's ORMF (e.g. effectiveness of internal controls, alignment of operational activities with the corporate strategy, potential for process errors, etc).

Woods concluded that the use of a balanced scorecard approach can significantly increase the embeddedness of risk management, including operational risk management. The benefit of such an approach is that risk management objectives are aligned with other performance objectives, including customer satisfaction, the effectiveness and efficiency of operational processes and the financial performance of an organization.

Tesco achieved the integration of risk management and other organization objectives through the use of a multi-spoked 'wheel' that highlighted a range of performance metrics grouped into five categories:

- customer (satisfaction and loyalty);

- community (internal and external);

- operations (efficiency and effectiveness);

- people (employee development and satisfaction);

- finance (sales, profit and return on investment).

Some of these metrics were qualitative. For example, the community metrics of 'being responsible, fair and honest' and 'being a good neighbour'. Others were quantitative such as the customer metric of queuing length and the financial metric of maximizing profits.

Woods found that staff at all levels of the organization were aware of the wheel, and the performance of their area in relation to the various metrics. They were also able to articulate the board's expectations in relation to the management of risk and the role that they played in meeting these expectations through the achievement of the performance targets assigned to each metric.

7.3 Indicators of effective embedding

To help monitor the degree of embeddedness of the ORMF it can be useful to monitor embedding indicators. These indicators may form part of routine risk-culture monitoring (see Chapter 4), or they may be reported separately. The following list of ORMF embeddedness indicators is intended to be illustrative rather than comprehensive. Some of these are quantitative metrics, others will require a qualitative evaluation:

- 'Pulling versus pushing' indicators that assess the relationship between front-line management and the operational risk function. For example:
  o the frequency with which front-line managers contact the risk function for advice and guidance, rather than the risk function initiating the interaction (a pulling indicator);
  o the number of risk assessments that have to be chased up because they are not up to date (a pushing indicator);
  o non-compliance with the operational risk policy identified by the risk function (pushing) versus non-compliance reported by front-line management (pulling); and
  o the number and duration of overdue operational risk management actions (pushing).
- Whether there is more focus on preventative controls (as opposed to detective/recovery) and leading (versus lagging) key risk indicators – demonstrating a shift from reactive to proactive management of operational risks (see Chapter 9).
- Whether discussions at risk governance committees (e.g. the audit and risk committee) are properly informed by the operational risk reports presented to them.
- Whether the operational risk profile is kept within agreed risk appetite or tolerance thresholds (Chapter 5).
- Evidence that front-line management are considering operational risk when making operational decisions (e.g. process changes, IT systems implementation or new product development).
- The perceived value of the ORMF, using opinion/satisfaction surveys.
- Comments from regulators, rating agencies or other external institutions regarding the embeddedness of the ORMF.

It is recommended that embedding indicators are reviewed on a quarterly basis. Not all of these indicators will change more frequently than this. Equally, less frequent monitoring might prevent adverse trends from being spotted and corrected in a timely fashion.

8. Conclusion

In this chapter we have discussed the components of an ORMF and the factors that can influence the embeddedness of such a framework. An organization's ORMF will not be effective if it is not embedded. Even a technically perfect ORMF will fail if it is not valued by its users, or is viewed as overly complex and bureaucratic.

Operational risk managers must ensure that they combine high levels of technical expertise with people management, influencing and negotiation skills. Significant effort must be devoted to building relations and promoting the benefits of an effective ORMF. That said, even the most skilled and experienced operational risk managers cannot succeed on their own. An organization's senior management and governing body must demonstrate that they are committed to the effective management of operational risk.

Reflective practice questions

1 Does your organization's ORMF contain all of the infrastructure elements and tools presented in Figure 2.1? If not, is there an explanation for the absence of an element or tool?

2 Does your operational risk management function combine technical expertise in areas like RCSA and soft (people) skills? Is the function valued by the wider organization?

3 Does the operational risk function work effectively with front-line management and the audit function? What could be done to build trust and further improve the working relationship?

4 Do you have risk champions in front-line functions? If yes, what are the benefits? If no, how might the implementation of risk champions improve the embeddedness of the ORMF?

5 Is the output from the ORMF (e.g. operational risk reports) used to support organizational decision making?

6 Have you assessed the embeddedness of your ORMF? If yes, what technique did you use? Was it effective? If no, when might you schedule such a review and what assessment technique would be best for your organization?

References

Ashby, S, Bryce, C and Ring, P (2019) Risk and performance: embedding risk management, ACCA Professional Insight Report, www.accaglobal.com/content/dam/ACCA_Global/professional-insights/embedding-risk/pi-embedding-risk-management.pdf (archived at https://perma.cc/Y2QL-3VEZ)

FCA and PRA (2015) The failure of HBOS plc (HBOS): A report by the Financial Conduct Authority and the Prudential Regulatory Authority, Bank of England, https://www.bankofengland.co.uk/-/media/boe/files/prudential-regulation/publication/hbos-complete-report (archived at https://perma.cc/JFN2-7YD2)

IIA (2020) Three Lines Model: An update of the three lines of defence, The Institute of Internal Auditors, https://na.theiia.org/about-ia/PublicDocuments/Three-Lines-Model-Updated.pdf (archived at https://perma.cc/4UTL-735Y)

Woods, M (2007) Linking risk management to strategic controls: A case study of Tesco plc, *International Journal of Risk Assessment and Management*, 7 (8), 1074–88

Categorizing operational risks

03

LEARNING OUTCOMES

- Explain why operational risks should be categorized.
- Know how to design and implement a categorization approach for operational risks that is customized to the needs of an organization.
- Compare some common approaches to categorizing operational risks.

1. Introduction

Operational risks are diverse. The effectiveness and efficiency of an organization's operations can be impacted by a wide range of possibilities. Some are human in origin (e.g. criminal activity, mistakes, design flaws, etc), others are natural events (weather, pandemics, etc). Many are a combination of the two.

Given the diversity of operational risk events, having an agreed approach to categorization is essential. Such an approach will help everyone in an organization to understand the scope of operational risk. In addition, it provides structure to activities such as risk assessments and reporting. It would be difficult to coordinate and consolidate these activities if there was no operational risk categorization approach or if each department or function within an organization used its own approach.

This chapter explores how to design and implement an effective approach to the categorization of operational risks. As ever there is no one 'best' approach to categorization. How an organization categorizes its operational risks is a personal choice. But there is sound practice that should be followed when selecting and using a particular approach to categorization.

2. Common risk types

Though the focus of this chapter is on the categorization of operational risks, it is important to remember that operational risk is one of several broad types of risk that can impact on organizations. In the financial services sector, it is common to distinguish the following risk types, as illustrated in Table 3.1.

Outside of the financial services sector there tends to be less emphasis on market, credit and liquidity risk. The UK Treasury's Orange Book provides an example:

Though categorization is essential to the effective management of risk in organizations, the distinction between risk types is rarely perfect. As a result, there will be occasions where exposures and events cut across different risk types or where an event attributed to one type of risk is the cause of a risk event in another. For example, the occurrence of an operational risk event (e.g. a labour shortage due to a pandemic) might precipitate a strategic risk (such as the inability to meet a sudden increase in consumer demand) and the combination could in turn cause a reputational impact. In view of this, any categorization of operational risks should not segregate or isolate exposures and must be conducted within a holistic framework for categorizing all of the risks to which an organization is exposed.

CASE STUDY 3.1   Revisiting the VW emissions scandal

The source of the VW emissions scandal was human/organizational misconduct, related to the design and use of a 'defeat device' designed to provide a misleading picture of a vehicle's emissions under test conditions. However, the scandal also damaged VW's reputation and impacted on its strategy.

Given the links to VW's reputation and strategy the scandal could be classified as either a reputation risk or strategic risk event. However, its source was operational in nature.

The solution to such boundary risks is rarely clear cut. One option is to classify the scandal according to the root cause event: human misconduct. But this would result in very few risks being classified as reputation in nature, for example. This is because reputation risks are usually the result of some underlying event, such as misconduct.

Another option is to accept that some risks cross categories and to ensure that the relevant experts in each risk type are involved in managing boundary risks. Having an organization-wide enterprise risk function and/or a chief risk officer (CRO) can help to achieve this. VW did not have a chief risk officer in 2015, only a chief compliance officer.

Table 3.1   Common risk types for financial institutions

Risk Type	Description
Credit	The risk that a counterparty may default of their obligations (a given financial claim is not paid in full) or have their credit rating downgraded.
Liquidity	The risk that an organization is unable to meet its financial liabilities as they fall due.
Market	The risks that arise due to fluctuations in the value of, or income from, the assets of an organization.
Operational	The effect of unpredictable outcomes on the efficiency and effectiveness of operations.
Reputation	Threats to the public perception of an organization and goodwill exhibited by its stakeholders.
Strategic	Risks that are created or affected by the chosen strategy of an organization.

Table 3.2   Risk types used by non-financial organizations (HM Treasury, 2020)

Risk Type	Categories	Description
Business	Commercial	Risks arising from weaknesses in the management of commercial partnerships, supply chains and contractual requirements, resulting in poor performance, inefficiency, poor value for money, fraud, and/or failure to meet business requirements/objectives.
	Strategy	Risks arising from identifying and pursuing a strategy, which is poorly defined, is based on flawed or inaccurate data or fails to support the delivery of commitments, plans or objectives due to a changing macro-environment (e.g. political, economic, social, technological, environment and legislative change).
Financial	Financial	Risks arising from not managing finances in accordance with requirements and financial constraints resulting in poor returns from investments, failure to manage assets/liabilities or to obtain value for money from the resources deployed, and/or non-compliant financial reporting.
Operational	Governance	Risks arising from unclear plans, priorities, authorities and accountabilities, and/or ineffective or disproportionate oversight of decision making and/or performance.

(*continued*)

Table 3.2   (Continued)

Risk Type	Categories	Description
	Information	Risks arising from a failure to produce robust, suitable and appropriate data/information and to exploit data/information to its full potential.
	Legal	Risks arising from a defective transaction, a claim being made (including a defence to a claim or a counterclaim) or some other legal event occurring that results in a liability or other loss, or a failure to take appropriate measures to meet legal or regulatory requirements or to protect assets (for example, intellectual property).
	Operations	Risks arising from inadequate, poorly designed or ineffective/inefficient internal processes resulting in fraud, error, impaired customer service (quality and/or quantity of service), non-compliance and/or poor value for money.
	People	Risks arising from ineffective leadership and engagement, suboptimal culture, inappropriate behaviours, the unavailability of sufficient capacity and capability, industrial action and/or non-compliance with relevant employment legislation/HR policies resulting in negative impact on performance.
	Property	Risks arising from property deficiencies or poorly designed or ineffective/ inefficient safety management resulting in non-compliance and/or harm and suffering to employees, contractors, service users or the public.
	Security	Risks arising from a failure to prevent unauthorized and/or inappropriate access to the estate and information, including cyber security and non-compliance with General Data Protection Regulation requirements.
	Technology	Risks arising from technology not delivering the expected services due to inadequate or deficient system/process development and performance or inadequate resilience.
Project	Project	Risks that change programmes and projects are not aligned with strategic priorities and do not successfully and safely deliver requirements and intended benefits to time, cost and quality.
Reputation	Reputation	Risks arising from adverse events, including ethical violations, a lack of sustainability, systemic or repeated failures or poor quality or a lack of innovation, leading to damages to reputation and or destruction of trust and relations.

3. Rationale for operational risk categorization

Operational risk exposures arise from the day-to-day operations of organizations. These operations span many activities and processes and require people, systems and equipment to perform them in an efficient and effective manner. Given the breadth of organizational activities and the diverse processes, people, systems and equipment required to fulfil them, the number of potential operational risk exposures is substantial.

In view of the wide scope of operational risk, categorization can help to organize the identification, assessment, monitoring and control of specific types of exposure, as well as the causes and effects of these exposures. Different categories of operational risk may require specific risk assessment techniques and control approaches. Equally, some may be insurable (liability claims and property damage), others not (regulatory fines).

The specific benefits are as follows:

- Identification: an operational risk categorization provides a 'menu' of potential risks, which can be used as a prompt in determining those that are relevant to an organization or its specific departments and functions. This should help prevent risks from being overlooked.

- Assessment: the use of consistent terms and descriptions facilitates comparisons between operational risks and supports data aggregation (especially where risks are sub-categorized).

- Monitoring and reporting: a common frame of reference enables more meaningful analysis and oversight of the outputs generated by an operational risk management framework. For example, management should be better able to prioritize resources to the most significant operational risks, compare risk exposures in different departments and functions, and set more granular targets, limits and thresholds.

- Control: given the scope of operational risk, different categories may require very different control responses. Hence by categorizing these risks customized control strategies may be developed.

4. Key principles for categorizing operational risks

No categorization is ever perfect. Numerous compromises and trade-offs are required. Additionally, the nature, scale and complexity of an organization will influence the approach that is selected.

However, it is essential, whatever categorization is chosen, to minimize the potential for gaps and overlaps. Overlaps will result in time-consuming debates about which category to assign specific exposures. Gaps in categorization are even more serious as they may lead to exposures being ignored until too late. Overlaps do at least mean that the exposure is being recognized but time-consuming bureaucratic debates on classification need to be avoided.

To help minimize the potential for gaps and overlaps there are a number of principles that should be used when categorizing operational risk exposures. These principles are explained below.

4.1 Risk categorizations should be based on established external approaches

The most commonly used external categorization approach for operational risk is provided by the Basel Committee on Banking Regulation (Table 3.3). Though this focuses on financial institutions it represents a good starting point for any operational risk categorization.

The risk categorization presented within the UK Treasury Orange Book (HM Treasury, 2020) and replicated in Table 3.2, provides an alternative approach. The Orange Book categorization is less detailed, but still represents a good starting point for any categorization.

Starting with a recognized external approach to operational risk categorization should help ensure that potential exposures are not missed. However, organizations need not follow an external categorization precisely; see section 4.2 below. This might mean adding new categories, changing the definitions of categories or changing how a category is worded.

4.2 Risk categorizations should be customized

Though an established external categorization provides a useful starting point for any categorization, organizations may need to adapt them. Adaptation may be required to suit the nature, scale and complexity of an organization's operations, along with the activities and objectives of its various departments and functions. Such adaptions will ensure that the language contained within a categorization makes sense to the user population.

Where organizations do decide to deviate from an external categorization it is recommended that a mapping exercise is completed to ensure that all relevant categories are included. It may also be that an organization is required to use an external approach (e.g. the Basel categorization in the case of financial institutions) for regulatory reporting. Here it is especially important that no category is missed out.

Table 3.3 Basel perational risk categorization

Event Type Category (Level 1)	Definition	Categories (Level 2)	Activity Examples (Level 3)
Internal Fraud	Losses due to acts of a type intended to defraud, misappropriate property or circumvent regulations, the law or company policy, excluding diversity/ discrimination events, which involves at least one internal party	Unauthorized Activity	• Transactions not reported (intentional) • Transaction type unauthorized (with monetary loss) • Mismarking of position (intentional)
		Theft and Fraud	• Fraud / credit fraud / worthless deposits • Theft / extortion / embezzlement / robbery • Misappropriation of assets • Malicious destruction of assets • Forgery • Check kiting • Smuggling Account takeover / impersonation etc • Tax non-compliance / evasion (wilful) • Bribes / kickbacks • Insider trading (not on firm's account)
External Fraud	Losses due to acts of a type intended to defraud, misappropriate property or circumvent the law, by a third party	Theft and Fraud	• Theft / robbery • Forgery • Check kiting
		Systems Security	• Hacking damage • Theft of information (with monetary loss)

Category	Description	Subcategory	Activity
Employment practices and workplace safety	Losses arising from acts inconsistent with employment, health or safety laws or agreements, from payment of personal injury claims, or from diversity / discrimination events	Employee Relations	• Compensation, benefit, termination issues • Organized labour activity
		Safe Environment	• General liability (slip and fall etc) • Employee health and safety rules events • Workers compensation
		Diversity and Discrimination	• All discrimination types
Clients, products and business practices	Losses arising from an unintentional or negligent failure to meet a professional obligation to specific clients (including fiduciary and suitability requirements), or from the nature or design of a product	Suitability, disclosure and fiduciary	• Fiduciary breaches / guideline violations • Suitability / disclosure issues (know-your-customer etc) • Retail customer disclosure violations • Breach of privacy • Aggressive sales • Account churning • Misuse of confidential information • Lender liability
		Improper business or market practices	• Antitrust Improper trade / market practices • Market manipulation • Insider trading (on firm's account) • Unlicensed activity • Money laundering

(continued)

Table 3.3 (Continued)

Event Type Category (Level 1)	Definition	Categories (Level 2)	Activity Examples (Level 3)
		Product flaws	• Product defects (unauthorized etc) • Model error
		Selection, sponsorship and exposure	• Failure to investigate client per guidelines • Exceeding client exposure limits
		Advisory activities	• Disputes over performance of advisory activities
Damage to physical assets	Losses arising from loss or damage to physical assets from natural disaster or other events	Disasters and other events	• Natural disaster losses • Human losses from external sources (terrorism, vandalism)
Business disruption and system failures	Losses arising from disruption of business or system failures	Systems	• Hardware • Software • Telecommunications • Utility outage / disruptions
Execution, delivery and process management	Losses from failed transaction processing or process management, from relations with trade counterparties and vendors	Transaction capture, execution and maintenance	• Miscommunication • Data entry, maintenance or loading error • Missed deadline or responsibility • Model / system mis-operation • Accounting error / entity attribution error • Other task mis-performance • Delivery failure • Collateral management failure • Reference data maintenance

Monitoring and reporting	• Failed mandatory reporting obligation • Inaccurate external report (loss incurred)
Customer intake and documentation	• Client permissions / disclaimers missing • Legal documents missing / incomplete
Customer / client account management	• Unapproved access given to accounts • Incorrect client records (loss incurred) • Negligent loss or damage of client assets
Trade counterparties	• Non-client counterparty mis-performance • Miscellaneous non-client counterparty disputes
Vendors and suppliers	• Outsourcing • Vendor disputes

CASE STUDY 3.2   Truro City Council (Cornwall, UK)

Like many local authorities in the UK, Truro City Council publishes its risk management strategy online (Truro City Council, 2020). This strategy includes the council's approach to risk categorization.

For operational risk Truro City Council lists seven risk types, summarized in Table 3.4.

Table 3.4   Operational risk categorization of Truro City Council

Professional	Risks associated with specific professions (accounting, social care, etc)
Financial	Risks associated with financial planning and control; plus, the adequacy of insurance cover
Legal	Potential for legislative breaches and compensation claims
Physical	Health and safety incidents affecting employees, residents and third parties; plus, damage caused by fires, floods, wind, etc
Contractual	Failure of contractors to deliver goods and services at the agreed cost or specification
Technological	Events relating to a reliance on technology; includes IT systems, equipment and machinery failures
Environmental	All forms of environmental pollution (chemical, noise, etc); plus, energy efficiency of the council's operations

Some of the operational risk categories chosen by Truro City Council are the same as those in the Orange Book (Table 3.2). Others are different. These differences can be explained by the nature of the work performed by the council. As stated in the strategy, the seven risk types were selected because these are the ones that managers and staff encounter in their day-to-day work.

4.3 Consultation is essential

The directors, managers and employees of an organization should be comfortable with any categorization. Specifically, they must be able to understand the terms and descriptions that are used, and the categorization must be usable and support the work that they do.

It is recommended that an initial, draft, categorization is developed by the operational risk function, using one of the established external categorizations as a foundation. Comments should then be invited from all those that will be involved in the use of the categorization (e.g. risk owners, governing body, internal audit, compliance, etc) to ensure that they understand the terms and descriptions used. They could also be invited to suggest omitted categories that may be relevant for the organization, but which are not captured by an external categorization. However, where this is done, care should be taken to check whether any additional categories are simply a rewording of an existing category, as well as whether they can be mapped back to one of the categories within the external approach used as a basis for the categorization.

4.4 Periodic review

An organization's operations and its associated operational risk exposures will change on a regular basis. It may also be that, through the use of a categorization, gaps and overlaps are identified that were not considered at the initial design stage. Equally, new types of risk may emerge, as was the case with cyber risk. Hence, to ensure that any categorization remains valid, periodic review is necessary. Usually this should be completed on an annual basis.

Care should be taken when changing a pre-existing categorization. Changes to a categorization may make it harder to track trends or interfere with historical data aggregation. When any change is made to a pre-existing category this should be mapped back to the previous categorization to allow data to be carried forward into subsequent risk assessments, for example. This is especially important where statistical tools and models are used to support risk assessment.

Adding new categories is easier, but it is important to double check whether a 'new' category is not simply a reimagining of a pre-existing one. Adding multiple new categories may also make the categorization unnecessarily complex, especially if they increase the potential for overlaps and misclassifications.

5. Designing an operational risk categorization

Designing an operational risk categorization requires great care. Errors at the design stage may make a categorization inefficient and time-consuming to use. Worse, it may result in important operational risks from being overlooked. This section outlines the key factors to consider when designing a categorization.

5.1 The basis of categorization: cause, event or effect?

Like any type of risk, operational risks are multifaceted, meaning that they are a combination of causes, events and effects. Figure 3.1 illustrates the relationship between them.

Figure 3.1   Cause, event and effect (author's own)

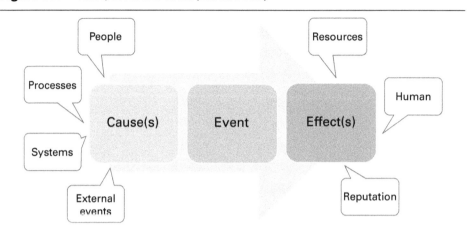

The Basel II definition of operational risk (see Chapter 1) demarcates operational risk on the basis of its causes: people, processes and systems, and external events. These causes may result in a wide range of operational risk events (fires, floods, theft, errors and omissions, etc). In turn these events have multiple effects (financial loss, physical injuries, etc). A categorization may be based on any one of these three facets of operational risk. However, it is not recommended to build a categorization based on all three – this could result in user confusion and result in many categorization gaps or overlaps.

Categorizations based on operational risk events are most common. The Basel categorization in Table 3.3 is event based, so financial institutions are often required to report their operational losses using this categorization, and therefore decide to use it elsewhere to ensure consistency. In addition, operational risk data is usually collected on a per-event basis (see Chapter 8). This is because reported operational risk events are the most visible manifestation of the presence of operational risk in an organization.

One of the advantages of an event-based approach is that it does not preclude the further sub-division of events into their constituent causes and effects. This allows an organization to better picture the relationships between causes, events and effects, highlighting potential correlations or concentrations of risk.

However, a downside of an event-based approach is that the associated categorization approach can become very detailed, in an attempt to reflect the totality of events that may occur. This requires careful consideration of the issue of granularity (see section 5.3, below).

Causal-based categorizations have an intuitive appeal because they represent the starting point for operational risk exposures and so may help make operational risk management more leading and proactive. However, effective classifications are hard to achieve in practice. Though the broad categories of causes are small, specific causes are numerous, often more numerous than potential events. The absence of established external approaches for categorizing operational risks according to their causes also makes them more challenging. The same arguments apply to effect-based categorizations (numerous sub-effects, especially non-financial effects, and no external categorization).

In most cases operational risks are best categorized on an event basis. However, where possible high-level sub-categorizations for their causes and effects should be used to complement an event-based categorization. This will allow an organization to better link causes, events and effects, and to identify and mitigate potentially dangerous patterns in these causes and effects.

CASE STUDY 3.3   The causes and effects of the Covid-19 pandemic on organizations

The Covid-19 pandemic is an event that illustrates how complex the causes and effects of an operational event may be. The underlying cause was external, the natural emergence of a new zoonotic virus (transmitted from animals to humans), but the spread of the virus is linked to a range of system, process and human failures (The Independent Panel, 2021). Pandemic preparedness was inconsistent and underfunded in many countries and the global pandemic alert system was too slow.

The net result was a fast-spreading global pandemic and government responses that all but stopped global travel and forced citizens to remain in their homes. For many organizations, these responses caused significant disruption to their operations, as they struggled to cope with things such as site closures, supply chain disruption and home working.

Hence the emergence of Covid-19 and the global failure to control its spread caused a large number of organizations to experience a major business disruption event. In addition, the preparedness of these organizations and their ability to adapt to the fast-changing implications of the pandemic also caused differences in the level and type of disruption that they experienced.

In terms of the effects of the pandemic on organizations these have been far-reaching also. There have been human, resource and reputation effects. Reputations have worsened or improved depending on the ability of organizations to maintain their operations (see Chapter 11 for more on operational resilience). Plus, from a financial perspective there have been winners and losers. Online and essential retailers such as supermarkets have profited, while the travel, tourism and hospitality sectors have suffered large losses. Then there are the human effects, both the loss of life from the virus and the mental health consequences of the various lockdowns and quarantine requirements – effects that impact on organizations through the loss of key staff, general staff shortages and reduced morale/productivity.

5.2 *Minimizing gaps and overlaps*

The minimization of gaps and overlaps requires trade-offs. A very detailed categorization should eliminate most gaps but may result in frequent overlaps and misclassification problems. In contrast, a less detailed classification should make it easier to categorize risks but could result in important risks being missed.

The best approach is to develop levels of classification. The initial level of classification is kept relatively broad, with additional layers added to provide further detail (see section 5.3 below). The advantages of such an approach is that all operational risk events should be classifiable, while the layers of detail help users to apportion events, thus preventing overlaps and gaps.

To further avoid gaps, it may appear tempting to include an 'other' category to capture risks that cannot be allocated to any other category. However, such a category can become overloaded with risks that could be categorized elsewhere. Rather than provide a catch-all 'other' category, where a discrete new category of risk emerges, it should be added to the categorization.

5.3 *Granularity*

Determining the level of detail in any operational risk categorization is an essential decision. Less granularity will make the categorization easier to manage and aggregate data for assessment and reporting purposes, but more detail will assist the focus of management and support mitigation. Some organizations adopt a compromise solution, which involves adding more granularity for critical categories but accepting less detail for categories of lower significance (in terms of volume and/or value). This avoids the trap of too few risks spread across too many categories, resulting in an inability to aggregate.

Various layers of granularity are possible. Table 3.5 summarizes the most common.

The Basel operational risk categorization in Table 3.3 illustrates the first three levels of granularity.

Not all organizations may elect to have granularity levels 2 or 3 in Table 3.5. But most will have level 4. This is to allow specific departments, functions, etc to customize the categorization to meet their specific needs, while ensuring that all risks can be mapped back to a level 1 category.

The advantage of levels 2 and 3 is that they add extra detail. This detail can help users to ensure that risks are categorized in a consistent manner. In addition, it can reduce the potential for risks being overlooked, because users have not considered a specific aspect of a risk event (e.g. internal as well as external hacking attacks).

Table 3.5   Levels of granularity for operational risk categorization

Level	Explanation
1	A small number of high-level labels reflecting, for example, common categories of events, the generic systems and processes of an organization, areas of regulatory concern or the organization's objectives. For example: acts of God (fires, etc), business continuity, IT systems, legal and regulatory, financial crime, etc.
2	The level-1 categories split into their logical component parts, depending on the specific manifestations of these events. For example, acts of God might be split into fires, floods, windstorms, etc; financial crime into internal and external fraud; or IT systems into hacking attacks and equipment failures.
3	Level-2 categories further sub-divided to reflect the operational activities that may occur within an organization's divisions, departments, or functions.
4	A detailed description of the level-2 or 3 (where present) operational risk events that may occur within a specific context (e.g. payroll, manufacturing, sales, etc).

5.4 Language

Getting the language right is essential to ensure consistency of use. This means providing clear and unambiguous definitions and descriptions for each category of risk. Non-technical language (so-called plain English) is recommended, as this will reduce the potential for any misunderstanding.

6. Implementation

This section outlines the factors that should be considered when implementing an operational risk categorization, along with some common challenges and how these challenges may be overcome.

6.1 Roles and responsibilities

An operational risk classification will influence many operational risk management activities across all of the departments and functions that make up an organization. Table 3.6 outlines the primary users of the classification and their responsibilities.

Table 3.6   The primary users of operational risk classifications

Role	Responsibilities
Governing body and senior managers	The governing body supported by senior management have responsibility for ensuring that a sound system of operational risk management is in place. This includes ensuring that an appropriate risk categorization is in place and working as intended.
Risk owners and other staff with operational risk management responsibilities	Risk owners are business managers with responsibility for the management of some or all operational risks in their area. Risk owners should ensure that they and their staff understand the operational risk categorization and that it is used correctly to support risk identification, reporting, etc. All other staff with operational risk management responsibilities must ensure that they understand the categorization and use it correctly.
Operational risk function	The operational risk function is responsible for the design of the operational risk management categorization and for ensuring that it is used consistently. To support the implementation of the categorization the operational risk function should ensure that it is clearly documented and that an appropriate description of each category is provided. Mechanisms for dealing with any boundary issues (see section 6.4) should also be explained. This documentation could be supported by training and awareness activities, to help ensure that all relevant staff understand the categorization and can use it effectively.
Internal audit	Internal audit is responsible for providing assurance to the governing body and supporting senior management that an operational risk categorization approach is fit for purpose and working as intended. Internal audit may choose to use the operational risk classification to support audit planning and to structure management actions in audit reports, linking each action to one or more category of operational risk. Where possible this approach is recommended, as it can help to embed the categorization approach and ensure a consistent approach to operational risk.

6.2 Ensuring consistent use

Consistency of use is key. If different managers or parts of the organization classify similar risks differently then it will be impossible to achieve an accurate organization-wide view of its operational risks.

A key challenge to consistency is that categories are rarely mutually exclusive. This means that the users of any operational risk categorization may find that a risk could be placed into two or more categories. For example, a fraud committed by a former employee might be classified as either an internal or external fraud.

A related challenge is that risk events can be related, with the occurrence of one event causing another to occur. For example, an external hacking attack might, in turn, result in a systems failure as well as data theft. Such an event could be categorized as an external fraud or cyber attack (the underlying cause) or as a systems failure or data theft event.

There are no easy or universal solutions to these categorization challenges. But it is essential to agree a consistent approach for them across an organization. As a general rule the following is recommended:

- Operational risk events should be categorized according to the underlying or original event. In the case of the above hacking attack example this means classifying the event as an external hacking (cyber) attack, rather than a systems failure or data theft event. However, the potential for such an event to impact on systems continuity and security should be noted and addressed in any management response.

- Procedures should be documented on how to resolve any classification difficulties. As a general rule, if managers are in any doubt about how an operational risk should be classified they should refer the matter to the operational risk function for a decision.

- These procedures should be supported by training on how to categorize operational risks in a consistent manner. Ideally this training should include local examples of risks and explain how they should be categorized.

- Where an IT system is used to support operational risk management, the risk categorization should be embedded within this system and include guidance on how to classify risks appropriately (e.g. drop-down descriptions of each risk category).

- As part of the periodic review process of the operational risk categorization, attention should be paid to problem categories, where management find it most difficult to allocate risks in a consistent manner. Where possible these categories should be amended, in consultation with management, to correct any issues.

6.3 *Reporting*

The structure of operational risk reports should reflect, where possible, the agreed operational risk categorization. This should ensure the accurate aggregation of operational risk data and help embed the categorization across the organization.

An operational risk categorization should also be used to adjust the level of detail provided in reports. As a general rule the governing body will require reports that summarize any significant exposures or loss events in relation to an organization's level-1 (see Table 3.5) operational risk categories; senior management significant exposures/loss events in relation to the level-2 categories and for departmental/functional managers' exposure to their local level 2 or 3, if used.

6.4 *Addressing boundary events*

A boundary event can be defined as one that becomes apparent in one risk type but has its causes in a different risk type, e.g. an insurance risk or credit risk loss that has arisen as a result of an underlying operational risk event (e.g. a process or control failure). For example, a creditor default is an example of credit risk, but the underlying cause may have been errors in the due diligence process, which meant that credit was provided to a counterparty with a poor credit rating.

Boundary events are inevitable for most organizations. They can be particularly problematic in organizations that have discrete risk functions (e.g. a credit risk management function and an operational risk management function). This is because arguments may occur over which function 'owns' the risk. It may also lead to a waste of management resources because it is double managed. Even worse, risks may be overlooked, with each function assuming that it is the other's responsibility.

Boundary events are less problematic in organizations that have mechanisms for coordinating the management of different risk types, such as an enterprise risk management framework or a holistic risk function led by a chief risk officer. Cross-discipline training can also help, where specialist risk functions learn about the work of their peers (e.g. operational risk training for the credit risk function and vice-versa – as can the establishment of a cross-disciplinary risk committee that discusses potential boundary events and apportions responsibility for their management to the relevant risk function.

7. Conclusion

Given the variety of operational risks it is important that they are organized in a consistent way. Well designed and implemented operational risk categorizations help to ensure consistency, prevent risks from being overlooked and reduce the potential for wasteful overlaps in management effort.

Though there is no one best way to categorize operational risks, designing and implementing an approach suited to the nature, scale and complexity of an organization's activities is essential. A sound operational risk categorization is the skeleton that supports the entire operational risk management framework. A weak approach to categorization will mean a weak framework, however effective the other elements are believed to be.

Reflective practice questions

1 Is your organization's operational risk categorization based on a respected external approach, such as the Basel or Orange book categorizations? If yes, have you reviewed these categorizations for relevance to your organization and made amendments where necessary?

2 Do you periodically review your operational risk categorization to check for gaps (omitted risks) and to mitigate identified overlaps?

3 What level of granularity do you use for your operational risk categorization? Would a more granular approach help to prevent risks from being omitted and support the aggregation of operational risk assessments for reporting purposes?

4 Is your operational risk categorization written in plain English and easy to understand?

5 Do the first line (front-line management), second line (risk functions) and third line (audit) all use the same operational risk categorization? If not, why?

6 How do you address boundary events? Is a documented procedure in place?

References

Note: Some of the sources included in this chapter have been listed previously. Only new sources are listed below.

The Independent Panel (2021) Covid-19: Make it the last pandemic, The Independent Panel for Pandemic Preparedness & Response, https://theindependentpanel.org/mainreport/ (archived at https://perma.cc/F9HH-F9GZ)

Truro City Council (2020) Risk management strategy revision 12, March, https://www.truro.gov.uk/_UserFiles/Files/Risk%20Management%20Strategy%20March%202020.pdf (archived at https://perma.cc/3WQZ-B8Y9)

Risk culture

04

LEARNING OUTCOMES

- Explain what risk culture is and why it matters from an operational risk perspective.
- Compare different approaches to assessing and monitoring risk culture.
- Know how to influence an organization's risk culture.

1. Introduction

Organizations contain people who work together to achieve common objectives. Wherever there are people there is culture, a social mechanism that helps them to collaborate and coordinate their activities. An organization's culture, and by extension its risk culture, are both a source of strength and weakness when it comes to the management of operational risk. An appropriate risk culture will ensure that staff accept the importance of effective operational risk management and behave in a manner consistent with the organization's operational risk policies, procedures and appetite. An inappropriate risk culture can both cause adverse operational risk events and intensify their impact.

This chapter explains how risk culture may be identified, assessed and influenced to help reduce the probability and impact of adverse operational risk events. It must be emphasized that there is no one optimal risk culture, nor are there universal characteristics for a 'strong' or 'weak' risk culture. However, it is important that organizations work to understand the operational risk management implications of their risk cultures and influence these cultures where appropriate.

CASE STUDY 4.1   The Barclays London Interbank Offer Rate (LIBOR) scandal

Corporate lawyer and investment banking expert Antony Salz was asked to complete an independent review into LIBOR rigging by Barclays' investment banking division (then known as Barclays Capital) between 2005 and 2009 (Salz, 2013). The review concluded that the underlying cause of the scandal was the inappropriate risk culture of Barclays Capital. In contrast, the review concluded that the risk cultures of Barclays' retail bank and credit card businesses were entirely appropriate for the activities they performed.

At the core of the inappropriate risk culture for Barclays Capital was a drive to win. The division looked to recruit people who were 'winners' and rewarded winning. Pay and bonuses were linked to short-term performance measures and money making was prioritized over serving the needs of clients and customers. In addition, the report noted that senior management in Barclays Capital did not want to hear bad news and encouraged staff to solve problems on their own.

As a result of this inappropriate risk culture, certain staff members within Barclays Capital took it upon themselves to report false rates on the interbank loans they had negotiated with other banks, a cheat-to-win strategy. Lower rates were reported in order to make Barclays appear stronger financially than it was, and so avoid regulatory intervention. For larger clearing banks like Barclays, interbank rates are individually negotiated 'over the counter' rates and the rate of interest paid is in part linked to the financial strength of a bank. The lower this financial strength, the higher the rate of interest, to reflect increased default risk. In turn, this false reporting skewed the headline LIBOR rate, Barclays being a large bank and a major player in the interbank lending market.

As the Salz report noted, the LIBOR scandal damaged the reputation of Barclays and the UK banking sector more generally. Barclays also faced fines of £290 million from UK and US regulators.

The Barclays LIBOR scandal highlights the consequences of an inappropriate risk culture. It also shows that it is wrong to blame such scandals solely on the actions of the immediate perpetrators. People work within risk cultures and their actions are heavily influenced by them. Ultimately it was the senior managers and directors in position at that time who failed to ensure that an appropriate risk culture was in place.

2. Understanding risk culture

Like any human–social construct, risk culture is a difficult concept to understand, let alone define. From a practical perspective the accuracy of one definition or another is unimportant, providing a common understanding is shared across the organization, especially in terms of what is included in risk culture and what is not. It is particularly important that senior management and the board understand what is in and out of scope, both to help manage their expectations and to minimize gaps and overlaps with other areas of work.

The Institute of Risk Management (IRM, 2021) defines risk culture as follows:

> A term describing the values, beliefs, knowledge, attitudes and understanding about risk shared by a group of people with a common purpose. This applies to all organizations – including private companies, public bodies, governments and not-for-profits.

This is as good a definition as any. One key strength is its inclusiveness, reflected in the range of terms used to describe risk culture (values, beliefs, etc). Another is the

Table 4.1   Defining characteristics of risk culture applied to operational risk management

Values	The values of the organization and how they may relate to and influence the management of operational risk. Many organizations state several values (e.g. putting the customer first or emphasizing sustainability over short-term profit) that they believe complement their mission and objective. These values may influence how staff perceive risk and risk management. Groups of people in different parts of the organization may also develop their own values, which may either reinforce or contradict group management activities, including operational risk management.
Beliefs	What people believe about the importance of operational risk and the benefits and costs of operational risk management. Some people may share positive, others negative, beliefs.
Knowledge	What people know about operational risk and how to manage it, in effect their competence for operational risk management. Some people may have a good knowledge of the range of operational risk events their area is exposed to and how to manage them, others may be less knowledgeable.
Attitudes	Most individuals have an attitude or preference towards specific types of risk, like operational risk. Some may be very risk averse, others risk preferring. In an organizational context, research shows that risk attitudes tend to align, at least within specific social groups. Attitudes can differ for certain types of risk, for example, people may be more averse to risks where they perceive a large potential downside (threats). In contrast they may be less averse to risks that are associated with opportunities, such as the potential for generating a profit.
Understanding	Knowledge is gained through education and training (learning), understanding comes with experience. Some people may have a better understanding of operational risk management because they are actively and regularly involved in the identification, assessment and control of operational risks.

emphasis on the human–social aspect of risk culture. Table 4.1 provides further detail, from an operational risk context, on the key terms used in this definition.

Building on Table 4.1, three elements require further emphasis:

- Risk culture is concerned with risk taking as well as risk control. All organizations must take risks to achieve their objectives, and this may include having to accept a degree of operational risk exposure. An organization's risk culture will influence whether people perceive an operational risk to be beneficial (e.g. associated with the pursuit of a potential opportunity) or a threat. It may also influence whether they perceive operational risk management activities to be a benefit or cost.

- Each of the characteristics within Table 4.1 exist on three levels (Figure 4.1):

Figure 4.1   Risk-culture iceberg (author's own)

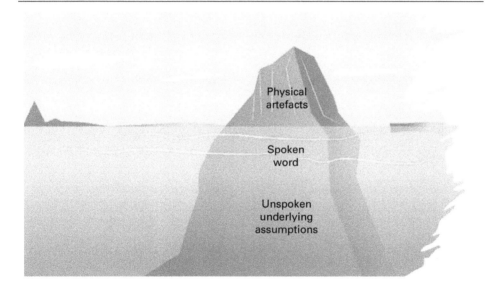

  o The top level relates to the structures (e.g. reporting and governance) and documentation that exists on operational risk management. For example, policies, procedures, terms of reference, minutes and reports. This level is the most visible and easiest to analyse. However, it represents only the tip of the risk-culture iceberg.

  o The middle level relates to what is said about operational risk and its management by people across the organization. One key element of this is 'tone from the top', but it includes the 'tune in the middle', meaning what staff below top management are saying and whether they are receptive to the top management 'tone'.

o The bottom level relates to assumptions and perceptions that are taken for granted, so much so that they are rarely verbalized. For example, people may have deep-seated and mutually reinforced views on specific operational risks or operational risk management activities. For example, they may refuse to accept the importance of certain risks (e.g. cyber or pandemic risks) or they may innately assume that operational risk management is a bureaucratic exercise that has limited business benefit.

- While organizations may wish to implement a consistent, enterprise-wide risk culture, they must recognize that sub-cultures often exist (as in the case of Barclays Capital and the LIBOR scandal, see Case Study 4.1). Sub-cultures emerge because people are most influenced, culturally, by those in proximity. Even in smaller organizations sub-cultures can exist, for example people in a specific department or geographic location. Sub-cultures are not necessarily a problem, especially where people have different roles, accountabilities and objectives. However, they can become dangerous where a specific group develops values, beliefs or attitudes that are contrary to those of the wider organization and the needs of its stakeholders. The assessment of risk cultures, including sub-cultures, is explained in the next section.

3. Assessing risk culture

Many organizations that choose to formalize their work on risk culture will assess it in some way. These assessments may be conducted by the operational risk function or a wider enterprise risk function, though it is also common for them to be conducted by internal audit as part of their assurance activities. Human resources staff may be involved, because of their knowledge and understanding of people and an organization's wider culture.

Assessing risk culture is fraught with challenges. Remember that risk culture is a human–social construct. Such constructs are complex, highly subject and difficult to assess in an accurate way. In addition, the conduct and interpretation of risk culture assessments may themselves be influenced by the risk culture of an organization.

CASE STUDY 4.2   Assessing risk culture in financial organizations

Power, Ashby and Palermo (2013) investigated the activities taken to assess and influence the risk cultures of a wide range of financial organizations. As part of this research, they developed a risk-culture questionnaire (see Appendix A) and offered this to financial organizations so that they could assess their risk culture. They then observed how these organizations completed the assessments and interpreted the results.

The researchers found that the interpretation of risk-culture assessments was endogenous, meaning that the prevailing risk culture of an organization influenced how management interpreted the results of a risk-culture survey.

For example, in one organization that completed the survey, they concluded that the results indicated that they were overly risk averse, and that decision making was overly consensual. This conclusion reflected fears at the time that the organization was slow to make operational risk management decisions and was so averse to operational risk that customer service was being affected. A careful, and neutral, review of the results did not indicate such conclusions.

Reflecting the complexity of risk culture there are various assessment approaches that can be adopted, each with their own strengths and weaknesses. Organizations should choose an assessment approach with care, to ensure that it is appropriate for their unique situation. They may also choose to combine two or more approaches to build a more complete picture of their risk culture.

Whatever the approach, or approaches, chosen organizations should remember that risk-culture assessments are never 100 per cent accurate. All they can do is provide a rough snapshot of an organization's risk culture at a particular point in time. This is analogous to the current 'mood' of the organization in relation to operational risk and its management, sometimes referred to as the risk climate (Sheedy, Griffin and Barbour 2017). Referring back to Figure 3.1 such assessments should provide a good picture of the current physical artefacts that can be observed at the surface of a risk culture, along with a reasonable, though less clear, indication of the spoken word. However, the unspoken, underlying assumptions of a risk culture are often too deeply embedded to be assessed and interpreted accurately.

3.1 Questionnaires

Questionnaires are a research instrument that use a specific set of questions to gather information from respondents. In the context of risk culture, questionnaires are used to gather information on the values, beliefs, attitudes and understanding of respondents in relation to risk and its management – information that is then aggregated and possibly subject to statistical analysis to arrive at an overall perspective on an organization's risk culture and potential risk sub-cultures. An example questionnaire is provided in Appendix A. This is the questionnaire used by Power, Ashby and Palermo (2013), as part of their risk-culture research project.

Care should be taken when designing a questionnaire. All the usual principles of good questionnaire design apply, for example, avoid leading questions, do not make the questionnaire too long, and ensure you collect a representative sample. In addition, think carefully about the specific aspects of an organization's risk culture that you wish to investigate. Most risk cultures are too multifaceted and complex to assess in one simple questionnaire. However, specific aspects of the risk culture may be targeted. For example:

- whether people share the aims and objectives for operational risk management outlined in the operational risk management policy;

- attitudes towards the operational risk function or specific operational risk tools and procedures (e.g. risk and control self-assessments);

- the presence of sub-cultures, by looking for differences in response between different functions, locations or levels of seniority;

- whether people believe that the organization is taking too much or too little operational risk; and

- whether people have adequate knowledge and understanding of operational risk (so-called risk awareness).

The advantages of questionnaires are that they can reach a significant number of people across the organization. Plus, the basic results are easy to compile, especially if using an online survey tool. However, questionnaires are time-consuming to construct and to complete. As a result, many organizations choose to complete them on a one-off basis or at best infrequently (every two to three years, for example). This limits their usefulness. Ideally, repeat surveys should be completed at least once a year. This allows the organization to see how its risk culture is evolving and analyse the effectiveness of any control measures.

When using a questionnaire to assess risk culture it is important to obtain a statistically representative sample of respondents. This means circulating to a significant number of people across the organization, in terms of geographic location, department, role function (e.g. first, second and third lines of defence) and seniority. This will help to stratify differences in responses and identify indications of counter sub-cultures. Alternatively, questionnaires could be targeted at specific locations, departments or role functions, especially where concerns exist about the nature of their sub-cultures. For example, where there is excessive operational risk taking, or evidence of ineffective control.

Finally, there is the potential for respondents to fill in questionnaires incorrectly, either because they are disengaged and in a rush to complete or because they deliberately enter false information to protest against a particular issue. The use of experts in questionnaire design can help to mitigate this problem. Trained experts can design questions to check the internal consistency (also known as the reliability) of responses. See Krosnick (2018) for some of the latest research on questionnaire design. For research in relation to risk-culture questionnaires see Sheedy, Griffin and Barbour (2017).

3.2 Interviews

Interviews should normally be conducted on a semi-structured basis. This means asking high-level, but non-leading questions that allow the interviewee freedom to highlight the information that they perceive to be important. Examples include:

- In the conduct of your role, what does operational risk mean to you?
- How would you explain the value of operational risk management to someone outside the organization?
- In your opinion what are the most important objectives for operational risk management?

These questions should be forwarded to the interviewee in advance, in the form of an agenda to allow them to prepare. If necessary, slightly more specific follow-up questions can be used to clarify responses. In all cases interviews should be recorded to allow subsequent analysis. Ideally, multiple interviews should be conducted in any one area to cross-check responses. Any discrepancies can then be followed up with the interviewees to determine the reasons behind them.

The advantage of interviews is that they provide a deeper, more complete picture, reflected in what people have said about the organization's risk culture during the interviews. Recorded interviews may also be transcribed and cross-analysed for common themes. This can be done by highlighting common themes or phrases that occur within several interviews.

The key problem with interviews is cost. To allow an adequate discussion interviews should last at least 30 minutes, preferably an hour. This means that they can take up a lot of time and resource. Hence it is better to use them in a targeted fashion. For example, to complement a questionnaire by interviewing a sample of the respondents to help clarify and add depth to their responses, or to examine a particular sub-culture that may be of concern.

There is no optimal number of interviews, though most academic studies of culture in organizations include 20–30. Usually interviews are conducted to a 'thematic saturation point'. This means that the points raised in the interviews become increasingly common, with little new information identified. It is also good practice to complete an initial set of interviews (say 10–20), analyse the results, refine the questions and repeat, to check if any new information is identified and/or to add detail and clarity to the original findings.

3.3 Focus groups

Focus groups can be conducted in a similar manner to interviews (semi-structured, open questions, provide an advance agenda, etc). The key advantage over interviews is that focus groups allow for a group discussion, helping to highlight common themes or issues regarding an organization's risk culture.

Ideally, two people should facilitate a focus group. One to take the lead on asking the questions and the other to observe and interject if they feel that an important point has not been discussed adequately, or to clarify meaning.

Focus groups can help to clarify the findings of a questionnaire or series of interviews. The agenda for such a focus group would include a presentation of the questionnaire or interview results, followed by an open discussion on the significance and meaning of these findings.

Using focus groups to discuss the results of other assessment tools can help mitigate the potential for interpretation bias. However, the composition and facilitation of such a focus group requires extreme care. It is important that such focus groups comprise a diverse cross-section of people (different departments, experience, age, gender, etc), to ensure that any local social biases are challenged. In addition, the facilitator must ensure that focus-group discussions are not dominated by particular individuals, such as the most senior manager or director.

See Krueger and Casey (2001) for more information on running focus groups.

CASE STUDY 4.3   Facilitating a focus group

A focus group is presented with the results of a risk-culture questionnaire. The Head of Customer Services concludes that the results indicate that staff are too averse to operational risk and devote an excessive amount of time to control activities. As a result, she believes that the risk culture is not sufficiently agile and customer focused, because of excessive bureaucracy. Several others agree, including the Chief Executive Officer (CEO).

The Head of Finance provides the opposite perspective. A debate ensues, chaired by the lead facilitator, who ensures that all attendees contribute equally. Following this debate, it is agreed that staff are excessively averse to certain types of operational risk, but that they do not appreciate the importance of others (e.g. internal fraud).

The benefit of this debate, and the presence of diverse views, is that a misinterpretation of the results of the questionnaire is avoided. Focus groups can be an excellent complement to risk-culture questionnaires, helping to add detail to questionnaire results and avoiding their misinterpretation.

3.4 Direct observation

In the performance of their duties operational risk professionals will encounter people from across their organization. This provides them with the opportunity to observe people's values, beliefs, attitudes, knowledge and understanding of risk and risk management. Though it may appear more subjective than a questionnaire or interview, direct observation is a powerful assessment tool for risk culture. Direct observation is used widely by professional risk-culture researchers such as anthropologists and psychologists (see Douglas and Wildavsky, 1983).

A simple approach to direct observation is to maintain a log of encounters with people from different locations or departments. It is not necessary to record names, to preserve the anonymity of people, just the date, location and department(s), as well as the number present. In the log, reflect on how the people you have encountered talk about risk and risk management (e.g. whether they view them in positive or negative terms), as well as their attitudes towards operational risk policies and procedures. It is also helpful to reflect on their body language: for example, whether they appeared relaxed or agitated when interacting with you.

It is recommended that when you start a log you record as many encounters with people as possible. As you build up a picture of your organization's risk culture and sub-cultures you will be able to reduce the number of entries, only recording new observations, especially those that challenge your existing assessment.

3.5 Third-party risk-culture assessment tools

Many consulting organizations offer risk-culture assessment tools. Most rely on questionnaires to survey staff; some combine this with semi-structured interviews.

There are three potential advantages of using a third-party tool:

- the tool should, in theory, have been developed by experienced professionals who know how to assess risk culture;
- they are outside the organization's risk culture, which should help prevent interpretation bias; and
- they can compare the results of an assessment with other, similar organizations and help to share good practice.

The main disadvantages are:

- they will only have limited exposure to an organization's risk culture, and will not understand it as deeply as in-house risk professionals;
- questionnaires may be generic, not customized for the organization;

- questionnaires sometimes focus on the management of risk culture, rather than the actual, underlying risk culture, and take the view that there is a single, optimal approach to managing risk culture, which is *not* the case.

When using a third party to assess risk culture it is recommended that both questionnaires and focus groups should be performed, at a minimum. Plus, the questionnaire should be customized to meet the unique circumstances of the organization. Never accept a pre-prepared questionnaire, always ask how it has been adapted to suit your organization.

Finally, care should be taken where a third party offers a risk-culture 'score' as an indication of the 'strength' of an organization's risk culture. Such scores are based on the false notion that there is an optimal approach to risk culture. There is no such optimal approach. Scores also reinforce the false notion that risk culture can be measured. Remember that risk-culture assessments are inherently subjective and provide only a rough snapshot of an organization's risk culture.

4. Monitoring risk culture: risk-culture metrics

Assessments of risk culture provide a point-in-time estimate. This can be useful when an organization is beginning to influence its risk culture in a more proactive way, or to help raise senior management and board awareness of risk culture. However, risk cultures change (Salz, 2013) and such change can occur at any time. Risk-culture metrics help organizations to track these changes on a more regular basis than could be achieved using most assessment tools.

Given the resource-intensive nature of risk-culture assessments, a cost-effective alternative is to combine occasional (e.g. annual, biennial, or even triennial) assessments with monthly or possibly quarterly risk-culture metric reports.

Table 4.2 provides a list of metrics that can be used to monitor risk culture. Most are metrics that should already be collected by organizations, only the application of each metric has changed. The advantage of using pre-existing metrics is that there are no additional costs of collection. Plus, there should be pre-existing trend data to help an organization track how its risk culture may have changed over time. This is not designed to be an exhaustive list but should provide a good starting point for organizations looking to begin tracking risk-culture metrics.

There is no maximum or minimum number of risk-culture metrics; organizations should choose the ones that are relevant to them at a particular point in time. However, it is recommended to keep risk-culture metric reports short, typically one to two pages, otherwise management will not have time to review them.

Table 4.2 Example risk-culture metrics

Metric Type	Description
Staff Turnover	High levels of staff turnover mean that significant numbers of new people are joining the organization, which will change the social mix and hence risk culture. High levels of turnover may also be a warning of moral issues, which may have a risk-culture element.
	In contrast, low levels of staff turnover increases the potential for 'group-think'. Group-think is a problem because false and inaccurate perceptions about risk and risk management will go unchallenged.
Staff Conduct	A fall or rise in staff grievances and disciplinaries may indicate a change in risk culture (negative or positive).
Policy Compliance	An increase in compliance is a positive risk-culture indicator, suggesting that attitudes and behaviours are improving and vice-versa.
Internal Audit	High or low levels of audit actions are not necessarily risk-culture indicators; even areas with an appropriate risk culture may have controls that need improving. However, long delays in the completion of audit actions may indicate behavioural issues or a lack of knowledge and understanding about the need for effective operational risk management.
Losses and Near-Misses	A sudden increase or decrease in losses and near-misses might be due to a change in risk culture. In addition, evaluations into the causes of losses and near-misses can include a search for cultural factors.
Risk Communication	One simple but powerful metric is the number of times that business functions contact the operational risk function for unsolicited advice. This indicates the perceived value of the operational risk function.

Where possible, it is good practice to compare metrics from different locations and departments. This will help to highlight risk sub-cultures. Regular input from relevant professionals, notably HR and audit, can also be used to support the monitoring of risk sub-cultures. In the course of their duties, they may well come across values, beliefs and attitudes that could be a cause for concern. The operational risk function should work to build good relations with these professionals to ensure that they report any concerns.

One way to select an appropriate set of metrics is to complete an initial risk-culture assessment, using one or more of the tools above. Then the results of this assessment can be used to help select an appropriate set of risk-culture metrics. The metrics selected might address specific aspects of concern identified during an assessment, such as potentially problematic beliefs or values relating to the overall risk culture or particular sub-cultures. It is good practice to consult on the selection of these metrics with relevant experts to ensure that they are appropriate. For example, consult with HR when selecting human-resource-related metrics, internal audit for audit metrics, etc. It is also good practice to share the selected set of metrics with senior management and the board to get their input. In some regulatory regimes they are held accountable for the monitoring and influencing of risk culture (see Chapter 12).

CASE STUDY 4.4 Selecting risk-culture metrics

The results of a risk-culture assessment reveals that the employees of an organization do not understand the value of operational risk management. They see it primarily as a compliance tool that does not contribute to the organization's performance. The survey also reveals a non-accountability culture, whereby people believe that operational risk is the sole responsibility of the operational risk function.

The organization takes steps to influence these findings and improve the appropriateness of its risk culture. To help monitor progress a number of risk-culture metrics are selected. Firstly, metrics are chosen to keep track of policy compliance (e.g. reported incidents of non-compliance). Secondly the internal audit function is asked to supply information on late audit actions to help identify the areas within the organization that are slowest to improve their operational risk management activities. Finally, the operational risk function starts to record the number of interactions they have with front-line management, comparing the number of interactions initiated by them and the number initiated by front-line management. The hope is that an increase in the number of interactions initiated by front-line management will signal improving levels of engagement and accountability.

5. Influencing risk culture: potential interventions

Organizations that assess and monitor their risk culture will usually take steps to influence it in some way. The aim is to mitigate inappropriate aspects of the risk culture and to promote more appropriate values, beliefs and attitudes.

The use of the term 'influence' is deliberate. Talk of managing risk culture implies a greater level of control than is usually the case. Risk cultures are human–social phenomena; this means that they will change over time, even without any organized interventions. Heavy-handed or overly formalized attempts to change a human–social phenomenon like risk culture will often fail. This is because such attempts interfere with the natural evolutionary cycle of the risk culture and can have significant unintended consequences, including amplifying the less appropriate aspects of a risk culture. Values, beliefs and attitudes are very hard to change.

To maximize success, measures should be targeted at specific aspects of the risk culture that an organization wants to change. Broad, far-reaching risk-culture change projects do not tend to succeed. Effective risk-culture change is incremental and takes great skill and time. Staff will resist large-scale, rapid change in most circumstances, but they are more likely to accept incremental influence. Such influencing measures should be complemented with regular monitoring of the risk-culture metrics to help track their effectiveness. It may well be that measures have to be refined several times before they have the desired result.

Organizations employ a range of influencing measures, some of the most common are explained below.

5.1 Strategy and leadership (including tone)

The strategy of an organization in terms of its vision, mission and objectives can have a significant effect on its risk culture and vice-versa. Organizations that promote an aggressive short-term growth or market share strategy are likely to find that its risk culture will change to accommodate this (i.e. the organization will become more risk seeking). Conversely an organization that promotes a conservative market follower strategy will tend to move towards a more risk-averse and risk-controlling culture.

Care should be taken to avoid implementing a strategy that conflicts with the prevailing culture. For example, organizations with a conservative, risk-averse culture should not suddenly adopt an aggressive profit- or growth-orientated strategy because its employees will find it difficult to implement such a strategy, as it will be at odds with their pre-existing beliefs and underlying assumptions about the objectives of their organization.

Leaders and managers throughout an organization have a significant effect on its risk culture. Top-level leaders will generally affect the organization's overall risk culture, while middle managers (department heads, etc) have a significant effect on the sub-cultures of an organization. Some ways in which leaders and managers can have a positive effect on risk culture include:

- Being visible and consistent in terms of what they say and do – acting in a way that supports the values of the organization as well as its policies and procedures.

- Sending out clear messages regarding their expectations about risk management and decision making, including having a clear operational risk appetite statement and operational risk management policy.

- Making it clear that all areas of risk management, including operational risk management, are important value-adding activities, not simply 'cost-centres'.

- Being open to challenge and resistant to problems such as 'group-think', whereby the top leadership become blind to or even actively hostile towards new information about their risk exposures and risk management strategy. Group-think can also result in overconfidence – via the belief 'that it will not happen here'.

5.2 Risk appetite and tolerance

An organization's risk appetite, including its appetite and/or tolerance for operational risk, will affect its risk culture. As with strategy, organizations with a high appetite and tolerance for risk are likely to promote a risk-seeking culture, while those with a low appetite/tolerance for risk will generally have a more risk-averse and controlling culture.

Significant changes to risk appetite and tolerance levels should be avoided. This is because people will find it hard to adjust, because the prevailing risk culture will reflect the previous appetite/tolerance level. To allow the culture to adjust, changes in appetite or tolerance levels should be gradual.

CASE STUDY 4.5   Demutualization of UK building societies: the case of Northern Rock

In the mid-1990s a number of UK building societies 'demutualized'. This meant cancelling their mutual status by offering free equity shares to existing mortgage and savings customers, the legal 'owners' of these mutual building societies.

One such organization was Northern Rock, which came to dominate the UK mortgage lending market prior to the 2007–08 global financial crisis. However, this dominance was obtained via a strategy of significantly increased risk taking (Linsley and Slack, 2013). As a result, the bank failed in 2008 and had to be rescued by the UK Government.

As demonstrated by Linsley and Slack (2013) the failure of Northern Rock was a complicated one, characterized by a number of risk-culture elements, including the historical cultural baggage of the organization as a risk-averse, socially responsible, caring organization, rooted in the UK building society movement. This baggage created cognitive dissonance (the mental discomfort encountered when trying to reconcile conflicting beliefs, values and attitudes), whereby the employees of Northern Rock could not reconcile the risk-averse, caring-oriented values that they once shared with the new high-risk/reward strategy chosen by the board and senior management.

5.3 HR policies and procedures

HR processes and management techniques have an important role to play in influencing risk culture. Tools include:

5.3.1 Ethical standards and codes of conduct

Ethical standards and codes should make clear the values, behaviours and attitudes that are expected in relation to the management of operational risk. For example, they can be used to promote a concern for effective governance and compliance. Equally they can promote a wider appreciation of the needs of different stakeholders (in terms of customer care, or concern for the wider physical and/or financial environment, for example) or to communicate unambiguous messages about the unacceptability of specific risk types, such as internal fraud.

CASE STUDY 4.6   Barclay's post-LIBOR code of conduct

One of the recommendations from the Salz review (Salz, 2013) was that Barclays should implement an organization-wide code of conduct for staff and put in measures to ensure compliance.

Barclays did this and now has 'The Barclays Way' (Barclays, 2021), which outlines the values of the bank and the behaviours that staff are expected to exhibit. The document covers things like Barclays' role in society, along with the treatment of customers and colleagues. In addition, the code has a section on risk, emphasizing the importance of good governance, internal control and maintaining high ethical standards.

Staff are expected to sign up to the code on an annual basis and speak up about any concerns they may have about compliance. A dedicated Raising Concerns Team is available to talk to staff about these concerns.

5.3.2 Recruitment and selection

Organizations wishing to change their risk culture may recruit new staff members (especially in relation to leadership and management positions) who are better aligned to the desired culture. The cultural alignment of a new staff member may be assessed using techniques such as role play, psychometric tests and competency-based interview questions.

5.3.3 Performance management and appraisals

How staff are rewarded and the appraisal criteria on which they receive these rewards can have a significant effect on risk culture. For example, large bonus payments may promote a culture of significant risk taking, while the potential for bonus clawbacks may promote a longer-term perspective on risk taking. Similarly rewards that are based on short-term performance criteria (e.g. sales or quarterly profits) may also promote a culture of excessive risk taking.

It is recommended that relevant professionals, from the operational risk function and/or the HR function, as appropriate, should be consulted about the organization's performance management and appraisal strategy to ensure that it promotes an appropriate risk culture.

To help promote an appropriate risk culture it is also recommended that:

- rewards are based on longer-term performance criteria, such as customer satisfaction and retention, or profits over periods longer than one year;

- rewards and appraisals should reflect concern for operational risk and its management, as well as profit and sales growth;

- mechanisms such as bonus clawbacks are implemented to highlight the consequences of inappropriate risk taking and control decisions;

- staff induction and ongoing training courses are used to raise awareness of operational risk, and acceptance of operational risk management policies and procedures.

5.4 Communication: formal and informal

Effective lines of communication, both formal and informal, are powerful risk-culture influencing tools. Activities include:

- Establishing a common language (taxonomy) for operational risk and its management, to help avoid any misunderstandings.

- In larger organizations, especially those that are geographically dispersed, ensuring that people do not feel disconnected and potentially develop their own destructive risk sub-cultures. This may involve regular phone or email contact with the central operational risk function – though ideally site visits to the locations in question, as well as encouraging staff from more distant locations to visit head office, should be encouraged.

- Establishing clear channels of communication to ensure that potential concerns are escalated as quickly as possible.

- Ensuring that staff feel they can trust management to listen to their concerns about operational risk and its management. The establishment of a 'just' culture, which encourages open, no-blame, reporting, while ensuring that accountability is maintained, is paramount. The establishment of an effective whistleblowing procedure is also important.

- Regularly reinforcing key operational risk management messages, via roadshows, presentations, webinars, cascade materials, etc.

5.5 Process and system design

An organization's processes and systems reflect and influence its risk culture. Significant changes to their nature, design or implementation can have a significant effect on the risk culture of an organization. Effective measures include:

- Ensuring that systems and processes do not become so automated that staff lose the ability to think for themselves and be creative (within clear boundaries) when the situation demands it.
- Designing flexible processes and systems that can adapt to changing risk and business environments, as necessary. This includes ensuring that the staff operating these systems and processes are flexible as well. Statements such as 'we have always done it like this here' are not part of effective risk-culture management.

5.6 Risk governance

The governance of an organization can have a significant effect on the management of its risk culture, especially in relation to the control of risk sub-cultures. Issues include:

- Long reporting lines, which can create a 'hierarchy of waste buckets' – whereby operational risk management information may be distorted or even hidden (to protect local agendas) as it moves up the chain.
- Complex department and divisional structures, which may facilitate the development of sub-cultures, especially in areas that are organizationally distant from the head office.
- Mergers and acquisitions, which will require especially careful risk-culture management, to help preserve those aspects of the merged cultures that the organization wishes to maintain and deal with any culture clashes. One way to address this is to move people around the new organization – creating secondments in other parts of the business, including secondments to the operational risk function.
- Embedding risk assessment and control responsibilities into the business – so that it is not just seen as the role of 'risk professionals'. One way to achieve this is to create risk champions – who act as a network of supporters for risk management across the business. Risk champions may focus only on operational risk, or a wider range of risks.
- Developing greater collaboration between the first and second lines of defence so that operational risk professionals actively support business decision making.

6. Conclusions

An organization's risk culture is an important component in its success or failure. Organizations that have an appropriate culture should be better able to balance risk and opportunity, achieving their objectives, while avoiding potentially destructive surprises along the way.

Risk culture is not a given and can be influenced. However, attempts to assess, monitor or control risk culture in a mechanistic or formulaic way will not succeed. Judgement and experience is always required, as is patience. Operational risk professionals need to trust their judgement and experience but remember that they cannot work alone on risk culture. The maintenance of an appropriate risk culture requires collaboration between a range of experts, including risk, HR, audit and corporate governance professionals.

Reflective practice questions

1 Has your organization implemented measures to assess its risk culture? Are these assessments repeated on an annual basis?

2 Have risk-culture metrics been implemented to support less frequent risk-culture assessments?

3 What measures have been implemented to prevent interpretation bias, when reviewing the output from risk-culture assessments or metric reports? For example, have you made use of facilitated focus groups or external, third-party experts?

4 Does your senior management/board discuss the organization's risk culture on a periodic basis? What measures have they implemented to address any concerns about the appropriateness of specific aspects of your organization's risk culture?

5 Do staff and management live the organization's code of conduct? What measures have been implemented to ensure that the code is taken seriously?

6 Do operational risk professionals work with other relevant experts (HR, audit, governance) to assess, monitor and influence risk culture?

APPENDIX A Example risk-culture questionnaire

Please indicate the extent to which you agree or disagree with the following statements (Q1–Q5):

1. In my area of responsibility (depending on your role this means your function, department or business)...

	Strongly disagree		Neither agree nor disagree			Strongly agree	
It is okay to raise 'red flags'	☐	☐	☐	☐	☐	☐	☐
I get 'early warning' signs about impending issues	☐	☐	☐	☐	☐	☐	☐
Most employees are not hesitant to take risks	☐	☐	☐	☐	☐	☐	☐
Mechanisms are in place to recognize judicious risk taking (e.g. awards)	☐	☐	☐	☐	☐	☐	☐
Risk taking has a positive effect on compensation and/or career advancement	☐	☐	☐	☐	☐	☐	☐
Mechanisms are in place to provide an inclusive environment for decision making	☐	☐	☐	☐	☐	☐	☐
Issues can be raised, even when they are 'bad news'	☐	☐	☐	☐	☐	☐	☐
I can choose the methods appropriate to a task	☐	☐	☐	☐	☐	☐	☐
I can determine how much time I spend on tasks	☐	☐	☐	☐	☐	☐	☐
I have opportunity for independence in how I do my job	☐	☐	☐	☐	☐	☐	☐

2. In my area of responsibility, effective processes are in place to…

	Strongly disagree			Neither agree nor disagree			Strongly agree
Stop projects that have turned 'bad' even if already well under way	☐	☐	☐	☐	☐	☐	☐
Provide an 'open-door' environment to discuss risk issues as they arise	☐	☐	☐	☐	☐	☐	☐
Identify areas that have become exposed to significantly increasing levels of risk	☐	☐	☐	☐	☐	☐	☐
Learn from past mistakes (e.g. analysis of losses and near-misses)	☐	☐	☐	☐	☐	☐	☐
Alert personnel responsible for risk management when risk issues arise	☐	☐	☐	☐	☐	☐	☐
Review risks as part of the regular management reporting cycle	☐	☐	☐	☐	☐	☐	☐
Escalate risk issues to the appropriate management level or committee	☐	☐	☐	☐	☐	☐	☐
Allocate ownership for specific risks	☐	☐	☐	☐	☐	☐	☐

3. In my area of responsibility, risk management activities are…

	Strongly disagree			Neither agree nor disagree			Strongly agree
Directed to avoid negative consequences	☐	☐	☐	☐	☐	☐	☐
Driven by prior incidents and losses	☐	☐	☐	☐	☐	☐	☐
Directed to realize positive outcomes	☐	☐	☐	☐	☐	☐	☐
Driven by business opportunities	☐	☐	☐	☐	☐	☐	☐
Implemented in response to regulatory requirements	☐	☐	☐	☐	☐	☐	☐

4. In my area of responsibility, emphasis is placed on…

	Strongly disagree		Neither agree nor disagree			Strongly agree	
Implementing procedural checks and controls	☐	☐	☐	☐	☐	☐	☐
Conforming to standards and certifications	☐	☐	☐	☐	☐	☐	☐
Addressing regulatory demands	☐	☐	☐	☐	☐	☐	☐
Setting limits and authorities for individuals or groups of individuals	☐	☐	☐	☐	☐	☐	☐
Reviewing limits and authorities for individuals or groups of individuals	☐	☐	☐	☐	☐	☐	☐
Verifying that employees are compliant with prevailing regulations	☐	☐	☐	☐	☐	☐	☐

5. In my area of responsibility, if things go wrong, effective processes are in place to…

	Strongly disagree		Neither agree nor disagree			Strongly agree	
Allocate individual responsibility for failures	☐	☐	☐	☐	☐	☐	☐
Explore the causes of errors	☐	☐	☐	☐	☐	☐	☐
Sanction personnel that made errors	☐	☐	☐	☐	☐	☐	☐
Provide a no-blame environment to discuss the causes of errors	☐	☐	☐	☐	☐	☐	☐
Establish disciplinary actions for errors caused by violations of policies/ procedures	☐	☐	☐	☐	☐	☐	☐

Please indicate the average percentage of working time spent on the following activities:

	0%			Around 50%			90% or more
Addressing regulatory requirements	☐	☐	☐	☐	☐	☐	☐
Discussing future business scenarios	☐	☐	☐	☐	☐	☐	☐
Working on compliance processes	☐	☐	☐	☐	☐	☐	☐
Discussing how to take advantage of business opportunities	☐	☐	☐	☐	☐	☐	☐
Preparing external disclosure documents (excluding financial statements)	☐	☐	☐	☐	☐	☐	☐
Devising alternative plans to the strategy currently pursued	☐	☐	☐	☐	☐	☐	☐

Please indicate, over the period of a month, how often on average you get in touch by email or phone with...

	Never			Weekly			Daily
Central risk personnel	☐	☐	☐	☐	☐	☐	☐
Local risk personnel (e.g. risk teams in my business unit/division)	☐	☐	☐	☐	☐	☐	☐
The head of my business unit/division	☐	☐	☐	☐	☐	☐	☐
My direct supervisor	☐	☐	☐	☐	☐	☐	☐

Please indicate, over the period of a month, how often on average you communicate in a one-to-one meeting with...

	Never			Weekly			Daily
Central risk personnel	☐	☐	☐	☐	☐	☐	☐
Local risk personnel (e.g. risk teams in my business unit/division)	☐	☐	☐	☐	☐	☐	☐
The head of my business unit/division	☐	☐	☐	☐	☐	☐	☐
My direct supervisor	☐	☐	☐	☐	☐	☐	☐

Please indicate, over the period of a month, how often on average you participate in group meetings with...

	Never			Weekly			Daily
Central risk personnel	☐	☐	☐	☐	☐	☐	☐
Local risk personnel (e.g. risk teams in my business unit/division)	☐	☐	☐	☐	☐	☐	☐
The head of my business unit/division	☐	☐	☐	☐	☐	☐	☐
My direct supervisor	☐	☐	☐	☐	☐	☐	☐

Compared to your prior experience (in your current company or other organizations), please indicate the extent of change in the following areas during the last two to three years:

	Decreased to a great extent		Stayed the same		Increased to a great extent		
The number of new products	☐	☐	☐	☐	☐	☐	☐
The number of jobs filled by people with little experience in the company	☐	☐	☐	☐	☐	☐	☐
The number of jobs filled by people with little experience in the industry	☐	☐	☐	☐	☐	☐	☐
Turnover in key managerial positions	☐	☐	☐	☐	☐	☐	☐
Aggressive and stretching goals from the top	☐	☐	☐	☐	☐	☐	☐
The use of formal performance rankings for the purpose of employee assessment	☐	☐	☐	☐	☐	☐	☐
Bonuses as a % of total compensation	☐	☐	☐	☐	☐	☐	☐
Regulatory requirements	☐	☐	☐	☐	☐	☐	☐
Compliance activities	☐	☐	☐	☐	☐	☐	☐
Loss of sensitive data	☐	☐	☐	☐	☐	☐	☐
Loss of key clients	☐	☐	☐	☐	☐	☐	☐
Information technology failures	☐	☐	☐	☐	☐	☐	☐
The number of customer complaints	☐	☐	☐	☐	☐	☐	☐
Disagreements with regulators	☐	☐	☐	☐	☐	☐	☐

References

Note: Some of the sources included in this chapter have been listed previously. Only new sources are listed below.

Barclays (2021) The Barclays way, https://home.barclays/citizenship/the-way-we-do-business/code-of-conduct/ (archived at https://perma.cc/6YJJ-BR2V)

Douglas, M and Wildavsky, A (1983) *Risk and Culture: An essay on the selection of technological and environmental dangers*, University of California Press, Berkeley CA

IRM (2021) Risk culture, IRM Thought Leadership, www.theirm.org/what-we-say/thought-leadership/risk-culture/ (archived at https://perma.cc/LAM6-SZYS)

Krosnick, J A (2018) Questionnaire design, *The Palgrave Handbook of Survey*, Palgrave Macmillan, Cham, pp 439–55

Krueger, R A and Casey, M A (2001) Designing and conducting focus group interviews, *Social Analysis, Selected Tools and Techniques*, World Bank Social Development Papers, 36, pp 4–23

Linsley, P M and Slack, R E (2013) Crisis management and an ethic of care: The case of Northern Rock Bank, *Journal of Business Ethics*, 113 (2), 285–95

Power, M, Ashby, S and Palermo, T (2013) Risk Culture in Financial Organizations: A research report, CARR-Analysis of Risk and Regulation

Salz, A (2013) Salz review: An independent review of Barclays' business practices, Barclays PLC, https://online.wsj.com/public/resources/documents/SalzReview04032013.pdf (archived at https://perma.cc/3WUA-4HYA)

Sheedy, E A, Griffin, B and Barbour, J P (2017) A framework and measure for examining risk climate in financial institutions, *Journal of Business and Psychology*, 32 (1), 101–16

Risk appetite 05

LEARNING OUTCOMES

- Explain what risk appetite is and why it matters from an operational risk perspective.
- Compare different approaches to determining and expressing operational risk appetite and tolerance.
- Know how to implement an effective operational risk appetite framework.

1. Introduction

Risk appetite is an area that attracts diverse views among operational risk professionals. Depending on the sector, scale and risk profile of an organization, operational risk-appetite approaches range in complexity and scope. Differences also exist in terminology, with some organizations preferring the term 'tolerance' over 'appetite' when referring to operational risks. For these reasons, this chapter does not recommend a one-size-fits-all solution. Rather, it outlines a range of good practices, from which operational risk professionals may choose what is appropriate for their organization.

Fundamentally risk appetite, whatever the risk that is focused upon, is about decision making. Every action or decision within an organization involves an element of risk. An organization must, therefore, be able to distinguish between risks that are likely to result in value-creating outcomes (e.g. profit, reputation, improved services, etc) versus those that may destroy value. By determining an appropriate appetite for risk and implementing a framework to ensure that this appetite is maintained, organizations can ensure that decision makers do not expose them to either too much, or too little, risk.

While the focus of this chapter is on operational risk, an organization's appetite for operational risk is part of a broader, enterprise-wide appetite for risk. Operational risk is important to all organizations, and it is essential that the board and senior management are engaged in its management. Effective governance and compliance require the management of risks that are typically operational in nature (e.g. fraud, health and safety and conduct-related risks). In addition, strategic decisions (e.g. new product development) often require exposure to operational risk and it is important that the board and senior management are cognisant of these risks and satisfied that the organization can take them in the pursuit of its objectives.

Organizations that implement a framework for determining and managing their operational risk appetite can achieve various benefits:

- Enable the board to exercise appropriate oversight and corporate governance by defining the nature and level of operational risks it considers acceptable (and unacceptable) and thus set appropriate boundaries for organizational activities and decisions.

- Provide a means of expressing senior management's attitude to operational risk, which can then be communicated throughout the organization to help promote a risk-aware culture.

- Establish a framework for operational risk decision making, to help determine which risks can be accepted/retained and which risks should be prevented or mitigated.

- Improve the allocation of risk management resources by bringing into focus higher-priority issues. Specifically, operational risk exposures or control weaknesses that are outside of appetite or tolerance.

- Ensure that the cost of operational risk management does not exceed the benefits.

- Align strategic goals and operational activities through optimizing the balance between business development/growth/returns and the operational risks inherent in pursuing those goals.

2. Key terms and definitions

There are no universal definitions of either risk appetite or risk tolerance. Agreeing a universal definition is especially difficult in the context of operational risk, given that they are generally framed as 'downside' risks, which can only result in a loss for an organization. This is despite the fact that such framing ignores that operational risks can have upside outcomes, for example where operational efficiency and effectiveness is greater than expected (see Chapter 1).

2.1 Risk appetite

In spite of these definitional difficulties, the operational risk function should ensure that their organization has a clear definition of operational risk appetite that is accepted and understood by its management and board of directors. A useful starting point is the IRM's definition of risk appetite from an enterprise-wide context (IRM, 2021): 'The amount and type of risk that an organization is willing to take in order to meet their strategic objectives.'

Organizations that take the view that operational risks can only be downside in nature could replace 'is willing to take' with 'is prepared to accept', or similar. However, this is not recommended. As explained in Chapter 1, operational risks are inherent in organizational activities and both operational risk events, and the measures taken to mitigate these events, can influence the efficiency and effectiveness of operations. Control measures taken to reduce operational risk exposures may sometimes have an even greater negative impact on efficiency and effectiveness than the adverse operational risk outcomes they are seeking to prevent, especially where they are expensive to implement, prolong operational processes, increase the complexity of systems or prevent activities from being undertaken. In short, operational risks must be taken if organizations are to achieve their strategic objectives, just like any other type of risk. In this context, organizations must be willing to take operational risks; the only pertinent question is how much and what types of operational risk are they willing to take?

CASE STUDY 5.1   The impact of excessive operational risk control

An organization decides that its exposure to IT systems security risks is unacceptable. As a result, it increases the level of control in relation to user account security. Users are required to change their passwords every week and are not allowed to repeat a previously used password. Passwords are also required to be at least 20 characters long and contain a mixture of alphanumeric and punctuation characters.

Upon implementation many users struggle to remember their passwords and the IT helpdesk is overloaded with password reset requests. This leads to lengthy reset delays and the efficiency and effectiveness of the organization's operations is affected.

A further problem with taking an acceptability perspective to risk appetite is that it can promote the view that operational risk management is a costly, bureaucratic activity that does not create value in organizations. This can impact on the level of embeddedness of an organization's operational risk management framework (see Chapter 2). Terms like 'willingness' promote a more positive, value-creating *and* protecting perspective for operational risk management – the message being that operational risks do need to be taken, but only in a mindful, risk-aware way, when the benefits exceed the costs.

Table 5.1   The RAG approach to risk prioritization

Status	Meaning	Required Action
Green	Acceptable	No immediate action required, except for routine monitoring
Amber	Tolerable	Investigate (to verify and understand the underlying causes) and consider ways to mitigate/avoid within a specified time period
Red	Unacceptable	Take immediate steps to mitigate or avoid

2.2 Risk tolerance

As explained above, an organization's appetite for operational risk will often reflect the balance that it maintains between the costs of controlling operational risk exposures versus the costs associated with adverse operational risk outcomes. This is a high-level strategic decision that will influence both the resources devoted to operational risk management and the level of operational risk that is present in organizational activities.

In contrast, the term 'risk tolerance' is typically used as a specific benchmark for the acceptability of specific, adverse, operational risk outcomes (e.g. the amount of internal or external fraud losses) or some other metric, such as a risk or control effectiveness indicator. In this regard an organization may decide that it is prepared to tolerate a specific number of operational errors or control weaknesses, because their elimination would not be cost effective.

Tolerance is often expressed using a red–amber–green (RAG)-based approach: the thresholds that determine when a risk exposure or metric moves from green to amber, and then from amber to red, reflect an organization's level of tolerance. The wider these thresholds, the greater the degree of tolerance.

Occasionally an organization may decide that it is not willing to tolerate something. Usually this is impossible to achieve for specific operational risk events, including highly undesirable ones like fraud or accidents at work. However, it is possible in relation to the effects that may be associated with these events, such as the potential for regulatory intervention and enforcement activities. For example, an organization can never reduce the number of workplace accidents to zero, but it can ensure that it does not breach health and safety rules. Hence it is possible to specify a zero tolerance for compliance breaches, though not for accidents.

Where both tolerance and appetite are used, organizations may either:

- Set tolerance limits and thresholds below the agreed appetite for operational risk. From a RAG perspective this means setting the appetite at the red level and tolerance at amber.

- Set tolerance limits above the agreed appetite for operational risk. Hence appetite would in effect reflect the amber threshold and the limit of tolerance the threshold for red.

The first approach is most appropriate in high-control environments, such as financial services. The primary benefit is that where a risk exposure (or related risk or control effectiveness indicator) exceeds the amber tolerance limit, it serves as an early warning of a potential appetite breach.

The second approach is most appropriate in more entrepreneurial environments where risk taking, including taking certain operational risks (e.g. new product development risks), is a necessary part of an organization's strategic objectives. The advantage of such an approach in this environment is that appetite for operational risk may be exceeded when there is a potential business benefit from doing so. However, it would be prudent for any such decision to receive board-level approval, especially where corporate governance rules require boards to oversee their organization's appetite for risk.

Whichever approach is selected, two fundamental principles remain – a level of exposure to operational risk that may be exceeded in exceptional circumstances, and a level that must not be exceeded under any circumstance. In terms of the latter, all organizations must not knowingly take operational risks that have a high probability of causing:

- death or injury;
- a breach of applicable laws and regulations;
- financial distress and bankruptcy.

2.3 Risk capacity

The concept of risk capacity is based on the notion that there is a maximum level of risk that an organization may expose itself to before it runs a significant risk of failure (e.g. bankruptcy). Hence risk capacity presents a level of risk exposure beyond which an organization should not exceed.

Risk capacity is usually determined by the financial strength of an organization, reflected in accounting metrics such as its credit rating, debt to equity ratio or capital ratios, such as the working capital ratio (total current assets divided by current liabilities) or the capital adequacy ratio of a financial institution (eligible capital as a percentage of risk-weighted assets).

From an operational risk perspective, it is rare for an organization to set a discrete capacity for operational risk. Risk capacity is an aggregate, enterprise-wide concept. However, where the concept of risk capacity is used, care should be taken to ensure that an organization's appetite for operational risk is not set high enough to breach this capacity, either on its own, or when combined with the agreed appetite levels for all other risk types.

2.4 Operational risk appetite framework

The term 'operational risk appetite framework' is often used as a catch-all for all of the processes, procedures, documents and outputs that form part of an organization's work on operational risk appetite.

The normal components of this framework include:

- A decision template, like the one provided in Appendix B.
- An operational risk appetite statement, which explains, in words, the organization's appetite for operational risk.
- Quantitative metrics that express, in numerical terms, the organization's appetite for operational risk.
- RAG tolerance limits for specific categories of operational risk, or the effectiveness of key operational risk controls.
- Documentation that outlines the processes and procedures for determining and reviewing operational risk appetite, including roles and responsibilities.
- Documentation that outlines the processes and procedures for addressing operational risk exposures that are considered to be outside of appetite.

3. Determining operational risk appetite and tolerance

Determining appropriate levels of operational risk appetite and tolerance, where necessary, involves a number of considerations, including the 'measures' of expression that should be used and the appropriate level of these measures. As is often the case, there is no one optimal approach, though there is sound practice. The key stages in the process are:

- agreeing who is responsible for determining operational risk appetite and tolerance;
- establishing how to express this operational risk appetite and tolerance;
- deciding on the appropriate levels of these methods of expression.

3.1 Roles and responsibilities for determining operational risk appetite and tolerance

3.1.1 The board

In jurisdictions like the UK, much of the rest of Europe, the United States and Canada, company law and associated corporate governance codes hold the board accountable for strategic direction and control. Determining an organization's operational risk appetite is an element of these activities.

There are two schools of thought on the role of boards in discharging their corporate governance accountabilities in relation to risk appetite, and operational risk appetite more specifically. The first is that the board should approve the work of the operational risk function. The second is that the board should determine an organization's risk appetite for itself, leaving only the setting of appropriate tolerance limits to the operational risk function.

The first approach takes the view that boards lack the time and experience to determine an organization's operational risk appetite. Instead, this work is delegated to the operational risk function, which is charged with bringing their work to the board for approval. In this regard boards still have an input into the process and can ensure that the work of the operational risk function is appropriate.

The premise for the second school of thought is that boards should play a more active role in the determination of operational risk appetite. A key reason for this is that the role of the board is to be forward looking, ensuring both appropriate strategic direction and internal control. In this regard, boards should have a good understanding of an organization's strategic priorities and the risks associated with these. Another reason is that the presentation of a prepared operational risk appetite to a board may result in anchoring effects (Furnham and Boo, 2011; Tversky and Kahneman, 1974). This means that though boards may make some minor tweaks and modifications, they are less likely to arrive at the same conclusions they would have done on their own.

For organizations struggling to decide between these two schools of thought a middle way is to have both the board and the operational risk function suggest an appropriate appetite for operational risk and to compare the results. This could then result in a valuable conversation between the board and the operational risk function about the appropriate degree of operational risk appetite and the rationale behind their thinking. It is also recommended that, even where the board takes control, the operational risk function should provide a decision framework for the board to help directors to determine the appropriate degree of operational risk appetite, such as that provided in Appendix B. In addition, the operational risk function could help to facilitate the work of the board. In this way they can use their expertise to ensure that important decision factors are not overlooked.

CASE STUDY 5.2   Working with the board to determine risk appetite

A large social enterprise was implementing an operational risk appetite framework for the first time. It decided that the board should play an active role in determining the appropriate degree of operational risk appetite.

The operational risk function designed a discussion and decision template similar to that in Appendix B. The operational risk function also facilitated the initial operational risk appetite workshop for the board, supported by a board member with experience in the management of operational risk. This workshop took place during a board away-day to ensure less time pressure. It was the first item on the agenda to further prevent the discussion from being rushed. In total the workshop lasted 90 minutes.

The session started with a presentation from the operational risk manager on the discussion and decision template. They also ensured that all board directors understood the concept of risk appetite and its importance from a corporate governance perspective.

After a few questions from the audience, the operational risk manager invited each board member to vote, secretly, on their preferences for the organization's appetite for the various operational risk strategic impacts. They could vote for one of four options each time, ranging from 'cautious' to 'significant'. An electronic voting system was used for this purpose.

The board members expressed their preferences for each of the operational risk strategic impacts in turn. In all cases a range of views were indicated; however, there was a clear majority view for each of the impacts. Board members that voted differently to the majority were invited to express their views. At all times the operational risk manager kept the discussion friendly and inclusive, providing their own perspective where appropriate.

Following the discussion board members voted a second time. This revealed a unanimous majority for each of the strategic impacts, in some cases this shifted from the previous majority view. For example, the appetite for financial impacts was set as 'cautious' (see terminology in Appendix B), compared to the initial vote for 'open-optimistic', while the appetite for human resource impacts was set at 'open-optimistic', compared to 'cautious'.

The specific responsibilities for operational risk appetite that should be allocated to the board include:

- Approve the contents of the organization's operational risk appetite framework. Ensure that the framework is consistent with the organization's strategic objectives, the needs of its stakeholders and relevant regulatory requirements.

- Ensure that any changes to the organization's strategic objectives, as well as any other strategic decisions, including new products or delivery channels, are consistent with the approved operational risk framework.

- Hold senior management accountable for the implementation of the operational risk appetite framework. Ensure that appropriate financial and other resources are devoted to assessing, monitoring and controlling the organization's operational risk profile to ensure that risk exposures are kept within appetite.

- Monitor the organization's operational risk profile on a regular (e.g. quarterly) basis, to ensure that any quantitative risk appetite/tolerance limits are not breached and to confirm compliance with any qualitative statements.

- Ensure that appropriate escalation procedures are in place so that the board can be notified promptly of any breaches that occur between the routine reviews.

- Where quantitative risk appetite/tolerance limits or qualitative statements are breached, ensure that appropriate action is taken to address each breach.

- Ensure that the organization's risk culture is appropriate and supports the operation of the operational risk appetite framework. This may include receiving reports on the organization's risk culture, including potential areas of concern and the actions being taken.

- Review the contents of the operational risk appetite framework on an annual basis, to ensure that it remains consistent with the organization's strategic objectives (and vice-versa), as well as the needs of stakeholders and regulatory requirements. This could include receiving independent assurance (from the internal audit function or an appropriately skilled third party) that the framework is effective and in line with regulatory expectations.

3.1.2 Front-line management

Managers across an organization will be involved in the day-to-day management of a wide variety of operational risks. Some may be designated risk or control owners to reflect their responsibilities for effective operational risk management.

Front-line managers do not, normally, get involved with determining an organization's appetite for operational risk, given that this is part of a board's governance responsibilities. However, they may be involved in determining RAG tolerance thresholds for specific operational risk exposures or risk and control metrics. Where they are involved in setting operational risk tolerances these should not contradict the overarching operational risk appetite.

The specific responsibilities for operational risk appetite that should be allocated to front-line managers include:

- Accountability for the management of risk within their area of responsibility, ensuring that their local operational risk profile does not breach the organization's appetite for operational risk.

- Ensure that any qualitative operational risk appetite statements (see section four this chapter), are embedded into day-to-day risk taking and control decisions.

This includes ensuring that all of their employees are aware of these statements and the need to comply with them.

- Establish, monitor and control adherence to local operational risk tolerance limits (e.g. limits for local risk, control and performance indicators), along with any local qualitative statements.

- Cooperate with the operational risk function and not interfere with their duties. This includes supporting the wider monitoring and reporting activities of the organization in relation to operational risk appetite, as well as, where required, actions taken to resolve any breaches of the organization's operational risk appetite and tolerance limits.

- Ensure that their local risk culture and remuneration arrangements are consistent with the organization's operational risk appetite and tolerance limits. Report any concerns to the operational risk function in the first instance.

- Escalate promptly any breaches of local tolerance limits, along with any potential breaches of the organization's overall appetite for operational risk.

3.1.3 The operational risk function or equivalent

The operational risk function has a dual role:

- supporting the work of the board (see above); and
- overseeing the work of business managers in determining RAG tolerance thresholds.

In overseeing the work of business managers, the operational risk function should balance the activities and objectives of specific business units, departments or functions with the operational risk appetite set by the board. Business managers should not set RAG tolerance limits that may facilitate decisions that are inconsistent with the board's appetite for operational risk (e.g. to set thresholds that promote excessive or insufficient risk taking and control). The operational risk function should challenge tolerance limits where they are concerned about consistency. Where applicable the risk or operational risk committee can be used to support this oversight.

CASE STUDY 5.3   Challenging RAG tolerance limits set by business managers

The business manager of a large customer-facing function reports a significant change in their RAG tolerance for external fraud events. They have decided to increase their function's tolerance for external fraud losses. The rationale is that this will help to improve efficiency, reducing the time taken on fraud-related due diligence (e.g. security questions) and increasing the availability of staff to address customer needs.

The operational risk function is concerned that this decision will exceed the board's appetite for external fraud risk. The head of operational risk starts by organizing a meeting with the business manager to understand further their rationale for the change in tolerance and explain the potential consequences for the wider organization. Then the operational risk function produces a paper for the board-delegated risk committee, explaining the situation and asking for a decision on whether to accept the change. The board risk committee decides that the change is too significant and would result in the organization's appetite for external fraud risk being exceeded. However, it does allow a slight increase in tolerance for external fraud losses and recommends to senior management that the external fraud controls of the customer-facing function should be reviewed to determine whether their efficiency and effectiveness could be improved. This ensures the appropriate control of external fraud risks without compromising customer service.

The specific responsibilities for operational risk appetite that should be allocated to the operational risk function include:

- Lead the development of the operational risk appetite framework, working with the board of directors and senior managers to ensure that this framework is consistent with the organization's objectives, stakeholder expectations and regulatory requirements.

- Establish a process to support the monitoring and reporting of the organization's risk profile in relation to its operational risk appetite and accompanying tolerance limits.

- Monitor the organization's operational risk profile to ensure that it remains consistent with its appetite for operational risk, involving the board and senior management where appropriate.

- Work with senior management to ensure that appropriate tolerance limits are set for all material categories of operational risk and, as appropriate, each business line/legal entity.

- Ensure that front-line management set the above tolerance limits in a manner that is consistent with the organization's appetite for operational risk.

- Ensure that the organization's operational risk management systems and processes provide effective support for the operation of the operational risk appetite framework.

- Act in a timely manner to ensure that operational risk exposures are managed in such a way to prevent the operational risk appetite/tolerance limits and qualitative statements being breached, and where limits or qualitative statements are breached to ensure that such breaches are rectified.

- Escalate to the board of directors any organization-wide risk appetite/tolerance limits that have been breached. Where possible, provide an early warning of limits that are close to being breached.

- Report any evidence of non-compliance with the organization's qualitative statements of operational risk appetite to the board risk committee or equivalent.

- Work with senior management to ensure that an organization has an appropriate risk culture to support the operation of the operational risk appetite framework and to ensure that decisions are made in a manner consistent with the organization's appetite for operational risk. This may include implementing measures to support the assessment/monitoring and management of the organization's risk culture where appropriate. It may also include reviewing remuneration arrangements to ensure that they are consistent with the organization's appetite for operational risk.

3.1.4 The internal audit function

Organizations that have separate risk and internal audit functions should not normally involve internal audit in the determination of operational risk appetites or tolerance thresholds. However, they may decide to use the internal audit function to review the process used for determining operational risk appetite and make recommendations for improvement, where necessary.

In smaller organizations, where the internal audit function may lack the necessary in-house expertise, a third-party agent, such as an experienced operational risk consultant, may be used to review the operational risk appetite framework.

The specific responsibilities for operational risk appetite that should be allocated to the internal audit function include:

- Assess, as appropriate, the design and implementation of the operational risk appetite framework, both on an organization-wide and local business unit/legal entity basis, where appropriate. Ensure that the operational risk appetite framework meets the needs of the organization and any regulatory requirements.

- Investigate whether breaches of risk appetite/tolerance limits and qualitative statements are appropriately escalated and resolved.

- As necessary, assess the performance of the tools/infrastructure elements that support the risk appetite framework – such as an organization's risk culture, risk management information systems and employee remuneration arrangements.

- Report promptly to the board of directors (usually via the audit committee) any deficiencies they have identified with the design and operation of the operational risk appetite framework.

- Report promptly any deficiencies they may identify in the management of the operational risk appetite framework on the part of front-line managers.

- Evaluate whether any of the above should be supported by external third-party audit expertise.

4. Expressing operational risk appetite and tolerance: qualitative versus quantitative

Operational risk appetite, along with tolerances for specific operational risk exposures or control effectiveness, may be expressed in a variety of different ways. Broadly these can be classified into qualitative and quantitative approaches.

4.1 Qualitative

Qualitative expressions rely on written statements that do not involve any quantification. They are useful where operational risks are difficult to quantify and to reinforce the relationship between operational risk and strategic/business management objectives. Qualitative statements can also be used to emphasize specific behaviours or attitudes, and in so doing help to control an organization's risk culture.

Specifically, qualitative expressions of appetite or tolerance can be used to reinforce several important messages, such as:

- To recognize that certain operational risks, however unwelcome, are unpreventable (e.g. terrorism, natural disasters, pandemics), though the effects of these exposures may still be mitigated through appropriate business continuity and crisis management.

- It is sensible to accept operational risks where the cost of mitigation/avoidance exceeds the expected loss, provided there is no risk of bankruptcy, enforcement or stakeholder harm.

- Risks will be accepted when the estimated losses are within prescribed tolerance levels.

- Behaviours deemed to be unacceptable, such as: knowingly breaking the law; breaching regulatory requirements or company policy; damaging the environment; providing poor customer service; or exposing people to physical harm.

- Risks deemed unacceptable, such as: operating within specific countries or selling certain products.

- The importance of maintaining a good reputation.

CASE STUDY 5.4   Qualitative risk appetite statements

An organization operating in the financial services sector decides to set a range of qualitative statements for operational risk appetite. These statements are grouped around four main elements:

1 continuity of operations;

2 financial sustainability;

3 growth;

4 compliance.

For each of these elements a number of qualitative statements are agreed. Example statements include:

- Continuity of operations:
  - The organization's goal is to reduce, as much as practicable, operational risks that threaten the continuity of its operations. Ensuring that customers can access services, at all times, with minimal delay, is paramount.
  - We will maintain a well-diversified range of outsource service providers and ensure that they have adequate business continuity arrangements and IT backup resources.
  - We will ensure that the actions or inactions of employees do not result in events that significantly disrupt the continuity of operations. We will achieve this through staff training and maintaining a risk-aware culture.
- Financial sustainability:
  - We will not expose the organization to any operational risks that threaten its current investment-grade credit rating.
  - We will maintain a contingency funding plan to ensure that appropriate funds are in place to mitigate the severe financial impact of unexpected operational risk events. This plan must be tested and updated on an annual basis.
  - We will ensure that appropriate provisions are put in place for expected future operational losses, where such losses may exceed £1 million.
- Growth:
  - Control before you grow: the organization should not grow faster than its operational controls can keep pace with. The efficiency and effectiveness of operations must not be compromised by extreme resource pressures caused by overly rapid growth.
  - Return on assets must be sufficient to compensate for the expected annual cost of operational risk exposures, plus an allowance for unexpected costs.

- o Entry into new products and markets must not occur before an assessment of the potential operational risks has been conducted.
- Compliance:
  - o We will, at all times, comply with the minimum capital requirements for operational risk. No decisions may be taken that could result in such a breach.
  - o We will, at all times, comply with applicable health and safety and environmental regulations.
  - o Honesty and openness is expected. Any concerns about the honesty and openness of behaviours should be reported to the whistleblowing team.

Many organizations situate specific qualitative statements like those in Case Study 5.4 within an overarching 'risk appetite statement'. Such a statement outlines, in words, an organization's overall appetite for operational risk. In essence these statements should outline the broad preference that an organization has for operational risk (e.g. risk averse, neutral, preferring), along with the key priorities for operational risk management (compliance, improving efficiency, maximize financial performance, etc). Key information on how the operational risk appetite framework functions may also be included in such a statement, but only where this is essential from a governance and control perspective. Additional information on the design of the operational risk appetite framework should be documented separately in a risk appetite framework document. The reason for this is to ensure that the operational risk appetite statement is clear, to the point, and no longer than necessary.

CASE STUDY 5.5   An example operational risk appetite statement

ABC Group PLC is committed to managing and controlling operational risk as an integral part of its business activities.

In order to free up investment capital to support ABC's strategic objectives, as well as to preserve its reputation and cash flows, the group's goal is to minimize operational risk exposures. However, it is recognized that most business operations cannot be carried out in a risk-free environment. The group also recognizes that it is not always cost effective to minimize operational risk exposures, especially where this may limit capital growth or the generation of increased cash flows.

To ensure an appropriate balance between operational risk and return, limits of authority apply for each business line when accepting operational risk exposures in current or new activities. Front-line managers will inform operational risk management whenever potential risks are identified that may exceed agreed tolerance limits. When exposure levels exceed these limits, the Operational Risk Management Committee may request that the business line takes additional action to mitigate these risks or to avoid risk by exiting the business/cancelling the activity. Only the board of directors is authorized to accept business that exceeds the stated appetite for operational risk.

4.2 Quantitative

Quantitative expressions of operational risk appetite involve hard data, i.e. numerical metrics. Normally these metrics are derived from existing sources of management information, such as performance, risk or control indicators (see Chapter 9).

Quantitative expressions tend to be risk category or control specific and thus are primarily an indication of operational risk tolerance, rather than overall appetite. Such measures can be accompanied by amber and red thresholds, so that it is clear when a tolerance breach has occurred or is imminent. The concept of setting zero-tolerance thresholds may seem impractical, but they can have a cultural purpose in reinforcing the message that it is not appropriate to accept avoidable losses without question. For example, some organizations set zero-tolerance limits for internal fraud losses and significant health and safety incidents. This does not mean that such losses will not occur but sends a clear signal that they should be reduced as much as is practicable. It also makes clear that when such losses/incidents occur they should be escalated. This should usually mean escalation to the board risk committee or equivalent, to reflect the seriousness of such events. The board risk committee can then decide whether action is required to reduce exposure further.

Strategic-level performance metrics that provide a broad expression of operational risk appetite in isolation are rare. One potential measure is the amount of economic or regulatory capital allocated to operational risk. Non-financial organizations do not tend to calculate or allocate capital to specific risk categories, but it is more common in financial services. Where capital is allocated to operational risk, an organization could express its appetite for operational risk in terms of a risk-specific capital buffer. For example, an organization may allocate a minimum of £10 million of capital to operational risk, plus a 10 per cent buffer (an additional £1 million) to allow for the fact that unexpected costs may exceed the minimum allocation. A larger buffer indicates a lower appetite for operational risk, because there will be less surplus (unallocated) capital to invest in new, but potentially risky, business ventures.

Risk- and control-specific operational risk tolerance metrics are common. Examples include:

- Delegated limits of authority beyond which subordinates must escalate for approval.

- Measures of system or process reliability, for example no more than xx per cent chance any business-critical system is unavailable for more than one day in any one year.

- Reported loss amounts based on budgeting, aggregate annual amount by business area/loss type and/or sensitivity, i.e. an adverse trend of 5 per cent may be acceptable, 10 per cent tolerable, but 15 per cent unacceptable. Note that thresholds may be set on a per-event basis, for specific risk categories over an agreed time period or on an aggregate basis for all operational risks. The aim is to cover both high-volume/low-value and low-volume/high-value types of events. Thresholds may also be used to support reporting and escalation processes, to help identify the level of management or executive attention.

- Risk/control assessment boundaries to distinguish acceptable/tolerable/unacceptable levels of exposure to specific risk types.

- Risk and control indicator amber and red thresholds, expressed in units that are appropriate for the indicator in question, i.e. numerical count, financial value, percentage or variance.

5. Deciding on the appropriate level of operational risk appetite and related tolerances

As explained above, the board of directors is ultimately responsible for deciding the appropriate level of operational risk appetite, while front-line management select tolerances for specific operational risks and controls that are consistent with the overall appetite.

In deciding on the level of operational risk appetite a board should consider three primary factors:

- The strategic objectives of the organization. For example, an organization looking to grow or maintain potential market share may decide to accept a greater level of operational risk.

- The risk preferences of key stakeholders. Where stakeholders are more averse to operational risk a lower level of appetite will be appropriate, and vice-versa.

- The financial strength of the organization. Weaker organizations should not normally have a high appetite for any sort of risk, given the potential for their crystallization to cause bankruptcy. Stronger organizations have more scope to take risk, including operational risks, because they should have the funds necessary to finance the costs associated with risk events.

When setting tolerance levels for specific operational risks or controls, front-line managers should ensure that these are consistent with the board's appetite for operational risk. Whenever tolerance limits are set that are inconsistent, especially if above the agreed appetite, this should be passed to the board (or board risk committee where present) for approval. Techniques that may be used to set tolerance thresholds include:

- looking at historic trends in data series to understand normal versus exceptional, and potentially less tolerable, values;
- benchmarking with similar organizations or industry standards, for example an inter-organization comparison of staff turnover or sickness absence or comparing systems availability to recommended standards of availability;
- benchmarking between different departments or functions within the organization.

Where trends or benchmarking information are not available, thresholds should be set using 'expert judgement', assumptions documented and signed off, and the thresholds refined as additional information becomes available.

CASE STUDY 5.6 Examples of how to set tolerance thresholds for operational risk exposures

Example 1

An organization wishes to set red and amber tolerance thresholds for staff turnover. High levels of turnover can be a signal of declining staff morale and new staff are more likely to make mistakes, so the organization is most concerned about a sudden increase. Monthly staff turnover usually averages 3 per cent with a normal deviation of 1 per cent (i.e. turnover tends to range between 2 per cent and 4 per cent). Once when the organization's turnover increased to 6 per cent for several months a morale issue was identified. Hence the organization decides to set the amber threshold at 4.5 per cent and red at 6 per cent.

Example 2

Red and amber tolerance thresholds need to be set for the availability of a new core system. Though extensive testing suggests that the system is very reliable, no historic data exists regarding the stability of the system in regular daily use. Management set red and amber limits based on their experience with other IT systems and user reactions to failures. Evidence suggests that a non-availability rate of less than 1 per cent is tolerable, but 2 per cent or more can disrupt business operations. Hence the amber threshold is set at 99 per cent availability and red at 98 per cent.

6. Implementing an operational risk appetite framework

Once an organization has determined, expressed and documented its appetite for operational risk, a variety of mechanisms are required to ensure that decisions taken across the organization are consistent with this appetite. In this section the key management mechanisms required to implement an effective operational risk appetite framework are discussed.

It cannot be emphasized enough that organizations and their decision makers must live their operational risk appetite. Agreeing operational risk appetite and associated tolerance limits is not an academic exercise. Neither should the results be limited to the board or senior management. The purpose is to direct and control real-world decisions and that means ensuring that all staff are aware of the organization's appetite for operational risk.

6.1 Communication

To ensure staff make appropriate decisions it is essential that an organization's operational risk appetite and associated tolerances are communicated across the whole organization. This will include communicating to staff involved in activities that necessarily involve an element of operational risk (e.g. the operation of systems, processes and procedures), as well as those involved in monitoring and controlling specific categories of operational risk exposures (e.g. HR and IT staff).

Organizations may communicate their overall appetite for operational risk using a range of methods, including staff induction and training, staff meetings, intranet resources and performance reviews. It is recommended that multiple channels are used to ensure the message is received and understood.

Tolerance thresholds for specific operational risks and controls should be communicated to all staff involved in the management of these risks and controls, especially risk and control owners, if used.

CASE STUDY 5.7   Communicating operational risk appetite

Following a major review of its operational risk appetite an organization undertook a range of measures to improve communication. This included:

- A senior representative from the operational risk function attended the quarterly induction sessions for new staff. They talked about the organization's appetite for operational risk and answered questions from new staff. In particular they emphasized a number of important qualitative statements relevant to all staff (the importance of effective internal control, escalating concerns, etc).

- Online operational risk appetite awareness training for existing staff, to emphasize the key qualitative statements.

- A three-hour classroom training session for relevant managers, explaining the changes to the organization's operational risk appetite and the rationale behind these changes. The training also emphasized the importance of ensuring that operational risk exposures are kept within appetite.

- Relationship management meetings with risk and control owners to ensure they understood the changes and to answer questions and address any concerns.

6.2 *Monitoring*

Procedures should be put in place to ensure that an organization's operational risk profile remains within its chosen appetite and tolerances for operational risk. The aim of these procedures is to ensure that the organization uses its operational risk management resources in the most efficient way, while preventing and mitigating the most significant operational risk management exposures.

There are two distinct steps involved in the design and implementation of procedures for monitoring operational risk appetite:

- Arranging for the required data to be reported by the appropriate party at an agreed frequency. From the outset it is important to take all reasonable steps to ensure the integrity of the data in respect of completeness, accuracy and timeliness. It is recommended that operational risk appetite and tolerance reporting is built into existing operational risk reports to save time producing new reports and to prevent overloading management. Such integration will also help management to understand the significance of a change in risk exposure, for example operational risks that increase in exposure, but remain within appetite or tolerance versus those that fall outside of the agreed operational risk appetite or tolerance thresholds.

- The second is the crucial stage of converting data to information by adding context and interpretation (e.g. how the data compares with business performance metrics, whether the data is suggesting the emergence of increased or reduced risk, i.e. whether movement is relatively positive or negative). This entails the identification and investigation of adverse variances and trends, and analysing the underlying causes. Some key considerations include, whether:

o recurring 'ambers' are reflecting a static or worsening position;

o a cluster of 'ambers' represents an overall 'red' in aggregate; and

o recurring 'greens' may suggest thresholds are not sufficiently sensitive and should be reviewed.

The monitoring of performance against qualitative statements of operational risk appetite or tolerance is more challenging but should be attempted where possible. One solution is to have regular conversations at board, risk committee and operational risk-function level about whether staff behaviours and organizational activities are consistent with these statements. Other relevant functions such as internal audit, HR and IT security may also be involved to gauge their opinion. The value of conversations about operational risk should not be underestimated. It can help to promote risk awareness and identify potential areas of concern.

More formal mechanisms to monitor performance against qualitative statements include internal audit reviews, information from staff performance reviews (where adherence to key qualitative statements could be assessed), and investigations into loss events, to determine whether they were partially the result of behaviours or actions included in qualitative statements (e.g. regulatory breaches).

6.3 Aggregation and reporting

Some of the challenges in aggregation and reporting arise from making sense of tolerance thresholds set in different parts of the organization.

Consider a large organizational group. If a specific business unit adopts group-wide tolerance thresholds it will, almost certainly, report a perpetual 'green' status because the scale of its operation is insufficient to breach these thresholds – thus there would never be any trigger for action anywhere in the organization. On the other hand, a 'red' status at business-unit level may be of little or no significance at group level and thus dilute the value of the 'unacceptable' flag at group senior management level.

A solution adopted by some organizations involves the recalibration of thresholds at different layers in the organization. Figure 5.1 provides an example.

The risk exposure on the left of this diagram belongs to Business 1, which represents 80 per cent of Division A, which in turn forms 80 per cent of the group. In this case the 'red' status at business level is of similar significance in the context of the division and group as a whole. The risk exposure on the right of this diagram

Figure 5.1   An approach to aggregating tolerance thresholds

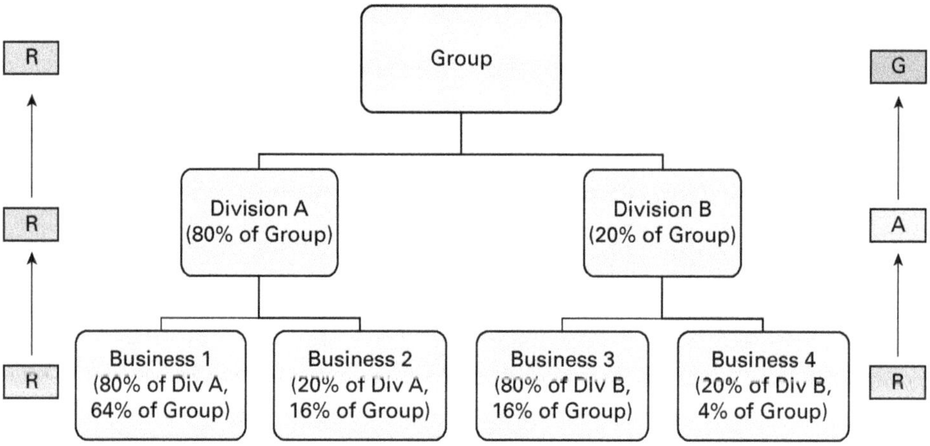

SOURCE IOR sound practice guidance paper

is also a 'red' risk at business level, because it is significant to the management of Business 4. However, since that business is a small part of Division B, which itself is a small part of the group, the significance reduces with the escalation up the organization.

Recalibration, at divisional and/or group levels, can be achieved by applying a weighting to the reported data according to the relative scale of the initiating business. However, weightings cannot be so low as to remove them from top-level scrutiny:

- the implications of poorly managed operational risk in one business may have a contagious effect on the reputation of the group as a whole; and

- weaknesses in operational risk management may be systemic, meaning that problems in one business may be a signal of issues elsewhere.

Therefore, the aggregate position needs to be managed on a common-sense basis. However good an aggregated reporting system may be, it does not remove the need for a qualitative and evaluative approach being adopted at the centre of an organizational group.

6.4 Management and decision making

An organization's operational risk appetite and associated tolerances should be used to drive action. Organizations should not accept exposures or control weaknesses that are outside of either its overall appetite for operational risk or agreed tolerance thresholds. Key decisions include:

- Whether it is appropriate to accept the breach for a limited time period. After weighing all the evidence, it may be the case that a breach could involve a truly one-off exception. In other cases, it may be appropriate to review and recalibrate previous tolerance levels if they are believed to be too conservative. It is recommended that such acceptances should be recorded and revisited regularly (e.g. on a quarterly basis).

- Taking steps to mitigate/avoid and prevent a recurrence. This is likely to be the most appropriate response to a breach of operational risk appetite or tolerance and will require approval to implement some additional or alternative control measures.

- Some intermediate management action – for example, conducting extended or more intense monitoring, undertaking additional root cause analysis, or investigating the cost/benefit of mitigation options.

It must be emphasized that operational risk exposures that exceed an organization's overall appetite for operational risk should be rectified as quickly as possible. Exposures that exceed appetite are unacceptable and risk the solvency and reputation of an organization.

Breaches of specific tolerance limits – especially as business unit, department or functional level – may be accepted for longer, so long as they do not risk the long-term survival of an organization. However, it is advisable to specify a maximum time period (e.g. one year) for acceptance. After this time, action should be taken either to reduce the exposure or to revise the tolerance limit.

7. Conclusions

Designing and implementing an operational risk appetite framework is challenging and time-consuming. However, it is hard to see how operational risk can be managed effectively without one. There is no optimal level of exposure to operational risk. Neither is it usually possible or desirable to reduce operational risk exposures to zero. As a result, organizations must decide upon and articulate their appetite for operational risk, making it clear which risks can be taken in the pursuit of organizational objectives, which risks should be reduced where cost effective, and the degree to which these positive and negative exposures can vary across the organization.

Operational risk appetite is an area where opinions can differ. Some operational risk professionals will accept that their organizations should be willing to take certain operational risks. Others are uncomfortable with such language, framing operational risks purely in terms of downside outcomes. Ultimately the choice is for them to make. However, what is clear is that organizations will not make effective operational risk management decisions without an understanding of the positive and negative aspects of operational risk exposures and their associated control mechanisms. So long as we all agree that most operational risk exposures cannot, should not, be reduced to zero, then there is a need to determine and express operational risk appetite.

Reflective practice questions

1   Does your organization talk about a willingness or preparedness to take operational risk in order to achieve its objectives? How did it arrive at this decision, and does it remain appropriate?

2   How involved is the board of your organization in determining operational risk appetite? Do board members play an active role or simply rubber-stamp the work of the operational risk function?

3   Do you use both qualitative risk appetite statements and quantitative metrics when expressing your appetite for operational risk?

4   Have you set loss tolerance thresholds for specific categories of operational risk, along with their associated risk, control and performance metrics?

5   How have you communicated your organization's operational risk appetite to staff?

6   Do you regularly compare your current operational risk profile to the agreed appetite? What action is taken when the agreed operational risk appetite is breached?

APPENDIX B Example operational risk appetite decision template

	1 Averse	2 Cautious	3 Open/Optimistic	4 Significant
Appetite Description	Avoidance of operational risk is a key objective.	Preference for safe options that have a low degree of operational risk and may only have limited potential for reward.	Prepared to consider all options and choose the one that is most likely to result in a positive return, even if this involves an element of operational risk.	Willing to be innovative and to choose options offering potentially higher business rewards (despite greater inherent operational risk).
Operational Risk Strategic Impacts	**Example behaviours when taking key decisions…**			
Financial • Income • Expenditure • Procurement • Fraud • Economic	• Avoidance of financial loss is a key objective. • No acceptance of budget variation. • Resources withdrawn from non-essential activities that expose the organization to operational risk.	• Prepared to accept the possibility of some limited financial loss for high gains. • Risk reduction remains the primary concern, especially where budgets may be put at risk.	• Prepared to invest for reward and minimize the possibility of financial loss by managing operational risks to a tolerable level. • Value and benefits considered (not just lowest risk). • Budget is not fixed and is allocated fluidly according to priority need. • Resources allocated in order to capitalize on potential opportunities.	• Prepared to invest for the best possible reward and accept the possibility of financial loss (although controls may be in place). • Budget is allocated according to the opportunity for highest return. • Resources allocated even where operational risks could impact on returns.

(continued)

	1 Averse	2 Cautious	3 Open/Optimistic	4 Significant
Regulatory and legal • Regulatory compliance • Governance • Legal challenge	• Avoid anything that could be challenged, even unsuccessfully. • Compliance driven/ overinvests in inspection. • Play safe always.	• Limited tolerance for taking risk. Want to be reasonably sure we would win any challenge or survive scrutiny. • Normal investment in compliance.	• Prepared to challenge generic regulation where there has been a proper appraisal of the options that can be justified in the context of the organization's specific/ differing operating environment.	• Chances of losing challenge are high and consequences serious, but success would return huge, standard-setting benefits. • Has the potential to attract adverse attention from the regulator.
Reputation and Customer Service • Reputation • Community	• Minimal tolerance for any decisions that could lead to challenge, adverse publicity or scrutiny.	• Tolerances for risk-taking limited to those events where there is little chance of any significant repercussion should failure occur.	• Appetite to take decisions to enhance reputation with some potential for exposure to additional publicity, but only where appropriate steps have been taken to minimize any exposure.	• Appetite to take decisions that are likely to bring challenge, but where potential benefits outweigh the risks.
Human Resources • Equalities • People • Social	• Protect staff. Maintain status quo as far as possible.	• Protect staff as much as possible.	• Flexible management of staff.	• Maximize efficiencies and cost savings.

References

Furnham, A and Boo, H C (2011) A literature review of the anchoring effect, *The Journal of Socioeconomics*, 40 (1), 35–42

IRM (2021) Risk appetite and tolerance, www.theirm.org/what-we-say/thought-leadership/risk-appetite-and-tolerance/ (archived at https://perma.cc/9DLM-9DN7)

Tversky, A and Kahneman, D (1974) Judgment under uncertainty: Heuristics and biases, *Science*, 185 (4157), 1124–31

Operational risk governance   06

LEARNING OUTCOMES

- Explain the role of operational risk governance and its importance for the success of organizations.
- Compare different approaches to the design and implementation of risk governance.
- Know how to implement effective operational risk governance arrangements.

1. Introduction

All organizations have in place governance arrangements to ensure that they are directed and controlled in a manner that is consistent with the expectations of their stakeholders (for example: shareholders, creditors, regulators, customers, employees and third parties). These governance arrangements should span all aspects of an organization's activities and operations, including the decisions made on its behalf by employees. The management of risk forms a central element of these arrangements. This includes the management of operational risk.

This chapter explores a range of sound practices for the governance of operational risk. The chapter is not intended as a replacement for existing governance codes and standards, such as the UK Corporate Governance Code (FRC, 2018) or the OECD's Principles of Corporate Governance (OECD, 2015). Instead, the aim is to highlight practices that may be employed to support the effective and appropriate management of operational risk, as part of the wider governance activities of an organization.

With sound practices for the governance of operational risk management an organization can ensure that its operational risk exposures are kept within appetite, maintain compliance with applicable laws and regulations (e.g. health and safety, environmental and solvency regulations) and ensure that internal policies and procedures for the management of operational risk are followed. More generally, effective operational risk governance should support the wider corporate governance and financial reporting activities of an organization through the control of 'people risks'. Sound practices for the governance of operational risk management can reduce the potential for inappropriate conduct on the part of directors, managers and employees, including wilful negligence and criminal activity.

CASE STUDY 6.1   Corporate governance and people risk

Research from the United States (Sahut, Peris-Otiz and Teulon, 2019) suggests that only one in four financial-market frauds are detected and that 15 per cent of US companies were engaged in fraudulent activities, such as financial misreporting, between 1996 and 2004. This research also estimates that the annual cost of internal fraud among large US companies is US $380 billion each year.

Internal fraud is a long-standing category of operational risk and a common example of people risk. Internal fraud is committed for a variety of complex reasons, ranging from greed, incompetence, a desire to punish or even to protect an organization (as in the case of the Barclays LIBOR scandal, see Chapter 4, Case Study 4.1). Sometimes internal fraud is committed by isolated individuals, other times groups of people. Almost always, a person's ability to commit fraud is the result of failures in corporate governance (Farber, 2005), which includes operational risk governance.

Given that many of the categories of risk that fall within the scope of operational risk management are forms of people risk (e.g. fraud, misreporting, mis-selling, non-compliance with policies and procedures, and health and safety risks) operational risk management and corporate governance are close relations. It would be impossible to have an embedded operational risk management framework without effective corporate governance arrangements, including arrangements for operational risk governance. Equally, effective corporate governance arrangements rely on an embedded operational risk management framework being in place.

2. The role of operational risk governance

Operational risk governance comprises the architecture (roles, responsibilities, policies, procedures, systems, structures and reporting arrangements) through which the management of operational risk is directed and controlled. The role of this architecture is to facilitate the oversight of operational risk management activities across an organization, to ensure that operational risk management decisions are made in a consistent manner and that these decisions do not interfere with the achievement of an organization's objectives. As such, operational risk governance is concerned with:

- providing assurance to the governing body of an organization that a sound system of internal controls for the management of operational risk is in place;
- escalating any concerns regarding the management of operational risk to the organization's governing body, especially where such concerns may threaten the achievement of an organization's objectives;
- ensuring that an organization's exposure to operational risk is kept within agreed appetite or tolerance limits (where relevant);
- maintaining compliance with external laws and regulations that relate to the management of operational risk;
- monitoring compliance with internal operational risk policies and procedures;
- allocating roles and responsibilities for the management of operational risk and ensuring that these roles and responsibilities are carried out correctly;
- the management of people and conduct-related risks, where the behaviours of directors, managers, employees and third-party contractors are incompatible with an organization's objectives.

The scope of operational risk governance spans a significant part of the wider operational risk management framework. But it is important to stress that they are not the same thing. As explained in Chapter 1, operational risk management is concerned with the organization of operational risks to help make operational risk management decisions that protect and create value. Operational risk governance is concerned with coordinating this decision making. In short, the role of operational risk governance is to ensure that operational risk management decisions are made in a consistent manner and that an appropriate balance is maintained between the expectations of all stakeholder groups.

CASE STUDY 6.2   Balancing the operational risk management expectations of different stakeholder groups

Balancing the expectations of different stakeholder groups can be challenging, especially when stakeholder groups have different preferences about their personal exposure to operational risk or the financial consequences of these exposures for organizations. A common dilemma is balancing the desire for short-term profit maximization (a priority for shareholders and the recipients of profit-related pay) versus the safety of employees, customers and third parties.

Sociologist Theo Nichols has been instrumental in the conduct of research on the value trade-off between safety and profit. He and others (see Nichols and Walters, 2013) have completed a wide range of empirical research in the area, which shows that organizations continue to struggle with this trade-off, especially in less-regulated jurisdictions. Ensuring the safest possible working environments can impact on the efficiency and effectiveness of operations, increasing equipment costs and reducing worker productivity, thus impacting on short-term profits. This is especially the case with chronic workplace-related illnesses, which may take years to manifest, perhaps after a worker has retired or moved to other work.

Law and regulation is a partial answer to this trade-off. Fines, legal liability laws and criminal sanctions against management can be a powerful deterrent to lax health and safety controls. However, increasingly the attitudes of traditionally profit-oriented stakeholders are changing, including those of shareholders. Concern for corporate social responsibility (an important component of corporate governance in the 21st century) has increased, especially as shareholders have learnt that corporate social responsibility supports the achievement of stable, long-term performance (Michelon, Rodrigue and Trevisan, 2020).

The key point here is that what is valued by stakeholders can change. Once shareholders and managers focused on short-term profits – increasingly this has shifted to a longer-term, more sustainable perspective. Corporate governance, in this case operational risk governance, plays an important role in helping organizations to understand these trends and ensure that their decision makers act in accordance with the changing wishes of stakeholders. In this case, it means giving greater priority to health and safety concerns. Even if this does impact on efficiency and effectiveness in the short term, the longer-term benefits more than outweigh the associated costs, especially if the reputation of the organization improves and shareholders reward the decision with a higher share price.

3. Elements of an operational risk governance architecture

An organization's operational risk governance architecture consists of multiple complementary elements, outlined below. It is essential that these elements work to support each other, otherwise gaps or weaknesses may emerge that permit inappropriate activities, decisions and behaviours.

The elements of this architecture span the formal and informal structures of an organization. Formal structures relate to the tangible policies, procedures, roles and tools that are used to govern the management of operational risk. Informal structures represent social relations and networks, including the organization's risk culture. Figure 6.1 illustrates the primary components of this formal and informal organization.

Figure 6.1   Formal and informal organization

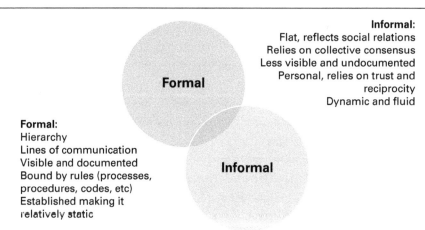

Formal:
Hierarchy
Lines of communication
Visible and documented
Bound by rules (processes,
procedures, codes, etc)
Established making it
relatively static

Informal:
Flat, reflects social relations
Relies on collective consensus
Less visible and undocumented
Personal, relies on trust and
reciprocity
Dynamic and fluid

Formal structures represent the cogs in the operational risk governance architecture of an organization. These cogs provide stability. They ensure that people understand what is expected of them and how to report issues of concern. However, they can be rigid and inflexible. The informal structures of an organization help to reduce these weaknesses. They act as the oil that smooths the operation of the formal cogs, ensuring that the efficiency and effectiveness of an organization's operations are maintained. In this regard both formal and informal structures are essential to effective operational risk governance.

CASE STUDY 6.3   Operational risk communication in a large financial conglomerate

A large financial conglomerate had multiple committees with responsibility for operational risk. This included business unit and divisional operational risk committees, plus a group operational risk committee and an enterprise risk committee.

The timing of these committees, coupled with the requirement for agendas/papers to be circulated one week in advance, meant that the formal communication structure was slow. Items deemed to be of group-wide concern at business-unit level could take two to three months to reach the enterprise risk committee.

To counter this problem a strong informal network of communication existed. Business-unit operational risk staff had regular, unscheduled discussions with their counterparts at the divisional and group levels. These discussions were aided by the fact that social gatherings were organized on a regular basis. This informal network ensured that items of concern could be escalated more quickly, bypassing the intermediate committees, where necessary.

3.1 Risk culture and operational risk governance

Risk culture is an essential element of the informal side of an organization's risk governance architecture.

From an operational risk governance perspective an organization's risk culture is both influenced by and reflected in the attitudes, behaviours and conduct of its managers and employees. In this regard it is important that the formal elements of an organization's operational risk governance architecture do not have a negative impact on its risk culture and vice-versa.

A key concern relates to how managers and employees perceive the relative costs and benefits of the formal operational risk governance structures used by an organization. Where the costs associated with these structures are perceived to be excessive (e.g. because they are perceived as bureaucratic or time-consuming) resentment and resistance can grow, reducing trust between the operational risk function and the wider organization. In turn this can prevent the effective embedding of operational risk management and may even lead to inappropriate conduct and behaviour.

CASE STUDY 6.4   Resistance to bureaucratic governance arrangements

A financial conglomerate was required to comply with corporate governance arrangements in multiple jurisdictions. This included the UK governance code and US Sarbanes-Oxley regulations.

The original arrangements for confirming compliance with all applicable governance regulations were piecemeal. This meant that separate compliance monitoring exercises were performed.

Resistance to these compliance monitoring exercises grew. Managers did not understand why they had to spend time reporting what was essentially the same information multiple times. This impacted on relations between front-line management and the various control functions of the conglomerate, including operational risk. As a result, breaches of operational risk policies and procedures increased. Front-line managers complained that they did not have the resources to ensure full compliance with these policies and procedures because of the time 'wasted' on compliance monitoring.

Following a review into the increase in breaches it was decided to implement an improved compliance monitoring process that did not require similar information to be reported multiple times. Relations between front-line management and the various control functions improved and the number of policy and procedure breaches reduced.

When designing and implementing formal governance structures for the management of operational risk, care should be taken to consider the potential impact of these structures on the risk culture of the organization. Solutions include:

- consulting with managers and employees on the business impact of any new operational risk governance arrangements (to assess the effect on operating costs, efficiency, etc);

- regularly reviewing formal governance arrangements, both to consider the need for new measures and to remove measures that are obsolete;

- involving managers and employees in the above reviews;

- working with colleagues in related control functions (e.g. HR, IT security, internal audit, compliance, etc) to minimize any overlap in governance arrangements.

3.2 Operational risk leadership

An organization's board of directors, or equivalent, is ultimately responsible for the governance of operational risk. In this regard the board is supported by a wider leadership team of executive directors and senior managers (sometimes referred to as the 'c-suite'), to whom responsibility for the implementation of effective governance arrangement for operational risk is usually delegated.

The board of directors and wider leadership team should:

- Set the operational risk governance standards by which the organization should operate. This will include agreeing the organization's appetite for operational risk and approving its operational risk management policy, along with any risk-specific policies (e.g. health and safety, IT security or environmental risk) that are important from an operational risk governance perspective.

- Demonstrate their commitment to the above standards, through what they say and do. This means that the board and wider leadership team must be seen to 'walk the walk', not just 'talk the talk' of operational risk governance. Employees are much more likely to follow an organization's operational risk governance arrangements if they perceive that the board and wider leadership team are also following them.

- Regularly monitor and review operational risk governance arrangements to ensure that they are functioning correctly. This should include building good relations with the operational risk function, including inviting representatives from the team to board (and other relevant) meetings (e.g. audit and risk committees), where appropriate.

- Ensure that improvements are made to an organization's operational risk governance arrangements, where necessary. This includes ensuring that any new/changed laws or regulations that relate to operational risk governance are complied with.

The board and wider leadership team embody both the formal and informal aspects of an organization's operational risk governance architecture and so represent a key intersection between the two. Board agenda items and papers are formal arrangements. In contrast, how the board and senior leadership team 'walk the walk' of an organization's operational risk governance arrangements is an informal mechanism. Building good personal relations with the operational risk function is also important.

CASE STUDY 6.5   Building formal and informal relations with the operational risk function

A medium-sized social enterprise, operating in the housing sector, has a board consisting of non-executive directors only. The enterprise is subject to governance regulation, which encompasses operational risk.

The board employs a number of formal and informal mechanisms to build relations with the operational risk manager. This includes:

- The operational risk manager attends the quarterly audit and risk committee to report on the organization's operational risk profile and to present papers for approval (e.g. annual reviews of the operational risk policy and business continuity arrangements).

- The operational risk manager facilitates a strategy-focused session on operational risk at most board away-days. This has included discussions about operational risk appetite, emerging operational risks and new areas of regulation (e.g. data protection).

- Occasional board briefings on topics relating to operational risk.

- Informal meetings between the operational risk manager and the audit and risk committee chair, the aim being to socialize and discuss recent developments in operational risk across the sector, rather than to focus on the operational risk management practices of the organization.

3.3 Modes of accountability

The operational risk governance structure of an organization should allocate clear and discrete responsibilities for the implementation, design and assurance of its operational risk management framework. These mechanisms are explained in Table 6.1.

Table 6.1   The three modes of accountability

Mechanism	Description
Implementation	Responsible for the day-to-day implementation of the operational risk management framework. This will usually include keeping operational risk exposures within agreed appetite or tolerance limits, ensuring compliance with the operational risk management policy, and ensuring that operational risk procedures are followed correctly (e.g. keeping risk and control assessments up to date, escalating loss events, etc).
Design	Responsible for the policies, procedures and tools that comprise an operational risk management framework. For more on the contents of an operational risk management framework refer to the IOR's paper on embedding operational risk.
Assurance	Reviews the implementation and design of the operational risk management framework. Provides assurance to the board or equivalent that the framework is appropriate and operating as intended.

However roles and responsibilities are allocated, all three modes of accountability should be present. Ideally no one person or function should have more than one mode of accountability, although in smaller organizations this can be difficult to achieve.

In terms of the application of the three modes of accountability a number of approaches are possible. This includes:

- the three lines of defence;
- the three lines model;
- the five lines of assurance.

3.3.1 The three lines of defence

This approach has been recognized for many years as sound practice for operational risk governance (IIA, 2015). In the financial services sector, many regulators require the implementation of the three lines of defence approach (see Chapter 12).

Two features distinguish the three lines of defence approach:

- The three modes of accountability are very clearly segregated. This means that individuals, and the functions or departments in which they are located, can only have one role (implementation, design or assurance). Usually so-called 'first-line' management are allocated responsibility for implementation; the (operational) risk function in the 'second line' has responsibility for design; and in the 'third line' internal audit is responsible for assurance.

- The individuals responsible for the design of the operational risk management framework (usually the central risk or operational risk management function) are allocated an additional oversight role. This means that they monitor those responsible for the implementation of the framework and take action to correct any errors or omissions.

One advantage claimed for the three lines of defence approach is that it mitigates the potential for conflicts of interest within individuals or functions by segregating the three modes of accountability. The argument being that the more segregated these functions are, the more likely it is that weaknesses in the design or implementation will be detected and corrected quickly.

Another claimed advantage of the approach is that by allocating an oversight role to the designers of the operational risk management framework, errors or omissions in implementation will be detected quickly, rather than relying on infrequent internal audits to identify concerns.

However, there are also some significant disadvantages with this approach, as highlighted by the Chartered Institute of Internal Auditors (IIA, 2020). Firstly, segregating the three modes of accountability, especially when physically segregating the individuals or functions responsible for them (e.g. by placing them in different locations), can lead to a serious breakdown in trust and cooperation. Trust and cooperation are built when colleagues can work together and help one another. When co-working is inhibited, this can very quickly result in resistance and even conflict, manifested in issues such as first-line managers not following the operational risk policy or procedures correctly, a failure to escalate issues of concern, or, in the extreme, reckless risk taking.

Secondly, a strict interpretation of the three lines approach can prevent those responsible for designing and assuring the operational risk management framework from helping those tasked with its implementation. First-line managers and their teams have many responsibilities and are rarely risk experts. This means that they often struggle to understand operational risk policies and procedures, and can find their implementation complex and time-consuming. Hence, without guidance and training from those experts in the design and assurance of operational risk management frameworks they are more likely to make mistakes and incur unnecessary resource costs.

In view of the advantages and disadvantages of a strict three lines approach, organizations should think carefully about implementing one. Where regulators require a strict three lines approach, one should be implemented. However, in other contexts, a strict three lines approach is rarely optimal.

3.3.2 The three lines model

Given the weaknesses that can be associated with a strict three lines of defence approach the Chartered Institute of Internal Auditors (IIA) launched a major revision of the approach in 2020, known as the three lines model (IIA, 2020). The model states that close collaboration should be maintained by the first and second lines in particular, although it argues that the third-line internal audit function should remain separate from the first and second lines. The three lines model also does away with the word 'defence'. This is because it promotes a negative view of risk. As explained in Chapter 1, risk exposures have positive upsides, as well as negative downsides. This includes operational risk exposures.

The three lines approach is built on the following core principles:

- Governance requires structures and processes that enable accountability, risk-based decision making and assurance.
- The governing body is accountable for effective governance but must delegate much of the day-to-day responsibilities to management.
- Management spans the first and second lines. These lines may be blended or separated.
- The first-line role involves the delivery of products and services and management of the associated risks.
- The second line assists the first line in the management of risk. This line may include risk, compliance and governance specialists. However, at all times the first line retains responsibility for the management of risk.
- The third line provides independent and objective assurance on the adequacy and effectiveness of governance and risk management. The third line must, at all times, retain independence.
- All lines must work together to create and protect value for the organization and its stakeholders.

3.3.3 The five lines of assurance

The five lines of assurance approach was originally proposed by Leech and Hanlon (2016). The approach differs from the three lines of defence and three lines model in that it makes more explicit the role of the board and an organization's executive directors in relation to risk governance.

Three of the lines within the five lines approach are very similar to the three lines approach. These are:

- work units, meaning business unit/function/department managers;
- specialist units, such as the operational risk function, compliance function and company secretary or governance professional;
- internal audit.

The remaining two lines are:

- the CEO, managing director and other senior directors and managers;
- the board of directors or trustees.

Within the five lines approach, the CEO or equivalent is responsible for building and maintaining a robust risk management framework, including operational risk. They ensure that the most significant value-creating and value-destroying risks to the organization's (strategic) objectives are managed. Responsibility for the management of these risks is assigned to senior directors and managers who act as the 'risk owners', ensuring that their teams identify, assess, monitor and control these risks in an effective manner.

Under a five lines approach the board has responsibility for ensuring that the other four lines are performing their roles in an appropriate way. The board also has responsibility for identifying, assessing, monitoring and controlling the risks associated with an organization's objectives, as well as other organization-wide issues such as succession planning, financial reporting and the performance of the CEO or equivalent. This means that the board is involved, directly, in the management of strategically significant operational risks and cannot delegate responsibility for their management, although the board can of course use the operational risk function, and other functions, to support its work.

3.3.4 The benefits of collaboration

Both the five lines of assurance and the three lines model emphasize the importance of collaboration across lines. The benefit of collaboration is that trust between those responsible for each of the three modes of accountability can be built (see Ashby, Bryce and Ring, 2019).

Improved collaboration can, as a result, help to prevent and mitigate operational risk events by removing potential causes and enhancing the associated control environment. In addition, it can help to improve operational risk governance, through improvements in the implementation, design and assurance of the operational risk management framework.

CASE STUDY 6.6 Building trust through collaboration

A financial services organization launched a new operational risk and control assessment approach, and supporting IT system. The initial first-line response to the approach and system was negative. Staff did not understand how to complete the assessments and in some cases they were required to repeat work.

Trust in the second-line operational risk function declined as a result. First-line managers resisted requests from the function and a perception grew that the function was bureaucratic and did not add value to the organization. Communication between the first and second lines reduced.

In response, the operational risk function reviewed its role. The organization had implemented a strict three lines of defence approach and only used the operational risk function for framework design and oversight purposes. Implementation of the new framework and system had, therefore, been left to first-line management supported by a small number of overworked operational risk champions. Senior management subsequently decided that the operational risk function should get more involved in supporting the work of first-line management. Subsequently second-line operational risk managers were assigned relationship management roles and began to support the risk and control assessment work being performed by the first line (attending risk assessment workshops, providing ad hoc advice and training and reviewing draft work, for example. This led to greater personal contact and the level of trust between the two lines improved. Various enhancements were made to the risk and control assessment approach as a result of this collaboration, and the user-friendliness of the IT system was improved. The second-line operational risk function also reported that first-line managers were more open about operational risk events and potential control deficiencies.

To help understand how collaboration can improve operational risk governance it is important to remember that while the operational risk and internal audit functions may contain technical experts in operational risk, it is first-line management that will typically have a superior understanding of the day-to-day operations of the organization. By combining this professional risk management expertise with the operational experience of first-line management, improvements can be made to existing operational risk governance and management frameworks, as identified in Case Study 6.6. This creates a virtuous circle of improved trust, enhanced organizational performance, and more efficient and effective operational risk governance. Such a virtuous circle cannot be achieved if the second and third line are segregated from first-line management.

It should be stressed that improved collaboration across the three lines does not imply that individuals or functions should have multiple roles, just that individuals and functions should collaborate. In terms of the operational risk function this could mean:

- Having a separate reporting line to first-line management and, where appropriate, internal audit.

- Maintaining good relations with both first-line management and internal audit. This should include regular formal and informal interaction, with an emphasis on working together for the benefit of the organization.

- Participating in meetings with first-line management to support the implementation of the operational risk management framework.

- Providing formal training and informal, ad hoc coaching to support the implementation of the operational risk management framework.

- Providing internal consulting services on operational risk, including decision support, although it should be made clear that the operational risk function cannot be held responsible for the outcomes of these decisions.

- Where possible, ensuring that the operational risk function is located close to those responsible for implementation and that they can be accessed easily. This includes physical and online access to the operational risk function.

3.4 Operational risk committees

Most operational risk governance infrastructures will include one or more committees with responsibility for overseeing the design, implementation and assurance of the operational risk framework.

In larger organizations separate operational risk committees may be created. This might include a number of divisional operational risk committees reporting into a group operational risk committee, chaired by the group head of operational risk or chief risk officer (CRO). In turn, the group operational risk committee may report to a group-wide, board-delegated risk committee or equivalent.

In smaller organizations there may be a single operational risk committee, or operational risk may form part of the terms of reference for a board-delegated enterprise risk committee, an audit and risk committee, or an audit committee.

At a minimum, the oversight of operational risk governance should be part of the terms of reference for at least one board-level committee. This might include the board or, more often, the board-delegated audit and risk or audit committee.

In relation to the governance of operational risk, the terms of reference for the relevant committees should include:

- Responsibility for overseeing the implementation and design of the operational risk management framework.

- In the case of an audit or audit and risk committee, responsibility for overseeing the assurance of the operational risk framework, including the review of:

  o any operational risk issues that may affect the satisfactory outcome of external financial audits or question the accuracy of financial reports;

  o operational loss events that are considered to be material for financial reporting purposes; and

- o internal audits that relate to operational risk management and approving the annual internal audit plan.
- Reviewing the operational risk policy on at least an annual basis and recommending approval (or not) of the policy to the governing body.
- Ensuring that appropriate action is taken to resolve any breaches of the operational risk policy or breaches of the associated procedures.
- Reviewing risk profile reports, including reports on operational risk events and the effectiveness of operational risk controls.
- Ensuring that operational risk exposures are kept within agreed appetite or tolerance limits, where relevant.

Though one or more committees may have delegated responsibilities for operational risk governance, the governing body must retain overall responsibility for the governance of operational risk. It is essential that appropriate arrangements are in place to keep the governing body informed of the work of these committees, especially that of the board-delegated risk and/or audit committees. The whole board must, at all times, be confident that a sound system of operational risk governance is in place across the organization.

Where a hierarchy of committees exists for operational risk it is important that escalation procedures are agreed to ensure that important risk exposures, events or concerns are reported in a timely fashion to the relevant level of management. Table 6.2 summarizes the relevant levels of importance for operational risk-related governance matters.

Table 6.2 Escalation of operational risk exposures, events or concerns

Board-delegated committee	All operational risk exposures or control weaknesses that threaten the achievement of organizational objectives or the integrity of its financial reporting.
Group-wide committee	Systemic risk exposures or control weaknesses that may affect multiple divisions or areas across the organization.
	Division-specific risk exposures or control weaknesses that may threaten the achievement of the organization's objectives.
Divisional committee	All risk exposures or control weaknesses that may impact on the efficient operations of the division or its ability to achieve performance targets.

4. Implementing operational risk governance

The success or failure of operational risk governance depends on how it is implemented. Effective implementation requires the allocation of clear and unambiguous roles and responsibilities for operational risk management, combined with appropriate policies and procedures, and reporting.

4.1 Roles and responsibilities

Roles and responsibilities will vary depending on the formal structure of operational risk governance (e.g. three lines of defence, three lines or five lines of assurance) and the nature, scale and complexity of an organization's activities.

Common roles in relation to operational risk governance are explained below.

4.1.1 Risk owners

Risk owners will typically be managers responsible for specific aspects of the day-to-day operations of the organization. All departments or functions will have one or more risk owners (e.g. finance, marketing, customer services, etc). This includes the risk function and/or operational risk function. For example, the head of operational risk is responsible for the health and safety of their staff, as a result they are the risk owner for health and safety risks in their function.

Risk owners are responsible for the management of one or more categories of risk in their area of responsibility. From an operational risk governance perspective, the owners of operational risks are responsible for the implementation of the operational risk management framework in their area of responsibility. This will include ensuring that they and their staff comply with the operational risk policy and associated procedures. Where applicable, they will also be responsible for ensuring that operational risk exposures are kept within appetite and or tolerance.

It is recommended that risk owners are allocated to each of the major categories of operational risk that a particular department or function is exposed to. For example, health and safety, fraud, cyber security, etc. Often the head of department or function takes on the responsibility of risk owner. Alternatively, ownership may be delegated to a number of specialist managers. Where ownership is delegated it should be made clear to the heads of department or function that they retain ultimate responsibility for the governance of operational risk management in their area.

4.1.2 The chief risk officer (CRO)

Some organizations appoint a CRO to lead their risk management work. Where a CRO is appointed they must have the authority necessary to ensure the effective governance of risk across their organization, including the governance of operational risk. To help achieve this, the CRO should also have direct access, whenever required, to the governing body and all board-delegated committees with responsibilities for the governance of operational risk.

In relation to operational risk the CRO is the individual with ultimate accountability for the design of the operational risk management framework and associated governance arrangements for ensuing that this framework is implemented appropriately across the organization. In this regard the CRO should ideally report to the chief executive officer (CEO), rather than the chief financial officer (CFO) or the chief operating officer (COO). This is to ensure fully independent reporting lines for the implementation and design of the operational risk management framework. Where it is not possible for the CRO to report directly to the CEO, an alternative may be for the CRO to report to the CFO, but only providing that the reporting line of the CRO and risk function remains independent from the day-to-day operations of the organization (e.g. sales, production, customer services, etc). In such a circumstance the CRO should retain direct access to the CEO and governing body in case of any reporting-line conflicts.

4.1.3 The risk management function

Most organizations will have a central risk function, sometimes called the enterprise risk function or group risk function, even if this function consists of only one full-time or part-time individual. In a larger organization a risk function may consist of different departments for specific risk types, including operational risk. In smaller organizations one or two individuals may cover multiple risk types.

The primary role of the risk function in most organizations is to design an appropriate risk management framework, which includes the framework for operational risk management. Depending on the nature of the organization's governance arrangements the risk function may also work to support and/or oversee the implementation of these frameworks (see section 3.3, this chapter).

It is essential that the risk function has sufficient authority to support effective operational risk governance. From an operational risk perspective, this should include:

- having access to the governing body regarding matters concerning the design of the operational risk management framework and the reporting/escalation of significant operational risks or control failures that threaten the achievement of an organization's objectives;

- working with the internal audit function to ensure that control weaknesses, including non-compliance with operational risk policies and procedures, are identified and rectified;

- working with compliance colleagues to ensure that rules and guidance relating to the management of operational risks are complied with.

As in the case of the CRO, the risk function must have an independent reporting line from managers responsible for implementing the operational risk management framework. This is to avoid any conflicts of interest between the responsibilities of risk owners and the risk management function.

4.1.4 Operational risk function

Not all organizations will have a discrete operational risk function. Where an operational risk function is present it must play a central role in the governance of operational risk management.

The operational risk function should have primary responsibility for the design of the operational risk management framework and for supporting its implementation by risk owners. The operational risk function may also support the work of the internal audit function on operational risk assurance.

Specific governance-related activities performed by the operational risk function include:

- supporting the work of the governing body and senior managers in relation to operational risk (e.g. providing advice, guidance, expert opinion, etc);
- supporting the activities of the risk committee or equivalent;
- monitoring the organization's operational risk profile and escalating any concerns about control weaknesses or exposures that exceed agreed appetite or tolerance limits;
- monitoring the risk culture of the organization and helping to influence this culture where necessary;
- drafting operational risk policies and procedures;
- working with risk owners to ensure that operational risk policies and procedures are implemented correctly (e.g. providing training, coaching, etc);
- reviewing and improving the operational risk management framework to ensure that it is user friendly and adds the maximum value for the organization and its management.

Ideally the governance of *all* categories of operational risk should fall within the responsibility of the operational risk function. This will ensure a consistent approach to the management of operational risk and avoid any gaps or overlaps.

However, in some organizations, areas like business continuity, health and safety, insurance or security (cyber or physical security) may fall outside the governance responsibilities of the operational risk function. Where this is the case it is important that the various functions work closely together. In addition, it is recommended that they have a common reporting line (e.g. the group head of risk or CRO).

As with the CRO and risk function, it is important that the operational risk function is able to maintain its independence from the day-to-day operational risk management decisions taken by risk owners. This should not, however, prevent the function from providing advice or guidance. The key is to maintain separate reporting lines and to ensure that policies and procedures make it clear that risk owners are accountable for all operational risk management decisions within their area of responsibility.

In large organizational groups, local (e.g. business unit, divisional or departmental) operational risk managers may be recruited to support the work of risk owners. The appointment of local operational risk managers can significantly improve the implementation of an operational risk management framework and is recommended when resources allow. It may also be that these local operational risk managers can help the group operational risk function to review and improve the design of the operational risk management framework and improve relations between risk owners and the group operational risk function. However, it is important to note that, from a governance perspective, the recruitment of local operational risk managers is no substitute for the establishment of a central, group-level, operational risk management function. Usually, local operational risk managers perform a first-line role; this means that a second-line group operational risk management function is required to coordinate operational risk management activities across the organization. Even where local operational risk managers are assigned second-line responsibilities it is important that their work is coordinated by a central function.

4.1.5 Other specialist control functions

Outside of the direct scope of operational risk there are a number of control-related functions that are relevant from an operational risk governance perspective. These include:

- accounting and finance;
- company secretariat (where relevant);
- compliance;
- human resources;
- IT services;
- legal services.

The operational risk function should work closely with these functions to maximize the effectiveness of operational risk governance. This might include sharing information, developing a common data-collecting and reporting system, providing input into each other's management frameworks, and regular relationship management meetings.

4.1.6 Audit

External and internal auditors (where relevant) have an important role to play in operational risk governance.

The most essential role is providing assurance to the governing body and senior management on the effectiveness of the organization's operational risk governance arrangements. This might include conducting audits of both the design and implementation of the operational risk management framework, as well as highlighting significant risk exposures or control weaknesses.

The operational risk function should maintain good relations with external and internal auditors. This should include reciprocal information sharing, ideally through the use of a common IT system; working together to ensure the effective oversight of the implementation of the operational risk management framework; and, if possible, requesting input from auditors into the design of the operational risk management framework, to ensure that it meets their needs.

Finally, it is imperative that the operational risk management function shares any concerns they may have about the integrity of the internal control environment. This includes sharing information to external audits about any operational risk events, exposures or control failures that could affect the integrity of the organization's financial reporting (e.g. frauds, disciplinary action taken against the senior staff in control functions, financial reporting errors, etc).

4.2 *Operational risk policy*

It is strongly recommended that organizations have either a dedicated operational risk management policy, or a general policy on risk management that explicitly includes the management of operational risks.

The benefit of an operational risk policy from a governance perspective is that it can make clear the organization's expectations for operational risk management, roles and responsibilities, and, where relevant, its appetite or tolerance for operational risk. Hence such a policy provides clear 'rules of the game', especially for risk owners tasked with the day-to-day management of operational risk.

An operational risk management policy should typically include:

- The purpose and scope of the policy. In particular this section should explain how the role and objectives of operational risk management supports the wider objectives of the organization (in terms of achieving profit, ensuring compliance, etc). This section should also make clear the categories of risk that fall within the remit of operational risk management.

- Key operational risk terms and definitions (e.g. distinguishing inherent and residual risk or explaining terms like 'risk events', 'near misses', etc). This helps to establish a common language for operational risk management.

- The governance structure for operational risk management (e.g. committee structure, risk function structure, etc).
- Roles and responsibilities (see section 4.1, this chapter).
- The overall design of the operational risk management framework (see Chapter 2). Specific aspects of this framework may subsequently be expanded upon in separate procedure documents.
- The organization's appetite or tolerance for operational risk.
- How any deviations from the policy may be authorized (e.g. whether or not they require approval from a board or executive committee).
- The frequency with which the policy is reviewed and the body responsible for its approval (ideally the board or a board-delegated operational risk committee, see section 3.4).

4.3 Performance management

Appropriate performance management arrangements that incentivize the implementation of effective operational risk management can enhance operational risk governance. However, extreme care is required to ensure that these arrangements do not result in unintended consequences, especially when financial incentives are offered. For example, a financial performance bonus based on the value of reported operational losses may result in the concealment of losses or underestimations of their value, to ensure the payment of the bonus.

Generally, it is better to design incentives based on the inputs into the operational risk management framework, rather than the outputs (e.g. the number and size of loss events). These inputs might include:

- completing risk assessments on time and in full;
- providing timely, accurate and complete information on risk exposures and control weaknesses;
- addressing internal audit actions within the specified time frame;
- living the values of the organization (in so far as they relate to operational risk management) and complying with any ethical code of conduct.

Monetary incentives should be kept small, if used. The higher the stakes, the greater the possibility that staff will attempt to game the system. Never underestimate the power of small-scale, even symbolic incentives. This might include an employee of the month or year award, for individuals who demonstrate good operational risk governance.

CASE STUDY 6.7   Implementing an operational risk incentive

A financial organization implemented a new incentive scheme to encourage acceptance of a revised operational risk assessment approach. Staff involved in the assessment work received a £50 gift voucher if it was completed on time and in full. The idea was to create a low-stakes incentive that prevented gaming of the scheme.

In addition, the organization launched a competition to name the new assessment approach. The winner was awarded a tablet device. The competition helped to create awareness of the approach and promote a sense of organization-wide ownership.

Another technique is to include operational risk management within a general performance management review and not provide explicit incentives. For example, the operational risk function could be asked to input into the annual performance reviews of risk owners, to help find ways to improve their practice (e.g. to identify training needs) and to set operational risk governance-related objectives.

Where performance incentives for operational risk management are offered it is important to consult with HR professionals, as well as the operational risk function, about their design. This should help to maximize their effectiveness and reduce the risk of gaming.

4.4 Reporting

Effective governance is impossible without information. From an operational risk perspective this requires information on the organization's operational risk profile, significant control weaknesses, and non-compliance with the operational risk policy and procedures. Further information on risk reporting is provided in the chapters on risk and control self-assessments and risk indicators (Chapters 7 and 9).

4.4.1 Internal reporting

To support the effective governance of operational risk, it is essential that operational risk profile reports are provided to the board-delegated committee with responsibility for operational risk management, as well as any supporting group and divisional operational risk management committees.

These reports should contain information on:

- the organization's exposure to operational risks that may threaten the achievement of its objectives, or which exceed agreed appetite or tolerance limits;

- significant control weaknesses, loss events or near misses;

- unauthorized breaches of the operational risk policy or significant breaches of procedures.

The significance of any operational risk exposures, control weaknesses and policy breaches should be agreed with the recipients of the reports. As a rule, a significant weakness is one that might have a material effect on the cash flows or balance sheet of an organization, damage its reputation, breach debt covenants, or result in legal or regulatory sanction.

4.4.2 External reporting

Good governance requires timely, accurate and complete reporting on an organization's risk exposures to its external stakeholders. Stakeholders need this information to make decisions regarding their relationship with the organization (e.g. whether to invest or not) and to satisfy themselves that the organization is working in their interests. The only caveat to this statement is commercial sensitivity. It is not in the interests of external shareholders to make public information that might provide a commercial advantage to rival organizations.

Various external stakeholders may require information on an organization's operational risk exposures. These include:

- shareholders;

- creditors;

- rating agencies;

- regulators;

- supplies;

- customers;

- employees.

The nature and sensitivity of this information will vary. It is particularly important to provide the fullest possible disclosure to rating agencies and regulators. Suppliers and especially commercial customers may also require detailed information on an organization's operational risk exposure, and the design of its operational risk management framework.

It is essential that the operational risk function is involved in all aspects of external reporting. This function has the best understanding of the framework and the organization's risk profile. Where the function is not involved (e.g. in the writing of the annual report and accounts) there is a danger that inaccurate or incomplete information might be reported.

4.5 Continual improvement

An organization should review, at least annually, the effectiveness of its operational risk governance. This might include:

- a review, update and reapproval of the operational risk management policy, including an evaluation of the effectiveness of the policy (e.g. number of unauthorized breaches, etc);
- where relevant, a review, update and reapproval of the operational risk appetite or tolerance statement and associated limits;
- consultation with risk owners and assurance functions to ensure that the governance arrangements continue to meet their needs.

Periodic (e.g. every two to three years) audits of the governance arrangements for operational risk are recommended. These may be conducted by the internal audit function or specialist consultants. The purpose of these audits should be to benchmark against peers to ensure that the arrangements remain up to date.

5. Conclusion

Effective operational risk governance, from the board of directors down, is essential for the survival and success of every organization. The operational risk governance architecture and activities described in this chapter should produce direct benefits to the organization. For example, the proper analysis of operational risk exposures and events should lead to fewer losses and near misses, reducing costs and enhancing efficiency. In so doing, governance activities should help to embed the management of operational risk across the organization, not be perceived as unnecessary 'red-tape'. Good governance never exists for its own sake, it must be value adding to be effective.

Reflective practice questions

1 Are you aware of the key formal and informal elements that comprise the operational risk governance architecture of your organization? What steps have you taken to manage both these formal and informal elements to improve operational risk governance?

2 Does the board of your organization regularly discuss the organization's operational risk profile and any exposures or control weaknesses of organization-wide significance?

3 Do you have a board-delegated committee with responsibility for operational risk? Is this reflected in the committee's terms of reference?

4 How do you implement the three modes of accountability for operational risk management: framework implementation, design and assurance?

5 What steps have you taken to improve trust and collaboration between staff working in each of the three modes of accountability?

6 Do you have a discrete operational risk function? Is this function responsible for the governance of all categories of operational risk?

7 How do you monitor the effectiveness of your operational risk policy and procedures?

References

Ashby, S, Bryce, C and Ring, P (2019) Risk and performance: Embedding risk management, ACCA Professional Insight Report, www.accaglobal.com/content/dam/ACCA_Global/professional-insights/embedding-risk/pi-embedding-risk-management.pdf/ (archived at https://perma.cc/Y8RV-E2QK)

Farber, D B (2005) Restoring trust after fraud: Does corporate governance matter?, *The Accounting Review*, 80 (2), 539–61

FRC (2018) UK Corporate Governance Code, Financial Reporting Council, www.frc.org.uk/directors/corporate-governance-and-stewardship/uk-corporate-governance-code (archived at https://perma.cc/7SU4-ZLNU)

IIA (2015) Internal audit, risk and corporate governance: The three lines of defence model, IIA Policy Paper, Chartered Institute of Internal Auditors, www.iia.org.uk/policy-and-research/position-papers/the-three-lines-of-defence/ (archived at https://perma.cc/BB93-CA9B)

IIA (2020) The IIA's three lines model: An update of the three lines of defence, IIA Policy Paper, Chartered Institute of Internal Auditors, https://global.theiia.org/about/about-internal-auditing/Pages/Three-Lines-Model.aspx (archived at https://perma.cc/SRU3-GU2Q)

Leech, T and Hanlon, L (2016) Three lines of defence versus five lines of assurance, *The Handbook of Board Governance: A comprehensive guide for public, private, and not-for-profit board members*, John Wiley & Sons, New Jersey, 335–55

Michelon, G, Rodrigue, M and Trevisan, E (2020) The marketization of a social movement: Activists, shareholders and CSR disclosure, *Accounting, Organizations and Society*, 80, 101074

Nichols, T and Walters, D (eds) (2013) *Work, Health and Environment Series: Safety or profit? International studies in governance, change and the work environment*, Baywood Publishing Co, New York

OECD (2015) G20/OECD principles of corporate governance, OECD Publishing, http://dx.doi.org/10.1787/9789264236882-en (archived at https://perma.cc/4NA8-W5SZ)

Sahut, J M, Peris-Ortiz, M and Teulon, F (2019) Corporate social responsibility and governance, *Journal of Management and Governance*, 23 (4), 901–12

Risk and control self-assessments 07

LEARNING OUTCOMES

- Know how to construct and assemble the components that comprise a risk and control self-assessment.
- Compare different approaches to the conduct of risk and control self-assessments (e.g. workshops versus questionnaires).
- Explain how to make effective use of the outputs from risk and control self-assessments to support decision making in organizations.

1. Introduction

The risk and control self-assessment (RCSA) is an integral part of most operational risk management frameworks. RCSAs provide a structured mechanism for estimating operational exposures and the effectiveness of controls. In so doing RCSAs help organizations to prioritize operational risk exposures; identify control weaknesses, along with control gaps and overlaps; and monitor the actions taken to address any weaknesses, gaps or overlaps.

This chapter will explore how to design and implement effective RCSAs. A well designed and implemented RCSA can help to embed operational risk management across an organization, improving management attitudes towards operational risk management and enhancing the overall risk culture. In contrast, an inefficient or unnecessarily complex RCSA can damage the reputation of the (operational) risk function and reinforce the perception that operational risk management is a bureaucratic, compliance-focused exercise that does not support the achievement of organizational objectives.

In addition, this chapter will explore how to make effective use of RCSAs to support decision making. Here, it cannot be emphasized enough that the output from RCSAs is about much more that the production of technical data. Though RCSAs can, and should, be used to help assess, even quantify where necessary, operational risk exposures, they are equally important as a mechanism for promoting open discussions about operational risk. Many operational risks are hard to identify, let alone quantify. This is because of a lack of accurate loss data and because new risks emerge on a regular basis. Equally, the effectiveness of specific controls can be hard to assess accurately. However, despite these difficulties, operational risks and their associated controls must not be ignored. Organizations that discuss, openly, their operational risks and the effectiveness of their associated controls should be better prepared for what the future holds, improving the proactivity of their operational risk management activities.

CASE STUDY 7.1   Using RCSAs to promote 'risk talk'

Research into the practice of risk management in organizations has highlighted the importance of 'risk talk' (Arena, Arnaboldi and Palermo, 2017; Mikes, 2016).

Risk talk is a structured mechanism for talking about risk issues, including operational risk-related threats and opportunities, and the efficiency and effectiveness of operational risk controls. Often this structure is provided by a tool such as RCSAs. In addition, opportunities must be created for the conduct of risk talk, such as through the organization of RCSA workshops. Expert facilitation by a relevant risk professional helps also.

The aim of risk talk is to come up with shared, unbiased, solutions for solving risk problems in organizations, solutions that are the result of balanced, evidence-based discussion, using the results of an RCSA, for example. Effective risk talk helps to reduce the potential for instinctual and ill-considered 'Systems 1' thinking and promotes slower, deliberate and logical 'Systems 2' thinking. Systems 2 thinking has been promoted as the best route to effective decision making in environments of risk and uncertainty (Kahneman, 2011).

An effective RCSA can also help support the governance and compliance activities of an organization. The results of an RCSA provide assurance to the governing body and regulators that an organization has in place a sound system for the management of operational risks. Equally RCSAs can support the work of internal and external auditors, helping them to prioritize audit attention and structure audit reports.

Finally, RCSAs can help to improve business efficiency. Weaknesses or gaps in controls can increase the chance of system and process failures and the impact of external events, increasing costs and the potential for disruption. In contrast, an excessive level of control can slow down systems and processes unnecessarily.

2. RCSA fundamentals

There are many ways to approach the design and implementation of an RCSA. Each organization should take time to review the options and select the approach that works best for the nature, scale and complexity of its activities, as well as its risk culture.

Given this variety, there are a number of fundamental decisions that need to be made. These decisions are discussed below.

2.1 Application and scope

The first fundamental decision is whether to require RCSAs for some or all of the operational risks to which an organization is exposed.

The common default option is to require that all identified operational risks should be subject to an RCSA. This ensures that the results of the RCSA are as comprehensive and complete as possible. However, given that the number of discrete operational risk exposures may number in the hundreds or thousands across the various business units, departments and functions of an organization, it can be a very time-consuming and expensive exercise.

Alternative options include:

1 Limiting the granularity of the RCSA. Organizations that categorize their operational risks may, for example, decide that they need only be completed for the 'level 1' risks in their categorization (see Chapter 3). This ensures that RCSAs are completed for all categories of operational risk but ensures that the number of assessments is limited. The downside of this approach is that it may lack sufficient detail for some users of RCSA information (e.g. internal audit, department management, etc).

2 Limiting the focus to the significant operational risk exposures that threaten the achievement of an organization's objectives. Such an approach will provide the information required by the governing body and senior management, but it will not help department or divisional management to manage their local operational risks effectively.

3 Limiting the focus to the significant operational risk exposures that threaten the achievement of department or function objectives. This ensures that department and divisional managers get the information they need to manage local risk exposures. In addition, an escalation process may be implemented to ensure that risks, significant enough to threaten the whole organization, are reported to the governing body/senior management.

Combinations of the above three approaches may be used to further refine the application and scope of an RCSA. For example, option 2 might be conducted using the level-1 risks in a categorization, option 3 the level 2-risks to increase granularity.

As in any risk management activity the costs and benefits of a more or less comprehensive RCSA approach must be considered. A fully comprehensive approach is not necessarily best, especially if it results in information overload and requires excessive amounts of time and effort to complete. RCSAs should only be used where they are value adding, meaning that the benefits must exceed the costs.

CASE STUDY 7.2   Using RCSAs for significant risks only

A large public-sector organization implemented a new RCSA approach. In the course of its day-to-day activities the various divisions and functions of this organization were exposed to a wide variety of operational risks. Health and safety risks, both for its employees and the general public, were especially numerous.

To help reduce the time taken on RCSAs the organization distinguished between what it termed 'business as usual' and 'significant' operational risks. Only significant operational risks were required to be assessed using the RCSA process. Business-as-usual operational risks were managed as part of the organization's various operational processes for the conduct of its activities. These operational processes included routine health and safety assessment activities such as fire safety assessments, display screen equipment assessments and vulnerable person risk assessments.

Significant operational risks were distinguished in terms of their impact on the organization as a whole. Such risks might have a material financial impact, damage the reputation or the organization or result in legal liability or compliance-related issues.

2.2 Process or event focus

Most RCSAs are conducted on an event basis. This means that they are linked to specific risk events such as: fire, fraud, injury, hacking attack, power failures, etc. Often these events are structured using some form of operational risk categorization, as explained in Chapter 3.

An alternative is the process basis. This approach involves mapping organizational processes and identifying potential points of failure within these processes (e.g. the potential for human error or systems failure). A process focus increases alignment between operational risk management and the day-to-day operations of an organization. In so doing it may be perceived as more relevant by management and can be used to link effective operational risk management to business process efficiency.

The downside of a process approach is the time required to map processes. The greater the detail, the more comprehensive will be the set of identified operational risk exposures. However, detailed process maps can take a considerable amount of time and expertise to complete accurately.

Where an organization has detailed process maps in place already, it is recommended that these are used as the basis for identifying operational risks for RCSAs. However, where such maps are not in place, the costs involved in creating them are likely to be excessive.

CASE STUDY 7.3   Implementing a process-based RCSA

A retail financial services organization decided to implement a process-based RCSA approach. One of the factors influencing this decision was that the organization was heavily reliant on a range of human-operated processes – processes that it wished to automate to increase the efficiency and effectiveness of its operations.

Mapping the organization's processes and identifying the operational risks and controls within them took over a year. One problem was a lack of experience across the organization in process mapping. However, once the mapping exercise was done the organization began to reap significant rewards.

As part of the exercise a range of automated control effectiveness tests were established for the operational risks identified in the various processes. The idea was to reduce the amount of staff time required for the completion of repeat RCSAs. In addition, automation increased the frequency and reliability of controls testing, providing a more up-to-date picture of the effectiveness of the organization's operational risk control environment and its residual (net of control) exposure to operational risk.

2.3 Roles and responsibilities

Like any operational risk tool, roles and responsibilities for the design, implementation and use of RCSAs need to be established.

Usually the RCSA process will be 'owned' by the operational risk function. This means that the operational risk function will be responsible for the design of the RCSA and for overseeing its implementation to ensure that the tool is used correctly. This may include documenting the RCSA process, providing coaching and training on how to conduct RCSAs, and facilitating RCSA workshops (see section 4.1.4 below).

Table 7.1 summarizes the other roles and responsibilities that can apply to the conduct and use of RCSAs.

Table 7.1   Other common roles and responsibilities for RCSAs

Role	Responsibility
Governing Body	Ensuring that an appropriate system of internal control is in place. This may include receiving assurance on the effectiveness of the RCSA approach and reviewing the results of Scars for significant operational risk exposures.
Senior Management	Responsible for supporting the work of the board. This includes ensuring that an effective RCSA approach is in place. Where present the chief risk officer (CRO) will have primary responsibility for overseeing the design and implementation of the RCSA.
Risk Owner	Responsible for the completion of RCSAs, ensuring that exposures are within appetite/tolerance, and that there are no significant weaknesses or gaps in controls. Risk owners may either complete the RCSA themselves or delegate the responsibility to suitably qualified individuals. Risk owners must also oversee the completion of any actions required to address control weaknesses or gaps.
Control Owner	Responsible for the design, implementation and maintenance of effective controls. Should provide information to risk owners on any weaknesses or gaps in controls. Should also ensure that action is taken to address any identified weaknesses in the controls they own.
Data Owner	Responsible for providing data to risk and control owners to enable them to complete the RCSA.
Internal Audit	Provide assurance on the design and implementation of the RCSA to senior management and the governing body.

Roles and role terminology may differ in organizations. Some may not use terms like risk, control, or data owner, for example. In all cases it is essential when using RCSAs to establish individuals responsible for the following:

- the production of timely, accurate and complete RCSAs;
- the identification of control weaknesses or gaps;
- providing the data required to complete effective RCSAs; and
- overseeing actions to address control weaknesses or gaps.

2.4   Frequency and timing

Once completed for the first time RCSAs should be reviewed on a regular basis to ensure that they remain up to date. An annual review and update is the most common frequency. But frequencies ranging from one month to one year are considered normal. It all depends on how dynamic an organization's operational risk profile is (i.e. how often exposures change), coupled with the degree of currency with which the organization wishes to maintain its RCSA. In a dynamic operational risk environment, annual assessments will become out of date quickly, for example.

Organizations may complement a full annual review with ad hoc updates for risks that change significantly within a year. That way RCSAs may be kept up to date, while keeping completion costs to a minimum.

Ideally RCSAs should be updated before annual reviews of organizational or departmental/divisional objectives and budgets. That way information from RCSAs can be fed into performance and budgetary reviews, helping to embed operational risk management within the strategic activities of an organization.

3.   Designing an RCSA

A well-designed RCSA tool is essential for success. Key is weighing the costs and benefits of additional comprehensiveness or complexity. The more elements that are added to an RCSA the longer it will take to complete, requiring more time and resources. This means that greater comprehensiveness or complexity is not always optimal.

Where an organization is implementing an RCSA for the first time, a minimalist and simple design is recommended. This will keep the completion costs low. Then as staff get used to the tool, and experience the benefits that can be obtained from the outputs of an RCSA, the comprehensiveness and complexity of the tool may be increased, gradually.

Always remember that there is no point having a highly sophisticated RCSA tool if people do not understand how to complete the tool or are unwilling to use it because it is overly resource intensive.

3.1   Common elements of an RCSA

Common elements of an RCSA are outlined below. Each of these elements represent a different aspect of an organization's operational risk exposures. Not all RCSAs will contain every element. As mentioned above, it is important to balance the benefits of an RCSA with the costs of completion, especially if they are to be updated regularly.

3.1.1 Risk (probability and impact) matrix

Most RCSAs include a qualitative assessment of risk exposure. These assessments rely on the views of people close to the risk in question. Usually, these views are translated into a two-dimensional risk matrix comprising ordinal scales for probability and impact. These scales typically range 1–3 (low, medium and high) up to 1–5. But any numerical range is possible. These are commonly referred to as 3x3, 4x4 or 5x5 risk matrices. Larger scales allow for greater differentiation between risks in terms of their priority for an organization. This can help to prevent clusters of seemingly high- or low-priority risks, allowing resources to be used more efficiently when controlling risks. However, the larger the scale the longer it can take for an assessment to be completed.

Some organizations prefer to use even-numbered matrices, others odd-numbered. An odd-numbered matrix includes a middle value (e.g. 3 in a scale of 5), while an even-numbered matrix does not. The concern with using an odd-numbered matrix is that users are more likely to select the middle value if they are unsure about the level of probability or impact. However, in cases of genuine debate, forcing users to select a higher or lower value that they would prefer is not necessarily optimal either.

CASE STUDY 7.4   Selecting an ordinal risk matrix

A university was designing a new RCSA tool. To help save time when completing assessments, a 3x3 risk matrix was selected. Tests of the tool indicated that users found it relatively easy to assign a low, medium or high value for probability and impact.

Acceptance of the new tool was high. Users found it quick and easy to use. However, the decision did result in a significant cluster of risks rated at 2 for probability and 2 for impact.

To help address this cluster the operational risk function commenced a challenge process. Risk owners were asked to provide evidence to justify the assessments, with a particular focus on the cluster of medium-level risks. This challenge process helped to stimulate debate about the university's risk exposures and resulted in a more dispersed priority order of operational risk exposures.

The key point about an ordinal scale is that data is shown in order of magnitude only, meaning that 2 is larger than 1. With an ordinal scale it is not possible to determine how much bigger 2 is than 1 because there is no standard of measurement for the differences between these two values. Sporting leagues are another example of ordinal scales. It is possible to say that the team at the top is the best team, but not how much better this team is relative to the others in the league. Table 7.2 illustrates a simple 3x3 ordinal scale risk matrix for probability and impact.

Table 7.2 Example ordinal scale 3x3 risk matrix

Probability		Impact			
1 Rare		**1** Low			
2 Possible		**2** Medium			
3 Frequent		**3** High			

	Impact				
		1	1	2	3
Probability	3	3	3	6	9
	2	2	2	4	6
	1	1	1	2	3

To assist in the use of ordinal scales, points of reference should be provided to help users decide on the appropriate scale of probability and impact. A simple example is provided in Table 7.3.

Table 7.3 Example points of reference for qualitative exposure assessments

Probability		Impact	
Rare	Chance of occurrence not expected to exceed once every 5 to 10 years	**Low**	Financial loss not expected to exceed 1% of cash flows and can be easily absorbed into day-to-day running costs
Possible	Chance of occurrence not expected to exceed once every 1 to 5 years	**Medium**	Financial loss between 1% to 5% of cash flows and may require moderate cost cutting

(continued)

Table 7.3   (Continued)

Probability		Impact	
Frequent	Chance of occurrence expected to exceed once per year	**High**	Financial loss exceeds 5% of cash flows and may require major cost cutting or the cancellation of strategic projects

Organizations should always determine their own points of reference for impact. These should be linked to the size of the organization (especially in terms of cash flows and assets and its strategic objectives). In terms of size, a loss of £1 million may be significant for a small organization, but insignificant for a large organization with a strong balance sheet. Financial values are the most common point of reference when estimating impact, but some organizations also include non-financial values like customer satisfaction or reputation. For factors like customer satisfaction or reputation one option is to look at the number of complaints or bad news stories. Another is to assign a financial equivalence value, such as a reputation event with an equivalent impact of £1 million, £10 million, etc.

It is recommended to start only with financial values and to add non-financial impacts later. A greater number of reference points should, in theory, improve the accuracy of the assessment, but it also increases the time required for completion.

In terms of probability, it is normal to link this to either probability ranges (e.g. 0.8–1 for high, 0.5–0.79 for medium, etc) or temporal frequency, in terms of the number of events every year or number of years. Table 7.3 provides an example that may be used as a starting point.

Though qualitative risk matrices are used widely it must be emphasized that, at best, they provide a rough estimate of an organization's operational risk exposures, at worst they can be biased and misleading (Cox, 2008). That said, recent research shows that the value of using risk matrices in tools like RCSAs is less about the production of risk exposure estimates and more about the conversations (risk-talk) that are stimulated by the use of these tools (Jordan, Mitterhofer and Jørgensen, 2018). From a practical perspective this implies that the results of RCSAs should never be assumed to be wholly accurate. But what they do offer is an opportunity to raise awareness of operational risk and to improve an organization's ability to both predict and respond to operational risk events.

3.1.2 Inherent risk exposure

Inherent risk refers to the level of risk exposure with no controls applied. It is also known as gross risk.

An assessment of inherent risk within an RCSA provides a baseline exposure score for the operational risk in question. One advantage is that it highlights the significance of a risk, should no controls be applied. A low level of inherent exposure suggests that the risk in question is of low significance and should require little management attention. In contrast, a high inherent exposure suggests that time and effort should be devoted to controlling the risk.

Organizations may decide that operational risks with a low level of inherent exposure do not require a full RCSA. There is little point spending time and resources assessing control effectiveness or identifying control gaps if inherent exposure is very low. Better to invest this time and resources on risks with higher inherent exposure scores.

The main problem with including inherent risk is how to determine inherent exposure. It is rare for risks to exist in an environment of zero control. Hence inherent assessments can be very conceptual and judgemental, increasing the potential for overestimates or underestimates of inherent exposure. Research into decision making under uncertainty has repeatedly shown that decision makers tend to overweight less-certain low probabilities and underweight medium to high probabilities (Tversky and Fox, 1995). Given the uncertain nature of inherent risk events, this means that inherent risk assessments will typically imply a higher level of risk than is actually the case.

3.1.3 Residual risk exposure

Residual risk is an assessment of the level of risk exposure with controls in place. It is also known as net risk.

An assessment of residual risk considers the number, type and effectiveness of the controls that are in place. In theory, a well-designed mix of effective controls should result in a low level of residual risk exposure, even if the level of inherent exposure is high (e.g. the risk of a nuclear power accident). This means that, where both inherent and residual risk are assessed, the difference between the level of inherent and residual risk shows the contribution that the assigned controls are making to reducing exposure.

Residual risk is easier to assess because it reflects the actual level of exposure given the controls that are in place at the current time. Hence it should be a more realistic assessment that is supported by actual experience in managing the risk, including, where available, historical loss data. It is hard to imagine how an RCSA could work without an assessment of residual risk exposure.

3.1.4 Causes

Operational risks are typically categorized on an event basis (see Chapter 3). This means that inherent and residual risk assessments usually refer to an organization's exposure to specific operational risk events (e.g. the probability and impact of an IT systems failure).

However, events rarely occur in isolation and may be caused by a range of factors. For example, an IT systems failure may be the result of a power cut, a hacking attempt or a faulty update, or a combination of all three.

Hence some RCSAs include information on the causes of risk events. This helps to provide further information to assist in probability assessments. It can also be used to help link controls to specific causes of risk events, and to check that controls are in place to address all of the most significant causes.

By linking events and especially controls to causes RCSAs can be made more prospective, helping organizations to better prevent future operational risk events. By collecting information on causes it can also be possible to link events, thus identifying how a particular cause or control failure in relation to a specific cause may precipitate a chain of operational risk events.

3.1.5 Effects

At the other end of the cause–event–effect chain are the effects of operational risk events. Operational risk events have a range of effects (e.g. financial, business disruption, reputational and physical). Equally the size of these effects can vary. For example, a small fire, contained to a limited area, compared to one that destroys a whole building or site.

Certain controls are designed to reduce the effects of operational risk events (e.g. insurance, sprinkler systems and business continuity plans). Hence some RCSAs collect information on effects to help link the relevant controls to these effects. For example, a sprinkler system will reduce the effect of a fire, but only if the system is well designed and maintained. Equally the establishment of an IT contingency site can help to reduce the effect of system failures, but only if the site is well maintained and tested on a regular basis.

By collecting information on effects, it is possible to determine whether an appropriate mix of controls are in place to address them, or whether there are gaps that need to be filled, for example effects for which no controls are currently in place.

3.1.6 Control effectiveness (individual)

By definition, an RCSA must include an assessment of the controls put in place to address the causes and effects of operational risk events. Ineffective controls will have little to no effect on an organization's exposure to operational risk. Worse, they may create a false sense of security, resulting in an underestimate of exposure.

There are two main ways to assess control effectiveness: a subjective assessment versus objective controls testing. Subjective assessments of control effectiveness use an ordinal scale similar to those used for probability and impact. The simplest is a two-point scale: 'effective' or 'ineffective', but scales of three points or more are common. Table 7.4 provides an example of a three-point scale.

Table 7.4 Example control effectiveness scale

	Control Effectiveness	Description
3	Substantial	Control is fully effective and working as intended
2	Adequate	Control is mostly effective, but there are minor flaws in its operation
1	Requires Improvement	Control is defective, there are significant flaws in its operation

Subjective assessments rely on management judgement, but it is recommended that they are supported by any available information, such as reported loss events or near misses (which may have been the result of a control failure) and internal audit reports.

Objective controls testing requires the identification and monitoring of control effectiveness indicators, usually referred to as 'control indicators' or 'key control indicators'. Examples of these indicators include:

- frequency with which business continuity plans are tested and updated, including whether tests or updates are overdue;
- the results of IT security penetration tests;
- results of portable appliance testing, and whether tests are overdue (or alternatively fire alarm and extinguisher testing);
- number of errors identified in financial transactions or reconciliations;
- identified breaches of policies and procedures.

Hence indicators may either be related directly to the operation of a control, or the frequency and reliability of any reviews conducted to test effectiveness. For more on the collection and use of control indicators please refer to Chapter 9.

3.1.7 Control effectiveness (overall)

It is rare for operational risks to have only one control. Typically, a variety of controls are required: some are causal controls, designed to prevent the event from occurring; others are effect based, designed to detect and mitigate the damaging effects of operational risk events. This range of cause- and effect-based controls are typically referred to as a risk event's 'control environment'.

Estimates of the overall effectiveness of the control environment for a particular operational risk event are less common than the assessment of specific controls but provide a valuable insight into whether a risk is over or undercontrolled. The identification of over or undercontrolled operational risk events is an important benefit of an effective RCSA, so the inclusion of an overall effectiveness assessment is strongly recommended.

Usually, assessments of overall control effectiveness are subjective and rely on a three-point scale:

1 Risk is undercontrolled, meaning that there are gaps in the control environment that need to be filled.

2 The overall level of control is appropriate, meaning that the control environment contains an appropriate mix of controls.

3 Risk is overcontrolled, meaning that some controls are unnecessary, and it may be possible to remove them.

Loss event and near miss data (see Chapter 8), coupled with internal audit reports, can provide valuable information on the overall effectiveness of the control environment. They may both highlight potential gaps in the control environment, while internal audits may sometimes identify obsolete controls.

3.1.8 Action planning

Most RCSAs will include fields to capture information on agreed action plans. Typically, these plans will address either deficiencies in existing controls, the implementation of new controls or the removal of obsolete or excessive controls.

It is important that agreed actions are: Specific, Measurable, Achievable, Realistic and Timebound (SMART) (see Table 7.5). This should ensure that actions are completed on time. It is also important to assign actions to an owner; usually the owner will be a manager with the necessary seniority to ensure the action is completed, preferably the control owner.

3.1.9 Other elements that can be included in RCSAs

The above elements are the most common in RCSAs, but that does not mean that they are the only ones. For example, some organizations may include information on:

Table 7.5 SMART actions

Specific	Set a specific target or goal for the action.
Measurable	By setting an action that is measurable it is possible to demonstrate in an objective manner that it is complete.
Achievable	Actions must be achievable to ensure that they are completed in a timely and effective manner.
Realistic	Controls and control environments are rarely 100% effective. Minor flaws may be considered tolerable, especially when the costs associated with increasing the level of control are high.
Timebound	Actions must be assigned an end date to ensure that they are completed in a timely manner.

- organizational objectives, to link specific operational risk events to objectives;
- risk descriptions, to add detail and context to the identified risk events;
- risk, control and performance indicators;
- loss event and near-miss data;
- identified internal audit issues and actions.

Care should be taken when adding new elements – at all times it is important to weigh the costs and benefits. As explained above, the more detailed and complex an RCSA is, the longer it will take to complete.

3.2 Designing the template

Two main options are available:

1 spreadsheet;

2 IT system.

Most organizations start by using a spreadsheet. An example is provided in Appendix C.

It is recommended that organizations use a spreadsheet approach for a few years before moving to a system. This will allow them to refine the design of the RCSA to ensure it is appropriate for the nature, scale and complexity of their activities, along with their risk culture.

It is not recommended that organizations purchase 'off the peg' RCSA systems that pre-determine the design of the RCSA approach. Such systems may not be compatible with the organization or its risk culture. It is important that any system can be customized, as fully as possible.

3.3 Top-down and bottom-up

RCSAs may be designed for top-down or bottom-up completion.

Top-down completion refers to RCSAs that are typically completed by senior management, including an organization's executive. A top-down RCSA will usually focus on strategic-level operational risks that may threaten the achievement of organizational objectives. Such risks are likely to have a significant financial, regulatory or reputational impact on an organization, and are usually organizational wide, though they may sometimes be specific to a department, division or function.

Bottom-up RCSAs focus on departmental or functional-level operational risks. They are primarily designed to be a local management tool, to help prevent/mitigate loss events and near misses and/or improve system and process efficiency.

Most organizations will design top-down and bottom-up RCSAs. The advantage of a top-down approach is that strategic-level risks can be cascaded down, and aligned to the risks, controls and actions identified in departments, divisions or function assessments. This can help to improve operational risk governance and ensure that organization-wide and local priorities are aligned.

The advantage of a bottom-up assessment is that local managers are able to focus on the risks and controls that are relevant to their area. Equally significant local risks may be escalated for top-level consideration, as may significant correlations between local-level risks in different areas.

Top-down and bottom-up RCSA templates must be consistent, using similar elements and terminology. This will facilitate the cascade of operational risk information up and down the organization. However, given the time limitations of senior managers it may be appropriate to develop a shorter, less complex template for them to complete.

4. Completing an RCSA: approaches and techniques

It is not recommended that RCSAs are completed by one person – such as the risk owner, or their delegate. The judgemental nature of most RCSAs means that subjective bias is very likely. Such bias may result in an over or underassessment of exposure and control effectiveness. In either case this will result in inaccurate information and wasted resources.

The best way to address bias is to involve a number of individuals in the RCSA process. That way the problem of individual biases should be mitigated, where the group is able to challenge them effectively. A further advantage of involving a number of individuals is to increase the range of expertise and experience involved. It is rare for any one individual to have all the information required to complete an RCSA effectively.

4.1 Workshop approach

A workshop approach to RCSA completion ensures human interaction and enables guidance to be provided by a risk professional during the process. Although it can be more time-consuming than the alternatives, the quality of the information generated by a workshop approach can be considerable. This is because of the range of skills, experience and expertise that should be present.

A workshop is a mechanism to get people engaged in talking about their risks, controls and any necessary improvements. Further potential benefits of a workshop approach include:

- raising awareness of operational risks and their associated controls;
- enabling the assessment and improvement of 'softer', hard-to-measure control mechanisms, e.g. communications, training and accountability; and
- providing an opportunity for the transfer of risk management skills across the organization.

4.1.1 Planning a workshop

Preparation is key to ensure a successful RCSA workshop. Guidance should be provided to the participants in advance of the workshop so that they fully understand the context and objectives of the exercise and indeed the contribution they are expected to make.

Table 7.6 summarizes common actions that should be taken to plan for a successful RCSA workshop.

Table 7.6 Planning topics and actions for an RCSA workshop

Topic	Action Required
Get executive support	Risk committee or equivalent should communicate its support for the workshops to risk and control owners.
	Relevant executive or senior manager for the area asked to attend the first five minutes of the workshop to communicate its importance. If attendance is not possible, ask them to contact the attendees via phone or email or produce a short introductory video.
Identify priority areas	Some departments or functions may have a more urgent need for workshops. This can be determined through the review of loss and near-miss data, internal audit reports or the identification of inherently high-risk areas.
Secure local support for the RCSA	Contact local management to ensure that they understand the process and benefits of an RCSA and address any concerns they may have. In particular secure their support for ensuring that any identified actions will be completed within the agreed timescales.
Review area processes and activities	Identify the key activities and processes performed by the area. It is important to understand the operations of an area to ensure that the right participants are selected. Where available review existing operational risk assessments and any loss or near-miss data.

(continued)

Table 7.6   (Continued)

Topic	Action Required
Identify and invite participants	Determine who should attend the workshop and confirm their attendance. If key attendees find that they are no longer available they should be asked to nominate a delegate.
Workshop scope and objectives	Agree the scope and objectives of the workshop with the participants. For example, it may be that only a specific category of operational risks will be considered (e.g. IT risks) or specific operational processes (e.g. customer processes).
	Sometimes risks are identified as part of the RCSA process. This means that the workshop will begin by identifying the relevant risks. However, it is recommended that the primary categories of risk (e.g. the relevant level-1 categories) are identified in advance. This will help to save time during the workshop.
Supply standard documentation (RCSA process and workshop agenda)	Ensure attendees understand what an RCSA is, the information required, and how the workshop will be performed.
Organize a facilitator	Workshops will require an expert facilitator skilled in RCSA. The facilitator should be impartial and may be a member of the (operational) risk function, a risk expert from another part of the organization or an external consultant.

4.1.2 Workshop attendees

The selection of attendees will depend on the scope of the workshop (e.g. risk categories to be covered, processes and activities under review, etc). As a general rule the following should attend:

- a local management representative, including, where specified, the relevant risk owner(s);
- where specified, all relevant control owners;
- where not represented by the relevant control owners, subject matter experts, covering key control areas like IT systems and security, customer relations, marketing, human resources, finance, etc; and
- an independent observer, such as a member of the risk function or a risk owner from another part of the organization.

As a general rule around 6–8 attendees are optimal, with 12 as a maximum. As workshops increase in size, facilitation becomes harder and there will be insufficient time to ensure that all voices are heard.

The role of the independent observer is to look for potential bias. The observer should only speak if they are concerned that a risk exposure or control effectiveness assessment is being over or underestimated.

Care should be taken when inviting managers to workshops, especially senior ones. Often managers need to attend because they are the relevant risk or control owners. However, there is a danger that they may dominate the discussion and/or discourage others from raising concerns. Here the role of the facilitator is key, along with the independent observer. They should be of sufficient seniority to ensure that management do not take over a workshop or use it to pursue a particular political agenda.

4.1.3 Structure and duration of the workshop

RCSAs can take several days to complete, especially when covering the full range of operational risks for the area in question. This presents challenges for the structure and timetabling of workshops. Even with regular breaks, sessions longer than two to three hours can result in fatigue, reducing focus and leading to inaccurate assessments.

To help maintain focus it is recommended that workshops are structured into distinct sections or modules. These modules may take place within one workshop or timetabled sequentially over a number of days.

Module 1: Describing the risks to be assessed and assessing inherent risk.

Module 2: Control identification and effectiveness and the assessment and residual risk exposure.

Module 3: Action planning and next steps.

By focusing discussion at the workshops on these core aspects (i.e. risks, controls and action planning), other additional requirements such as control testing, agreeing action due dates, or allocating and amending risk and control ownership, can be finalized outside of the workshops. In all cases, it is critical to remember that responsibility for, and ownership of, the business objectives, processes, risks and controls and their proper identification lies with local management. The workshop is merely a tool designed to assist them in discharging that responsibility effectively.

4.1.4 Facilitation

The use of a skilled facilitator helps to reduce subjectivity and bias and identify potential conflicts of interest and political manoeuvring (e.g. over or understating a risk to influence resource budgets).

Some organizations prefer to facilitate their own internal RCSAs, others will use external facilitators. When using internal facilitators, it is permissible to use experts from the risk or audit functions, providing it is made clear that ownership of the assessment and its outcomes rests fully with local management (e.g. the relevant risk and control owners).

The role of the facilitator requires a specific skill set, as outlined in Table 7.7.

4.1.5 Validation

To help combat assessment bias it is recommended that the output from similar workshops are compared. This should help to reveal significant outliers in terms of responses. Usually, this work should be completed by the (operational) risk function.

For example, it should be possible to compare risk and control assessments for similar risks across departments and functions. Where an assessment of a particular risk or type of control differs significantly, a discussion should be had with the relevant managers to confirm whether there are good reasons for these differences.

Note that care should be taken when asking for amendments to RCSAs. The operational risk function must, at all times, ensure that RCSAs are owned by the managers (e.g. risk owners) responsible for them. This may sometimes require tolerance of assessments that are slightly biased. But a flag should be placed on such assessments to ensure that this is signalled, especially when reporting RCSA output to senior management.

4.2 Questionnaires

Questionnaires can be used to collect some or all of the information required for an RCSA. Questionnaires may be used as a substitute for a workshop, to help save time and resources. But they are most effective when combined with workshops. Here the

Table 7.7   The role of a facilitator

Role	Skills
Maintain momentum and ensure the agenda is followed	Active listening
Ensure that the RCSA process is followed	Create a safe space for discussion, ensure that all perspectives are valued
Challenge potential bias or conflicts of interest	Assert authority and control to maintain discipline
Involve all attendees in the discussion	Summarize discussions clearly and accurately and set priorities
Ensure a balanced discussion	Detailed knowledge and experience of the RCSA process
Ensure that decisions, actions, and any disagreements are recorded (may use a note-taker to support this)	

initial thoughts of RCSA participants can be collected via the use of a questionnaire and a workshop can be used to discuss the findings.

It is also possible to use questionnaires to reach a wider audience than the few who may be invited to a workshop. This should reduce the chance that risks or controls are omitted, and help to control individual biases.

4.2.1 Questionnaire scope

Questionnaires may be designed for specific categories of operational risk (e.g. fraud or IT risks) or they may attempt to capture information on all risks. There are advantages and disadvantages for both. A more focused questionnaire will be shorter and take less time to complete, reducing the risk of respondent fatigue and increasing the accuracy of responses. However, where a number of focused questionnaires are required to complete an RCSA it is recommended that they are spaced over a number of months in order to prevent complaints about questionnaire overload. Alternatively, different-focused questionnaires can be sent to different samples of respondents. This can be especially effective where each sample is selected on the basis of subject expertise (e.g. IT risks survey is sent to the relevant IT experts and the main IT system users, etc).

Equally, questionnaires may be exploratory in nature (e.g. using open questions to identify new risks or controls) or confirmatory. Usually questionnaires are confirmatory, meaning that they start with a particular set of risks and controls in mind.

For confirmatory questionnaires it is recommended that a consistent operational risk categorization is used across the organization (see Chapter 3) and that standardized lists of controls are produced for the organization, preferably linking each risk category to a specific sub-set of these standardized controls. This will provide a consistent structure for the questionnaire and allow responses to be compared easily.

4.2.2 Questionnaire content

At a minimum, a questionnaire should ask questions on the following:

- estimated level of inherent risk;
- estimated control effectiveness (individual and the overall environment if this is part of the RCSA);
- estimated level of residual risk;
- recommended actions to improve control effectiveness.

The questionnaire should be kept as short as possible. The longer the questionnaire the greater the chance that respondents will either give up answering or provide random responses.

Socio-demographic questions (e.g. age, gender, etc) are not usually necessary so should be omitted to reduce the length of the questionnaire. The only potentially relevant questions are the department or function in which an individual works and their level of seniority.

4.2.3 Designing a questionnaire

Questions can be standard or non-standard:

- Standard questions are written centrally, usually by the operational risk function. These will address the minimum content identified above.

- Non-standard questions are written locally by the relevant management to address specific operational risk and control issues or concerns.

Where management buy-in remains a concern, it may be better to adopt a non-standard approach, giving greater ownership of the questionnaire design to local management. However, this will make it harder to aggregate and compare responses. Ideally local managers should be asked to include a number of standard questions and then be given the freedom to add further questions if they wish.

Closed questions should be structured so they can be answered using either an even-numbered Likert-type 'agree' or 'not agree' scale (e.g. 1 for Strongly Agree, 4 for Strongly Disagree) or a binary 'Yes' or 'No'. This will ensure that respondents do not 'sit on the fence' and provide the middle value for most responses (e.g. 3 for a 5–point scale).

Use of a 'Not Applicable' option is permissible, but only when respondents are able to justify this with an explanation (e.g. a particular control is not currently used in their area).

Open questions are encouraged, especially to justify choices like 'Not Applicable' or 'No'. Open questions might also be used to help add context, for example to explain why a control is believed to be effective or not effective.

4.3 Other approaches

Workshops and questionnaires are the most common techniques, but there are others that may be considered. Table 7.8 summarizes three alternative options.

5. Integrating an RCSA into the operational risk management framework

RCSA is not a stand-alone process. To be effective it must be integrated into the wider operational risk management framework. This means using other elements of the framework to provide information to support the completion of RCSAs. It also involves using the output from RCSAs to support other elements, notably operational risk reporting.

Table 7.8 Other RCSA data collection approaches

Technique	Description
Structured What-If Technique	Structured what-if technique (SWIFT) is a systematic team-oriented technique most commonly used for the assessment of health and safety and environmental-related risks and controls in areas like chemical processing and manufacturing, but it can be applied in many other ways. The technique uses a series of structured 'what-if' and 'how-could'-type questions to consider how deviations from the normal operation of systems, processes and controls may result in risk events.
	Brainstorming is supported by checklists to help focus the discussion. SWIFT relies on expert input and the use of a 'SWIFT leader' to structure the discussion. The SWIFT recorder keeps an online record of the discussion on a standard log sheet.
	There is no single standard approach to SWIFT – one of its strengths is that it is flexible and can be modified to suit each individual application.
	SWIFT is an expensive technique to use, because of the time and people involved. But it is more likely to address all relevant risk events and controls. This is why it is most commonly used in hazardous sectors such as chemical processing or nuclear power generation.
	For an application of SWIFT in the context of operational risk assessments see Card, Ward and Clarkson (2012). The paper focuses on the healthcare sector but is equally applicable to other sectors.
Delphi Technique	The Delphi technique is an information-gathering tool that is used as a way to reach a consensus of experts on a subject (Hsu and Sandford, 2007), in this case the completion of RCSAs. Each expert participates anonymously, and a facilitator uses a questionnaire to solicit ideas about the important points related to the subject. The responses are summarized and recirculated to the experts for further comment. Consensus may be reached in a few rounds of this process.
	In relation to RCSA the Delphi technique helps reduce bias and keeps any one person from having undue influence on the assessment. A range of experts can be used including risk management specialists, other functional specialists (IT, HR, governance, etc) and department and functional management (e.g. operations managers, accountants, etc).
	Anonymity is key because it encourages the experts to be as honest and open as possible. Studies have shown that the technique can be very effective at predicting future outcomes, but it also very time-consuming, especially if consensus is hard to reach.

(continued)

Table 7.8 (Continued)

Technique	Description
Root Cause Analysis	Root cause analysis assumes that operational risk events have multiple causes. For example, a fire-risk event needs: material to burn, a spark and oxygen before it can cause damage. Root cause analysis adds depth to an RCSA through an exploration of how and why an event may occur, the emphasis being on future prevention by improving existing controls or adding new ones to address previously unforeseen causes.

Root cause analysis approaches vary, but most are based on four principles:

- identify the causes of an event;
- establish the timeline from normal operations to a risk event;
- distinguish between root causes and more immediate causes;
- use the results to help assess exposure and control effectiveness.

Often the causes of an event, as well as the order in which the causes may arise, are identified using the 'five whys' technique. This asks 'why' questions such as:

- Why did a fire occur? Because combustible material started to burn.
- Why did the material burn? Because a spark caught the material alight.
- Why did the spark occur? Because an electrical fault occurred in the building's wiring.
- Why did the electrical fault occur? Because the wiring was old.
- Why was the wiring old? Because the wiring had not been safety inspected.

More or less 'why' questions than five may be used to get to the root cause, but usually it is possible to get to the underlying process failure in five questions. Further questions could still be used in this example to identify why a safety inspection has not been carried out, for example.

Root cause analysis is time consuming, and it is rarely practical or cost-effective to use it for all RCSAs, but it is a good technique to use when assessing the most significant operational risks across an organization. For a detailed discussion of the tools and techniques associated with root cause analysis see Andersen and Fagerhaug (2006). |

5.1 Linking to internal and external loss data

External and internal operational loss data (see Chapter 8) can be used to support RCSAs in two ways:

- to support the assessment of residual risk and control effectiveness; and
- to validate residual risk and control effectiveness assessments.

The size and frequency of actual loss events provides an indication of what may occur in the future, assuming current trends remain the same. Equally, operational loss events can often be linked to specific control failures or gaps in the control environment, providing information on control effectiveness.

Where RCSA results differ significantly from the available internal or external loss data, additional validation work may be required. This work should consider both the accuracy of the RCSA output and the effectiveness of loss data collection. For example, it may be that a high level of predicted residual exposure, relative to reported loss events, is the result of assessment bias, or it could be that the loss data is incomplete.

5.2 Scenario analysis

Significant control weaknesses and risk exposures identified through the RCSA are a valuable source of input for scenario analysis (see Chapter 10). Similarly, the process of defining and assessing operational risk scenarios may lead to the identification of new exposures and control weaknesses not captured within the RCSA.

Scenario analysis can be especially helpful when assessing inherent risk, where captured. By considering the potential causes and consequences of major control failures a structured approach to the analysis of scenarios can result in more robust inherent risk exposure estimates.

It is rarely practical or cost effective to use scenario analysis for every inherent risk assessment. But it can be a useful tool for validating especially high inherent risk scores.

5.3 Reporting RCSA results

There are various ways to report the results of RCSAs. Usually, a combination of different formats will be required – according to the audience for the report:

- Narrative reports (descriptions of the various risk exposures and any control weaknesses, may be presented in the form of a risk register).
- Heat maps and red–amber–green (RAG) traffic-light reports.
- Dashboards (risk, control effectiveness and performance indicators, usually presented using trend diagrams, pie charts, etc).

- Benefits log (a log of any improvements made to the control environment, such as enhanced control effectiveness, removal of obsolete controls, etc, and the effects of these in terms of reduced operating costs, improved efficiency, etc).

As a general rule, the more senior (high level) the audience, the less detail should be reported. For the governing body and senior management, the focus should be on the most significant areas of risk/control weakness that have the greatest potential to damage the organization and prevent it from achieving its objectives.

Conversely, reporting for line managers can contain more detail, as the additional information may be helpful to them in determining the best course of action and for the purposes of detailed monitoring of progress of action plans against agreed milestones and deliverables. Also, whatever the level of the audience, emphasis should be placed on keeping it pertinent and relevant to the audience for which it is intended.

The maintenance of a benefits log is highly recommended. These logs can be used to improve buy-in across the organization, thus improving the timeliness and accuracy of RCSAs. Such a log provides a tangible record of why RCSAs are a worthwhile exercise that can add value to the business.

CASE STUDY 7.5   Populating a benefits log

A retail financial services organization was encountering resistance to the implementation of a new RCSA tool. To help combat this resistance a benefits log was created. The log recorded any control weaknesses that were identified and corrected, plus any excessive controls that were removed, to enhance the efficiency of operational processes. The recorded benefits included:

- improvements to cash handling procedures, thus reducing risk of theft;

- a change of supplier, where sensitive data was discovered in one of its vehicles overnight as part of a controls testing process;

- the removal of outdated manual controls (e.g. the use of a company seal stamp for certain legal documents), where these were superseded by automated procedures;

- the identification of previously unknown system interdependencies;

- improvements to the credit scoring model due to the discovery of unreliable data on personal bankruptcies.

By recording and reporting these benefits, support for the new RCSA approach improved. Management were able to see how the approach was improving the efficiency and effectiveness of their operations.

5.4 Action planning

RCSA outputs are a valuable source of information for the development of operational risk action plans. Such plans might include improving the effectiveness of existing controls, removing obsolete controls, or introducing new controls to address gaps in the control environment.

Actions must always be justified on cost/benefit grounds – just because a control could be made more 'effective' or a new control added, does not mean that the time and effort required to achieve this is necessary. For example, it is not worth spending £1 million to fix a control gap that is assessed as representing a risk of loss of £100,000. Equally it must always be remembered that increasing the level of control can reduce the efficiency of systems and processes, and may even result in unforeseen new risks. For example, significantly increasing the frequency of password changes for IT access may result in staff writing down and then losing their passwords.

When deciding on the nature of an action plan it is helpful to remember the four common responses to risk exposures:

1 Acceptance – no further action is taken, either because the residual risk exposure is within appetite, or the cost of additional control is excessive relative to the benefits earned.

2 Mitigation – this will involve enhancing the level of control (improving control effectiveness or introducing new controls) to reduce the likelihood (loss prevention) and/or the impact of the risk (loss reduction).

3 Transfer – this may involve financial risk transfer to an insurer, or the physical transfer of risk to an external service provider (e.g. the use of a specialist contractor for the removal/processing of hazardous materials).

4 Avoidance – where changes are made to an activity, process or system to reduce inherent risk exposure.

All action plans must specify what is to be done, by whom and by when. Progress against completing action plans should be monitored until completion. Depending on the significance of the action, progress may be monitored by the governing body, a board-delegated committee, the (operational) risk function or local management.

In relation to the physical transfer of risk, regulations in certain sectors, such as financial services, do not permit the transfer of certain operational risks to external service providers (e.g. risks that may impact on the financial or physical wellbeing of the organization's customers). It is recommended that readers check their local requirements before attempting to use external service providers for operational risk transfer purposes. Even in the absence of such regulations it is good practice to maintain appropriate oversight over the work of external service providers to ensure that they do not take inappropriate levels of risk. For example, by ensuring that they do not take health and safety shortcuts.

5.5 *Internal audit planning and reporting*

The use of RCSA output by internal audit can confer a number of advantages:

- By taking on more responsibility for the maintenance of the control environment auditees should better understand the purpose of operational risk management and the benefits of effective assessment and control.

- Providing additional information to support audit work (e.g. the validation of control effectiveness estimates).

- Exposure assessments can be used to support a risk-based approach to internal audit.

It is also recommended that the internal audit function should review, periodically, the effectiveness of the RCSA to ensure that it remains effective and proportionate.

6. Conclusion

This chapter has explained how to design and implement effective RCSAs. The RCSA tool is an important part of most operational risk management frameworks. However, if poorly designed and implemented the outputs can do more harm than good. Like any operational risk management tool, the RCSA must be value adding, not a bureaucratic, compliance-oriented, box-ticking exercise. Excessive complexity or prescription can result in a process where the costs exceed the benefits. Remember that the output from an RCSA is not the end of the process. Rather it is just the start of meaningful conversations about operational risk. Such risk talk should be designed to promote a considered, reflective attitude towards operational risk exposures that reduce, as much as possible, the potential for instinctual bias.

Reflective practice questions

1   How complex is your RCSA tool? Do users find it overly time-consuming to complete?

2   Do you review the effectiveness of your RCSA tool on an annual basis? As part of this review do you compare the costs and benefits associated with using your RCSA tool?

3   How do you use the output from your RCSA? Is this output used primarily for compliance and internal control purposes or to support strategic and operational decisions?

4 Do you use your RCSA to help reduce excessive control as well as control weaknesses?

5 How do you mitigate the potential for assessment bias? Do you use tools like workshops and RCSA challenge processes to overcome bias?

6 Would you consider using techniques like Root Cause Analysis and SWIFT to improve the quality of the output from your RCSA?

Appendix C: Example RCSA templates

Examples of RCSA templates are provided below.

1. Example Excel-based template (with the minimum recommended fields)

More fields may be added, see section 3.1 above.

ID	Risk Description	Risk Owner	Inherent Risk	Key Controls	Control Owner(s)	Residual Risk	Within Appetite?	Action Required?
12c	Significant disruption to normal business operating environment	M Smith	High	Business Continuity plans in place Plans tested and updated annually Telephone call cascade tested quarterly	J Brown	Medium	No	Yes
13a	Breach of client data confidentiality	F Jones	High	Data Security policy in place and regularly reviewed Independent monitoring of adherence to policy Escalation of non-compliance Breach register	S Thomas	Low	Yes	No

2. Example RCSA action plan (with the minimum number of fields)

ID	Risk Description	Residual Risk	Action Required	Action Owner	Target Date	Expected Residual Risk
Outside Appetite						
12c	Significant disruption to normal business operating environment	Medium	Introduce desktop walkthrough exercises twice a year	J Brown	30/09/20	Low

References

Arena, M, Arnaboldi, M and Palermo, T (2017) The dynamics of (dis) integrated risk management: A comparative field study, *Accounting, Organizations and Society*, 62, 65–81

Andersen, B and Fagerhaug, T (2006) *Root Cause Analysis: Simplified tools and techniques*, 2nd edn, Quality Press, Milwaukee

Card, A J, Ward, J R and Clarkson, P J (2012) Beyond FMEA: The structured what if technique (SWIFT), *Journal of Healthcare Risk Management*, 31 (4), 23–9

Cox, A L (2008) What's wrong with risk matrices?, *Risk Analysis: An international journal*, 28 (2), 497–512

Hsu, C C and Sandford, B A (2007) The Delphi technique: Making sense of consensus, *Practical Assessment, Research, and Evaluation*, 12 (1), 10

Jordan, S, Mitterhofer, H and Jørgensen, L (2018) The interdiscursive appeal of risk matrices: Collective symbols, flexibility normalism and the interplay of 'risk' and 'uncertainty', *Accounting, Organizations and Society*, 67, 34–55

Kahneman, D (2011) *Thinking, Fast and Slow*, Macmillan, New York

Mikes, A (2016) The triumph of the humble chief risk officer, in M Power (ed), *Riskwork: Essays on the organizational life of risk management*, Oxford University Press, Oxford, pp 253–73

Tversky, A and Fox, C R (1995) Weighing risk and uncertainty, *Psychological Review*, 102 (2), 269

Operational loss events   08

LEARNING OUTCOMES

- Explain the benefits associated with collecting external and internal operational loss event data.
- Know how to design and implement an operational loss event data collect tool.
- Know how to use an operational loss event data collection tool to support risk reporting and decision making.

1. Introduction

Operational loss event data collection, analysis and reporting is the backbone of a sound framework for the management of operational risk. Data on actual events provides a tangible source of information on the probability and impact of operational risks, helping to reduce the subjectivity of operational risk assessments and reports. Data also provides organizations with the opportunity to learn from past events, where effective hindsight can promote more accurate foresight.

This chapter explains how to design and implement processes and procedures for the collection and use of internal operational loss event data and for the use of external loss event data, where appropriate. As a general rule the more data that can be collected, the better. A large dataset will cover a greater range of potential events, improving the statistical accuracy of the reports produced using this data. External data can help a lot in this regard, adding to the smaller number of internal events that are likely to be recorded. However, the usefulness of external data can depend on its relevance for the organization in question. Different organizations can experience different degrees of operational risk exposure, meaning that data from other organizations is not always comparable.

In this chapter the emphasis will be on operational *losses*. Current practice focuses on the collection of downside, loss outcomes only. It is theoretically possible to collect data on the upside outcomes of operational risk exposures (e.g. the potential for an unexpected efficiency improvement), but in practice such events are all but impossible to identify. Loss events normally have a tangible impact on the bottom-line finances of an organization. Efficiency gains will provide gradual gains over time. Benefit logs are one way to collect information on the upside outcomes of operational risk exposures.

2. Operational loss data: a brief statistical primer

From a statistical perspective historical data on operational risk loss events can be illustrated graphically using what are known as probability density functions (PDFs) and cumulative distribution functions (CDFs). A PDF charts the probability that the impact of a given operational loss event will take a value equal to a specific amount. For example, a PDF might reveal that there is a 0.1 (10 per cent) probability of a loss equal to or less than £10 million and that the probability of a loss equal to or less than £100 million is 0.01 (1 per cent), and so on. A CDF sums all of the potential probabilities and impacts for a given distribution, illustrating the range of loss events that could occur at a given level of probability (see Figure 8.1).

The distribution of PDFs and CDFs in the context of operational risk can take a variety of forms (Chapelle et al, 2008). Figure 8.1 illustrates two simple examples of an exponential PDF and CDF. An exponential function assumes that the probability of more extreme outcomes will fall at an increasing rate.

By using historical loss data to construct PDFs and CDFs, probabilities for observed impacts can be determined. The more data that is available the more complete

Figure 8.1   Simple exponential probability density and cumulative distribution functions (author's own)

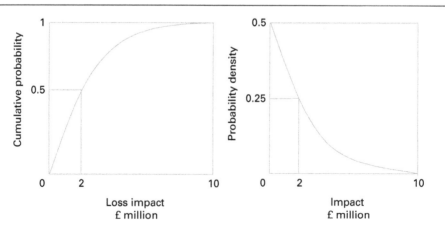

will be the distributions, allowing for increasingly precise estimates of probabilities. The PDF example in Figure 8.1 shows that the probability of a loss equal to £2 million is 0.25 (25 per cent). The CDF further reveals that the cumulative probability of a loss equal to £2 million or less is 0.5 (50 per cent). Note that with an exponential CDF the density function line gets very flat as it approaches its apex, this reflects the increasingly low level of probability associated with more extreme outcomes (this is clear from the PDF example).

Being able to construct distributions like this helps to reduce uncertainty, allowing for more objective decision making. In Chapter 1 the concept of Knightian uncertainty was discussed (see pages 4–5). Knightian uncertainty exists when there is insufficient information on probability and impact, preventing the construction of distributions like a PDF or CDF. By collecting data on probability and impact, uncertainty is transformed into known risks – risks that can, in theory, be managed in a more objective and reliable way.

However, there are two important caveats to this assertion. Operational loss data is rarely sufficient to allow the construction of a complete PDF or CDF, although it is possible to approximate distributions with partial data, using statistical tools like Monte Carlo Analysis. For more on the construction of probability and impact distributions for operational loss events see Cruz (2004).

More seriously, in a dynamic (changing) operational risk environment, historical data may not provide a reliable indicator for the future.

CASE STUDY 8.1   Pandemic risk and Covid-19

Pandemics are nothing new. Neither is the fact that pandemics can impact on the operations and supply chains of organizations. Pandemics such as SARS (Severe Acute Respiratory Syndrome) in 2002–04, MERS (Middle East Respiratory Syndrome) in 2012 and Ebola in 2013–16, caused global concern and prompted many organizations to improve their operational risk management practices to address future pandemics.

The rapid spread of Covid-19 shocked many governments and organizations. Organizations were doubly surprised by the unprecedented measures taken to control the spread, which included travel bans, household lockdowns and the closure of non-essential businesses.

Based on the available historical evidence few would have predicted that the operational impact of the Covid-19 virus would have been as large as it has been. In this regard the pandemic is an important lesson for organizations – expect the unexpected and be ready to manage impacts far greater than imagined previously.

Hence, even where plentiful amounts of operational loss event data are available, it must be remembered that the potential to construct forward-looking PDFs and CDFs using this data is limited. Large amounts of loss data are of limited statistical use if the world of operational risk is changing.

3. Comparing the benefits of internal and external event data

The collection of internal operational loss event data allows an organization to build a picture of its actual exposure to operational risk. The timelier the collection of this data the more real-time will be this picture. Similarly, the more comprehensive the data collection, the more accurate will be this picture.

Internal event data can be used to support a range of activities within the operational risk management process. Table 8.1 summarizes the key benefits.

External databases may be used to supplement internal data. In a given year, or even over decades, few organizations will experience the full range of operational loss events that they are exposed to. This is especially the case in relation to rare, low-probability, high-impact events, sometimes referred to as 'tail' events, because they are at the far tail of the PDF for the risk event in question. External data allows organizations to incorporate the events experienced by their peers, increasing the available sample size for data analysis, and enhancing the benefits identified in Table 8.1.

Sources of external data fall mainly into two types, and the data available from each type differs in a number of regards.Consortium-based data sources rely on contributors who pay a subscription and are required to share data among the membership. There are strict reporting criteria, which ensure that each member reports all events that are covered by the consortium agreement, but member identities are protected by a level of obfuscation. In most cases, the number of data elements is much higher than from public data sources, since members must report all loss events to the consortium, including those that are perhaps less newsworthy and receive little or no coverage in the financial press.

The primary benefits of consortium data are its comprehensiveness, accuracy and relevance for members. Consortia take care to group organizations, to ensure that the data supplied by the other members is relevant. In this regard consortium data can often be combined with internal data in a statistically robust manner. However, subscription costs can be high, and members must comply with the strict reporting requirements.

Public source-based data sources filter and analyse public and specialist news sources and republish the data in a form suitable for operational risk analysis. Such sources only have access to the more newsworthy cases, but usually add further

Table 8.1 Using internal data to support the operational risk management process

Process Objective	Benefit of Internal Loss Event Data
Identification	Loss events may reveal new operational risk exposures not previously identified. New exposures may arise as a result of social and technological change, for example new types of cyber risks associated with developments in hardware or social media.
Assessment	Provide information to support the assessment of probability and impact. The more loss event data that is available, the more complete will be the picture of the potential distribution of operational loss events in terms of probability and impact (i.e. the PDF and CDF for the risk in question).
Monitoring	Provides information on current exposure level and control effectiveness. Trends in recorded loss data can be used to determine whether current exposures are increasing or decreasing.
Control	Can be used to help assess control effectiveness. Loss events provide a live test of controls. They may also reveal information on potential control gaps and how controls may be improved in the future. Most loss events, especially larger events, will be linked to the full or partial failure of one or more control.

information about each event, including specifics about which organization incurred the loss, and the details of the control failures, contributory factors and aftermath of the event. Various operational risk management advisory organizations provide public source data services for a fee (e.g. the RiskBusiness Newsflash Library, www. RiskBusiness.com).

Public source databases are usually cheaper and there are no reciprocal reporting requirements. However, the public nature of the data means that it is unlikely to be as accurate or complete. Nevertheless, public data can provide a valuable source of information on low-probability, high-impact risk events, as these are the ones that tend to reach the media. They may also reveal emerging operational risks, where events have occurred in other organizations (e.g. new types of cyber risk).

Consortium data is most common in the financial services sector. Here organizations like ORIC International, ORX and the Global Operations and Loss Database (GOLD) provide specialist datasets for banks and insurers. Outside of the financial services sector, corporate insurance providers and brokers sometimes provide external operational loss data to clients, but there is no commercially available consortium product.

4. The elements of operational loss events: key concepts to consider when designing a loss collection tool

Reflecting the multifaceted nature of operational loss events there are a number of concepts that must be understood before designing and implementing an effective loss event collection process. This section explores the concepts that comprise this multifaceted nature.

Not all operational loss event databases will include all of these concepts. As with RCSAs the more comprehensive and complex an operational loss event database, the greater will be the implementation costs. Hence a balance must always be maintained between the desire for a fully comprehensive operational loss database and the costs associated with populating and maintaining this resource.

That said, it is important that operational risk professionals understand the full range of concepts that could be considered. This allows them to make a positive, informed choice about what to include or exclude.

4.1 Actual events and near misses

By definition, operational loss event data collection requires information on actual loss events. An operational loss event is an event where an organization has suffered some form of adverse impact, usually financial, though human and reputation impacts may also be recorded. These impacts may be direct or indirect (see below).

In addition to collecting data on loss events some organizations choose to go further and collect information on 'near misses'. A near miss is an operational risk event that occurred, but which did not result in an adverse impact of any kind. Losses may either have been averted because of good fortune or the effectiveness of certain controls. For example, a payment to a supplier may have been made twice, but the supplier reported the error, and the money was returned. Similarly, a post-payment account reconciliation may have revealed the error.

Information on near misses can be very valuable. They provide an early warning signal of events that may result in losses in the future. Research in the area shows that a series of near misses will often occur prior to a major operational loss. Hence if organizations can collect information on them, they may help to avert major losses in the future. Equally, near-miss information provides information on control effectiveness.

CASE STUDY 8.2   Near misses as a signal for future disasters

Research into organizational crises and disasters has revealed that large-scale operational loss events are usually preceded by a number of small-scale near misses (Elliott, Smith and McGuinnes, 2000; Tinsley, Dillon and Madsen, 2011). If organizations are able to detect these near-misses and take corrective action (e.g. by enhancing the control environment), then there is a good chance that they may avoid disaster. If they do not, then the potential for disaster remains high.

A tragic example of the dangers associated with ignoring near misses was the King's Cross Fire in 1987. Wooden escalators caught fire, resulting in a major incident that cost 31 lives and injured 100 more people.

The cause of the fire was a discarded match (used to light a cigarette) that was dropped beneath an escalator. Rubbish routinely collected beneath the escalators, and this caught fire. Initially the fire appeared minor, but it suddenly erupted into a 'flashover' that spread fire and smoke into the ticket hall.

Prior to the fire, smouldering incidents were known to occur. Discarded matches and cigarettes routinely caused minor fires under escalators. The inquiry into the fire (Fennell, 1988) criticized London Underground for complacency towards fire safety. Because there had never been a fire-related fatality, concern for fire was low and staff were given little or no training on fire safety. Fire safety was much improved after the incident, making the London Underground one of the safest mass-transportation systems in the world. Had management taken note of the many smouldering events that had taken place before the fire, and improved safety earlier, the lives lost and injuries that resulted would have been prevented.

4.2 Date and time of the event

Recording the date and time of an event allows an organization to build historical trend data, revealing how exposures are changing over time.

It is common to collect data on two time points: the time that the event was first detected and the time that the event ceased. Many operational loss events will last days, even weeks, months or years. For example, legal liability claims often take years to resolve, especially when linked to the effects of long-term illness like cancer or asbestosis.

In terms of the start of an event, some organizations go further than the date of first detection and look for the date that the event first manifested, which may be some time before it was detected. For example, pollution may occur on a site, but not be detected for some weeks, months or even years. Identifying the very first date an event manifested can be a time-consuming exercise that requires considerable detective work. However, it can facilitate things like insurance claims and may help an organization to improve its ability to detect events in a timely fashion in the future. Plus, where an event is found to have occurred in an earlier accounting year it may be appropriate to amend the accounts, especially if it impacted on reported profits, and hence corporation tax, for example.

4.3 Location

Along with recording the date and time of an operational loss event, it is essential to collect data on the location of the event. For larger, more dispersed, organizations this is especially important, as it allows them to build a 'geographical' profile of loss events. Where a geographical area has a higher proportion of the total losses than might be expected, adjusting for its size/significance (e.g. adjusting for the number of employees, operational output, etc), this may indicate control or operational risk governance weaknesses or an inappropriate operational risk culture.

Location includes the physical location of an event (e.g. the establishment or site in which the event occurred) and the business unit(s), function(s) or department(s) from which the event originated (e.g. Finance, Operations, HR, etc). For larger establishments or sites, it may be appropriate to record the building, room or production line in which an event has occurred. This will help to provide more granular information on where operational loss events occur. For example, it may be that fires are more prevalent in a particular building because of some local weakness in fire safety, or there may be some undetected fault in a specific production line.

4.4 Operational risk category

Allocating an event to a specific category of operational risk (see Chapter 3) is an essential part of any operational risk loss data collection and reporting process. By allocating events to pre-determined operational risk categories, it is possible to build a picture of the near-current risk profile of an organization. This can then be used to identify categories of high exposure and prioritize resources accordingly.

4.5 Causes

All operational loss events have causes, often multiple causes. These causes may form chains, consisting of proximate, intermediate and underlying causes, as illustrated in Figure 8.2.

Figure 8.2   Example causal chain (author's own)

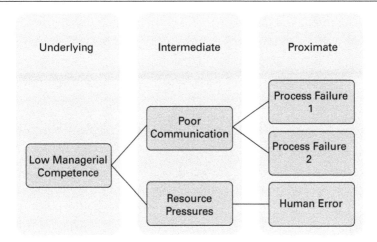

Causal chains may span multiple layers of causes, sometimes more than three. However, it is rare to collect this level of detail when collecting data on operational loss events. Many organizations simply collect information on the primary causal category (e.g. people, process failure, systems failure or external event). Others may use more granular categories, facilitating a more accurate picture of the causal chain, but increasing the complexity and cost of data collection. By way of a compromise, it is good practice to investigate the causal chains of large-scale losses, but not for low-impact events, when the effort is less justifiable on cost-benefit grounds.

4.6 Control failures

Control failures may be treated as causes, or the data may be collected separately to allow for a more granular investigation of the chain of causes and control failures that can precede operational loss events. Most operational loss events will involve the failure of one or more controls. Hence such events can be a valuable source of information on control effectiveness. By understanding how and why controls failed, targeted action plans can be created to help prevent similar failures in the future.

In addition to revealing potential failures, operational loss events may highlight effective controls, especially in relation to detective and mitigative controls. Effective detective controls will have helped the organization to realize that an event was oc-curring. Mitigative controls may have helped to reduce the impact of the event.

4.7 Direct and indirect impacts

Determining the impact of an operational risk loss event on an organization takes into consideration two elements, direct and indirect impacts.

Direct impacts occur as a natural consequence of an event and can usually be traced to a specific asset, product or service, or department/function. For example, an event that causes asset damage will result in an immediate write-down in the value of these assets and may also involve repair or replacement costs, assuming that the damaged assets are not abandoned. Operational loss events may also involve some form of 'clean-up' cost, such as the removal of pollutants. Equally, loss events will typically require staff time to manage, possibly resulting in overtime payments.

Indirect impacts tend to arise from the special circumstance of an event and will depend on things like whether customers are affected, or if the continuity of the organization is disrupted. A common example of indirect impacts is a loss of sales or market share. Regulatory fines are another example, since these are usually only incurred if an event was the result of a significant control failure.

Usually, direct impacts are relatively straightforward to ascertain, especially financial impacts, because of their relatively quick effect on cash flows. In contrast, indirect impacts may not be immediately identifiable and may only come to light some time after an event is recorded.

CASE STUDY 8.3   Toyota and the Aisin fire

In 1997 a fire shut down a factory owned by Aisin Seiki Co, a gearbox-parts subsidiary of Toyota. The fire was notable because the parts were vital to the production of almost all Toyota vehicles. Because of Toyota's use of modern 'just-in-time' manufacturing techniques, the company was reported as having only four hours' supply of the crucial part (Nishiguchi and Beaudet, 1998).

Luckily, Toyota was able to avoid a lengthy shutdown in the production of its vehicles, because of the close working relationship it had with other suppliers. Using plans provided by Aisin Seiki, these suppliers were able to resume production of the part within days of the fire.

The cost of repairing the Aisin Seiki factory and replacing the lost machinery reflects a major part of the direct costs of the incident. Also accounted for as direct costs are the engineering and overtime costs incurred by the other suppliers that reproduced the part in record time. The interruption in vehicle production represents the indirect costs of the event, costs that would have been much higher had the other suppliers not rallied round Toyota and produced the part.

4.8 Financial and non-financial impacts

Operational loss events have both financial and non-financial impacts. As indicated above, financial impacts may be direct or indirect and relate to the costs associated with replacing lost assets, clean-up, liability claims, fines, etc.

Non-financial impacts are a form of indirect cost that does not have a quantifiable financial impact, or the financial impact is impossible to estimate in a reliable manner. Examples of non-financial impacts include but are not limited to reputational damage, loss of goodwill and customer confidence. Such impacts can be assessed using a defined range – e.g. low, medium, high – calibrated by reference to an appropriate measure such as, for a service impact, the number of customers involved and the duration of the loss of service.

Typically, non-financial impacts are incurred sometime after the specific operational loss event (e.g. a fire, hacking attack, etc). Often the severity of these impacts are linked to how well an organization is able to contain any operational disruption. Extended disruption can lead to negative press reporting and dissatisfied customers. In the case of Toyota and the Aisin fire these non-financial impacts were limited. Had vehicle production been disrupted for several weeks, they could have been significant.

In time, once an event has ended, it may be possible to place a financial value on non-financial impacts like reputation damage or a loss of consumer confidence. For example, sales prior to an event might be compared to sales after. However, care is required when making such estimates. Variables like consumer sales may be impacted by a wide range of factors and isolating the effects of a specific operational loss event may not be possible in all cases.

5. Implementation

Though organizations should strive for timely and comprehensive operational loss event datasets there are trade-offs. Implementation can be costly and divert resources from other activities; the more data an organization attempts to collect, the greater will be the implementation costs. As discussed in Chapter 2 on embedding operational risk management frameworks, a high-cost approach to operational risk management can induce resistance from staff, especially when resources are diverted from activities they perceive as higher priority.

To help maximize the benefits and minimize the costs of operational loss event data collection there are a number of important implementation factors to consider. These are outlined below.

5.1 Aligning loss data collection with the wider operational risk management framework

To maximize their effectiveness, processes for collecting operational loss event data must be incorporated into the processes and procedures that are used to manage operational risk. This should include:

- Ensuring that the organization's governance arrangements support the collection of operational loss event data. This may include internal audits of collection processes and compliance with these processes; allocation of roles and responsibilities for data collection and reporting; procedures for the escalation of events, according to their severity.

- Aligning any reporting or escalation thresholds with the organization's overall appetite or tolerance for operational risk. For more on reporting thresholds see section 5.2 below.

- Ensuring that the classification of recorded risk events is consistent with the organization's operational risk categorization approach.

- Consideration of how the organization's risk culture may impact on the collection or analysis of reported events. For example, the risk culture of an organization may affect the willingness of staff to report losses.

CASE STUDY 8.4   The problem of a blame culture

A health sector organization attempted to implement an operational loss event reporting process. Upon implementation the operational risk function was surprised about the low number of loss events reported.

An investigation revealed that staff were unwilling to report operational loss events because management tended to blame them for the occurrence of such events. Hence staff kept events a secret where possible, to avoid blame. It was also identified that senior management were unwilling to hear bad news and complained to their direct reports when a significant number of loss events were recorded.

The organization took action to address the problem of a blame culture. The CRO worked with senior management to change the 'tone from the top' and training was implemented for managers in the importance of a no-blame culture. The number of operational loss events reported increased as a result.

When implementing an internal loss data collection process, it is essential to avoid a blame culture: such cultures can discourage open and honest reporting.

This is of particular significance when internal loss events are used as a basis for adjusting individual performance/reward arrangements and may be the subject of challenge from regulators. Some organizations have addressed this challenge by aligning reward to adherence to risk management procedures, e.g. submission of complete, accurate and timely loss event reports. They may equally apply a penalty (such as a reduction in expected bonus payments) in response to inappropriate behaviour by the accountable individual.

In larger organizations it is common practice to publish league tables of business unit and or site performance in respect of loss events, but this can result in peer pressure to reduce or even avoid reporting. Conversely such information can be used to promote continuous improvement, i.e. the event details providing an opportunity to avoid a potentially more damaging reoccurrence by addressing vulnerabilities in procedures and controls.

A communication strategy is key to driving an effective loss event reporting culture, identifying the diverse audiences from senior executives to junior operational staff and the corresponding messages, level of detail and method of delivery. In all cases the objective is to achieve awareness and then understanding in order to achieve commitment to appropriate action, and this can be more successful if emphasis is placed on the advantages and benefits of open and honest reporting.

5.2 Determining the right number of data fields

When considering the use of a specific data field care must be taken to weigh the benefits and costs of collection. It is important to remember that more is not necessarily better when it comes to data fields. Adding fields will increase the time taken to populate and manage an operational loss event database.

Table 8.2 summarizes the recommended minimum data fields required for an effective operational loss event database.

Section four of this chapter covers a range of other fields that could be added where the benefits outweigh the costs. This might include demarcating underlying and proximate causes or collecting data on indirect financial and non-financial impacts.

As a general rule it is recommended to start with the minimum fields in Table 8.2. Additional fields may then be added, where necessary, once staff get used to the data collection and management process. In all cases, additional fields should only be added where they are justified on cost-benefit grounds.

Table 8.2   Minimum recommended data fields

Data Field	Explanation
Business area(s) affected and their location	The business units, functions and/or departments that experienced the event.
Location	Organizations with multiple sites should record which of these sites were impacted.
Business activities affected	The activities, processes and operations that were affected by the operational loss event.
Event type	Using the organization's operational risk categorization approach.
Dates and times	The date and time that the event was detected and when the event was closed.
Description of the event	A short explanation of the event that occurred.
Causes	The circumstances that helped to cause the event. This may be refined once the event is closed, following a detailed root-cause analysis.
Impacts and recoveries	The direct financial impact of the event and any recoveries (e.g. compensation payments received, insurance claims, etc).
Actions	This may include short- and longer-term actions. Short-term actions are those taken to help mitigate the impact of the event (e.g. goodwill payments to customers). Long-term actions are those designed to prevent similar future events (e.g. improvements to control effectiveness).

5.3 Data capture thresholds

Ideally data should be captured on all operational loss events, to ensure a comprehensive dataset. In practice, such a goal can be overly costly, and organizations may choose to compromise by only collecting data on events for which financial impacts exceed a certain value threshold.

Thresholds may be set at any amount, for example, for events with an impact that exceeds £500, £5,000 or £50,000. The threshold chosen by an organization should reflect its size and appetite for operational risk. Large organizations with a high appetite for operational risk may choose a high threshold. Smaller organizations with a lower appetite may choose a smaller one.

Organizations implementing operational loss event data capture for the first time may choose a relatively high data-capture threshold, to help reduce initial collection costs. Over time, as users become accustomed to the process, the threshold can be reduced.

5.4 Categorizing and connecting operational loss events

There are two potential issues regarding categorization. Firstly, it can be difficult to distinguish between a loss and a near miss, especially when the level of financial impact is limited (though the non-financial effects may be much higher). Secondly, loss events are not always easy to separate into discrete risk event categories, especially when they are the result of multiple, connected elements (e.g. a chain of events leading up to a major operational loss).

In terms of distinguishing between losses and near misses, it is important to have a clear and consistent definition of the two. In general, a near miss can be defined as an event that does not result in any financial or non-financial loss, either because of good fortune or the effective application of specific controls. In contrast, a loss event will have a negative financial impact and/or adverse non-financial impacts also.

At times, events may come to light that have a potential adverse financial or non-financial impact, but at the time of detection this may be unclear. Such events should be classified as loss events in the first instance and may be reclassified as near misses if the impacts do not occur. Equally, financial or non-financial impacts may be adjusted up or down as new information comes to light.

Where a number of events are related (e.g. by the same underlying cause or control failure) but occur over an extended time frame it is helpful to aggregate these and treat them as a single event for the purposes of action planning and analysis.

By aggregating operational loss events it is possible to explore how they are connected. One common source of connection is where the occurrence of one loss event causes another and so on. By understanding and addressing these chains of causation an organization can significantly improve the effectiveness of its operational risk management activities. For example, by focusing resources on key underlying cause or control issues.

CASE STUDY 8.5   BP Deepwater Horizon oil spill

The BP Deepwater Horizon oil-well spill began on 20 April 2010 and the well was declared sealed on 19 September 2010. However, further oil slicks were reported in 2011, 2012 and 2013.

Due to the prolonged nature of the spill, along with adverse effects from the response and clean-up activities, extensive damage to marine and wildlife habitats was reported, which in turn impacted on the fishing and tourism industries. This damage continued to be reported for many years after the initial spill (Beyer et al, 2016).

From a loss data collection perspective all reported oil spills, along with every incident of habitat damage, clean-up cost, compensation payment and so on should be linked to the underlying event, the initial oil spill.

5.5 Data integrity and validation

Operational loss event data should be as timely, accurate and complete as possible. Out-of-date, inaccurate or partial data may provide a misleading picture of an organization's exposure to operational risk and the effectiveness of its controls:

- Timeliness: data should be collected and reported as soon as possible after the identification of an operational loss event. To ensure timeliness, setting a time limit for the recording of new data is recommended. This time limit should reflect the nature, scale and complexity of an organization, as well as its appetite for operational risk and risk culture. Some organizations may require data to be recorded within one working day; others require five working days or more. In all cases the operational risk function should consult with those required to supply the data to ensure that timescales are realistic and to maximize 'buy-in'.

- Accuracy: operational loss event data is rarely perfect, especially in the early stages of the event when the total impact may not be known with certainty. Steps should be taken to ensure that recorded data is as accurate as possible and that it is updated when any new information comes to light. To maximize accuracy, validation processes should be put in place, though usually these should only be employed when an event is closed, and all of the available data has been collected. This may include comparing data from similar events across business lines, departments or functions, and comparison with external events or internal audits of local data collection processes.

- Completeness: all required fields should be completed for each loss event and information on all eligible events should be collected. This may include all operational loss events or events for which the financial impact exceeds the agreed reporting threshold. Information may also be collected on near misses, though it is rare that all near misses will be captured. The fact that near misses do not have a financial or non-financial impact makes them harder to detect.

It would be very difficult, if not impossible, and require significant time and effort, to validate all direct financial losses, for example, by comparing loss estimates to the available accounting records.

This is partly because financial impacts of events tend to be charged to a variety of expenditure accounts and also, possibly, income accounts (e.g. in respect of a re-fund of commission earned). There is also the challenge presented by direct and in-direct financial impacts being accumulated over a period of time.

In practice most organizations who attempt validation take an '80/20' approach, focusing on what is readily identifiable in accounts and aiming to fully validate only the largest individual events.

5.6 Implementing an operational loss event database

Where data on operational loss events is recorded it is normal to store this data in some form of database. This might be a simple in-house database, using an application like Microsoft Access. Alternatively, a specialist operational loss event database may be used.

Many providers of operational risk assessment systems offer specialist loss event data collection and reporting applications. Some may form part of a standard risk assessment package; others are cost option add-ons.

Whatever the form of database that is chosen the following essential elements must be present:

- Data security – all data must be stored securely, with appropriate encryption and access controls. In addition, compliance with applicable data protection laws is essential. This is especially important where personal details are collected (e.g. names and addresses).

- User-friendliness – the system must be easy to use, to help minimize the amount of time required to record, manage or report data.

- Adaptability – the system should adapt to the needs of an organization, using the operational risk management vocabulary and event categorizations that staff are used to, for example.

- Compatibility – with the other systems used by an organization, especially its operational risk assessment and reporting systems.

5.7 Roles and responsibilities for recording operational loss events

It is unlikely that the operational risk function will populate the operational loss event database. Instead, the function will rely on staff across the organization to supply information on events that have occurred in their area. This means that roles and responsibilities for the recording of events must be established.

Where an organization has risk owners it is common to hold them accountable for the timely, accurate and complete reporting of operational loss events, though they may delegate the responsibility for recording losses to other members of staff. Alternatively, organizations that make use of risk champions might use them to record events. Where neither is present, an individual should be nominated in each business unit, department or function to record operational loss events.

In line with appropriate operational risk governance (see Chapter 6) the operational risk function should normally be accountable for overseeing the recording of operational loss events (e.g. timeliness, accuracy, completeness, etc). In addition, the internal audit function should periodically check that the recording process is operating as intended and that operational loss events are not going unrecorded.

5.8 Escalation

Procedures should be agreed for the escalation of recorded operational loss events. Ideally these should be signed off by the board or a board-delegated committee with responsibility for operational risk management. Where possible these procedures should be aligned with the organization's appetite for operational risk and any associated tolerances for the value of operational losses (see Chapter 5).

By way of an example an escalation process might look like this:

1 Losses below £5,000 are not reported outside the relevant local area.

2 Losses £5,000 or over are reported to the operational risk function.

3 Losses £50,000 or over are reported to relevant senior management (e.g. divisional director, business unit head).

4 Losses £250,000 or over are reported to the organization's executive directors.

5 Losses £500,000 or over are reported to the board-delegated risk committee or equivalent.

6 Losses £1 million or over are reported immediately to the board.

While upon initial reporting an event may not look to breach a particular threshold, care should be taken to recheck this once new data is received.

5.9 Taking action

Operational loss events will require some form of response. Table 8.3 summarizes the main options.

It is important to distinguish between actions taken to manage a current operational loss event and those taken to address potential future events. Actions taken to manage a current event will tend to have short timescales. Those taken to address future events may have longer timescales and may only be agreed once current events have been closed (i.e. when all available information has been collected).

5.10 Closing operational loss events

The most obvious point at which to cease tracking and updating a loss event record is when the agreed action plan has been completed.

However, if there is protracted recovery involved, some organizations will defer closure until the recovery is complete and the final net loss can be determined. Others take a pragmatic approach and set a time limit on the expectation of recovery – for example, the end of the current accounting period. This avoids the prospect of retaining open events on an almost indefinite basis.

Table 8.3   Operational loss event options for action

Acceptance	Acceptance of the event because it is considered to be within the organization's appetite for operational risk.
Mitigation	Reduce the financial or non-financial impacts of the current event (e.g. public relations activities, goodwill payments, out-of-court settlements, etc).
	Actions taken to reduce the financial or non-financial impacts of future events.
Transfer	Post-event (retroactive) insurance purchases for the current event. Increase the level of insurance for future events.
Funding	Creation of provisions draw down on loan agreements or rights issues in the event of a large-scale loss.
Prevention	Actions taken to prevent similar events from occurring in the future.

6. Using operational loss event data

Operational loss event data may be used for a variety of purposes, including:

- as an input for operational risk assessment activities and to validate these assessments;
- to help organizations learn from past events (insight) and to support governance activities (oversight);
- as statistical data for quantitative risk models.

In this section the various ways in which operational loss event data can be used are discussed.

6.1 Supporting operational risk assessments

Operational loss event data provides information on an organization's current, actual exposure to operational risk. In turn this information may be used to help estimate an organization's future level of exposure and to validate past assessments. In particular, operational loss event data may be used to support the following tools and activities:

- Risk and control self-assessment (see Chapter 7), by validating probability and impact estimates, providing information on control effectiveness, and identifying risks not currently subject to assessment.
- The identification and use of risk and control indicators (see Chapter 9). Loss amount trends by risk category is a valuable indicator in its own right. Similarly, recorded incidents of control failures could be used as a control indicator. It may also be possible to compare the number and value of reported losses to risk and control indicator trends. This can help to identify the most predictive indicators. It may also identify indicators that are not effective predictors and that can be removed.
- Scenario analysis (see Chapter 10), where actual event data can be used to inform estimates of probability and impact, as well as provide information on how controls might fail. Individual operational loss events could be 'magnified' to examine how a larger-scale event might impact on the organization. Equally, elements could be taken from a number of reported events to create a more severe scenario. External loss data can be especially useful for severe scenario generation, because of the greater number of low-probabilities, high-impact operational loss events that should be present.
- Additionally, where data is collected on the causes of operational loss events this could be used to construct potential causal chains for scenarios.

6.2 Using loss data to support the determination of operational risk appetite and/or tolerance levels

Organizations will be better able to determine and maintain appropriate operational risk appetite and/or tolerance levels when they have actual loss data on which to make decisions.

One of the factors contributing to the setting of tolerance thresholds for operational risk appetite is consideration of an organization's own historic performance. For example, operational loss event data from the previous 12 months (to account for any seasonal fluctuations) could be translated into more meaningful and current tolerance thresholds:

- The mean of recorded data could be adopted as the threshold for moving from green/acceptable to amber/tolerable on the basis it indicates variation from the norm (e.g. historic levels of expected loss) and is worthy of investigation.

- The worst recorded position could represent the threshold for moving from amber to red/unacceptable if there is no appetite for the position to be worse in future than previously experienced.

Furthermore, the interpretation and use of internal loss event data can be used to support the following activities:

- Real event data can be used to monitor actual loss experience versus the organization's desired tolerance levels for losses. If the impact of a loss event is within the stated tolerance level then it less likely to demand a response (other than continued monitoring) – i.e. it may be accepted as a cost of business.

- If the impact of a loss event is at a level that can be sustained, and if the cost of mitigating is prohibitive then it is likely the exposure will be accepted. In effect, this may represent an increase in appetite/tolerance.

- Where an event has had significant consequences and breaches existing appetite/tolerance thresholds it is likely to demand mitigating action.

6.3 Using external data to benchmark internal loss data

Analysis of internal incidents can be enhanced through comparisons with external data. It is possible to undertake benchmarking where the external loss data can be sorted by type of organization and risk category. The benchmarking may include comparisons of event frequencies and average loss. This can highlight a need to enhance controls: if an organization is susceptible to more frequent or higher-value losses compared with its peers for specific risk categories. Alternatively, if losses are below the industry average and within appetite/tolerance it may be possible to justify a reduction in control, saving costs and improving efficiency.

Comparison of the frequency/value of internal losses against external loss data may also identify failings in current reporting processes, for example, where business areas within the organization are under-reporting losses. This can then be addressed by an internal review or the testing of reporting processes and may identify additional training requirements. The failure to capture internal incidents is a significant risk to organizations because failing controls or processes that are not identified as a result of loss event reporting may ultimately lead to an event that threatens the organization (see Case Study 8.2). Alternatively, a string of high-frequency, low-value losses can lead to customer impacts (e.g. rising dissatisfaction) and reputational/regulatory issues if they are not addressed.

A further way of using external data to benchmark the quality of internal loss reporting procedures is where the external data includes information on the date of event and date of discovery/reporting. Where incidents in the external database have on average a shorter period between discovery and reporting than the organization does, it may need to introduce stricter reporting timetables, escalation procedures or refresh training to ensure its internal loss data reporting is up to date, enabling management actions to be undertaken on a timely basis.

6.4 Using operational loss data to support the identification of emerging risks

For a fully effective risk assessment process it is essential that an organization considers the complete range of risks that it may be exposed to. It is only by identifying all of its risks, and selecting the most significant, that it can ensure it is protected by a complete and effective framework of controls.

The use of loss data, especially external loss data, can help the organization to understand the nature of risks that it is exposed to. An important benefit of external loss data is that it may reveal risks that an organization is exposed to, but which have not previously impacted the organization. In this way, external loss data enables an understanding of emerging risks (including trends in volumes and nature/severity of impacts).

In addition, through using external data that provides causal information, an organization can be better informed on the nature of the required control framework to mitigate specific risk types, even though it may not have previously suffered any losses for that risk. The knowledge gained from the external loss database of the control failures leading to events suffered by other firms can help management determine cost-effective control measures where improvements to the control framework are identified under the risk and control self-assessment process.

Similarly, where the external database provides breakdowns of impacts arising from events, this can help the organization determine where additional investment in controls may be beneficial.

6.5 Supporting risk governance

Operational loss data can be used to help improve an organization's awareness and understanding of operational risk, including the consequences of ineffective operational risk management. In addition, it is a valuable source of data that can be used to help improve oversight and assurance activities, including the work of the operational risk function, internal audit, compliance and governing body.

As part of the governance of operational risk management, whether by committees or a second-line-of-defence risk function, internal loss event data can provide the basis for oversight of the framework as a whole by:

- providing senior management and boards with current information on the organization's actual risk profile;
- verifying/validating outputs of information generated by other framework components, such as RCSAs;
- assessing the extent to which outputs from loss events are used as inputs in the identification and assessment of risks in other framework components;
- reviewing the effectiveness of the control framework – both from the perspective of control failure contributing to a loss event and also from a near miss suggesting some degree of control success.

Where internal loss data is collected it is strongly recommended that it is incorporated into operational risk oversight reports, especially reports provided to the board-delegated risk committee or equivalent, as well as the audit committee.

6.6 Supporting operational risk training and awareness

Internal and external loss event data, when collated and interpreted, can be used to enhance staff awareness of the nature and impact of loss events, using real-world information to demonstrate the consequences of inadequate operational risk control. This is a powerful message, particularly if coupled with lessons learnt from reviews of major loss events. Details can be provided as to how and where the loss event started, how things went wrong, what processes and controls may have failed, the various impacts, actual costs and the subsequent actions taken to prevent or mitigate a recurrence. There is also an opportunity to review any measures put in place to strengthen the control environment as a response to the loss event.

In addition, an organization can utilize its internal and external loss event data to:

- demonstrate how various smaller loss events might aggregate resulting in a large-scale or complex impact;
- reinforce the message that a particular type of event in one part of the organization (or in another organization in the case of external data) could occur elsewhere.

Such insights can help staff to understand and respond to future warning signs of potential major losses ahead and ensure that action is taken to help prevent/mitigate such losses.

6.7 Thematic reviews

By monitoring external events, new or emerging risk types or unusual (by nature or size) events (e.g. the Icelandic volcanic ash cloud or Covid-19) can trigger thematic reviews within the organization, often along the lines of 'Could that happen here?' or 'If that happened here, how robust would our controls be in mitigating the impacts?'

By reporting the external events and undertaking specific actions, the awareness of management and other staff to the possibility of a significant event is heightened and clear remedial actions to enhance the control framework can be described and monitored.

6.8 Risk modelling

External and internal loss data may both be used to support risk modelling, especially in relation to the estimation of probability and impact. As ever, the greater the quantity and quality of the available data, the more robust will be any resulting statistical analysis. In particular, it should always be remembered that the loss data available to an organization, however timely, accurate and complete it may be, will only represent a sample of the full distribution of potential events. In addition, the available data is by definition historic, and there are no guarantees that past trends will necessarily continue.

Where loss data is used as an input for risk models it is recommended that periodic comparisons of actual losses versus predicted are conducted. This will allow the model to be refined in the light of ongoing experience.

7. Conclusions

This chapter has covered how to design and implement an effective operational loss event data collection and management tool. Though costly and disruptive, operational loss events provide an opportunity to learn. Often they are not one-off events and do not occur in isolation. By collecting loss event data, organizations are able to exploit this opportunity to the full, enriching their operational risk management framework in the process. Combining internal loss data with external data further increases the amount of data, allowing organizations to learn from the losses of others, especially low-probability, high-impact tail events that are rare in any one organization.

Perfection in loss data capture is rarely needed. The priority is to start analysing and learning from past events, especially when they reveal factors (e.g. control weaknesses or inappropriate human/cultural behaviours) in need of improvement. The goal is to build a greater understanding of the causes, control weaknesses and effects that influence the probability and impact of operational loss events, and to highlight the value of operational risk management in mitigating these losses.

Reflective practice questions

1   Has your organization begun collecting operational loss event data? Does this include data on near misses?

2   When considering the required data fields and loss reporting threshold (the minimum loss size that must be recorded) did you weigh the costs and benefits of additional complexity and comprehensiveness?

3   As your operational loss collection tool has become established have you considered reducing the loss reporting threshold to capture a greater proportion of operational loss events?

4   Do you collect information on the causes and non-financial effects of operational loss events? Do you use this information to support risk assessment activities, such as scenario analysis?

5   To whom is operational loss event data reported? Do you report local data to local management and organization-wide data to senior management and the board?

6   What action is taken in response to loss event reporting? Have controls been improved and have the probability and impact of similar loss events in the future been reduced?

References

Beyer, J, Trannum, H C, Bakke, T, Hodson, P V and Collier, T K (2016) Environmental effects of the Deepwater Horizon oil spill: A review, *Marine Pollution Bulletin*, 110 (1), 28–51

Chapelle, A, Crama, Y, Hübner, G and Peters, J P (2008) Practical methods for measuring and managing operational risk in the financial sector: A clinical study, *Journal of Banking & Finance*, 32 (6), 1049–61

Cruz, M (ed) (2004) *Operational Risk Modelling and Analysis: Theory and practice*, Risk books, London

Elliott, D, Smith, D and McGuinnes, M (2000) Exploring the failure to learn: Crises and the barriers to learning, *Review of Business*, 21 (3/4), 17

Fennell, D (1988) Investigation into the King's Cross Underground fire, Department of Transport, UK, www.railwaysarchive.co.uk/documents/DoT_KX1987.pdf (archived at https://perma.cc/NM3A-P7FM)

Nishiguchi, T and Beaudet, A (1998) The Toyota group and the Aisin fire, *Sloan Management Review*, 40 (1), 49

Tinsley, C H, Dillon, R L and Madsen, P M (2011) How to avoid catastrophe, *Harvard Business Review*, 89 (4), 90–7

Operational risk indicators   09

LEARNING OUTCOMES

- Explain the benefits associated with using operational risk indicators.
- Be able to distinguish between risk, control and performance indicators and explain the criteria for key indicators.
- Know how to use risk, control and performance indicators to support operational risk reporting and decision making.

1. Introduction

Risk indicators, commonly, though incorrectly, known as 'key risk indicators' or 'KRIs' (see section 2.4, this chapter) are an important operational risk management tool. As with any type of risk, operational risk exposures are dynamic and change on a frequent basis. Operational risk indicators offer a cost-effective means to keep track of potential changes in exposure.

All organizations use operational risk indicators in some form or another. Management rely on a range of indicators to help them do their jobs and make effective decisions. This includes metrics relating to the performance of people, processes and systems, along with the impact of external events – four elements that define the scope of operational risk. These indicators are monitored by management at different levels within an organization, right up to the executive and board of directors.

This chapter explains how to design and implement processes and procedures for the use of operational risk indicators to support decision making in organizations. A well-managed operational risk indicator process can provide an up-to-date picture of how an organization's operational risk profile is changing over time, both in relation to changes in underlying exposures and the effectiveness of its controls and overall management environment. Indeed, it is hard to imagine how an organization could manage its operations effectively without effective operational risk indicator processes and procedures. It would be impossible to drive a car or fly a plane without a range of risk metrics; the same is true when managing an organization.

CASE STUDY 9.1   Risk indicators in a social housing organization

Social housing organizations build and/or buy homes to rent at below the private market rent, usually 50 per cent below this rent. This makes homes more affordable. In addition, many social housing providers offer long-term leases, increasing the security of tenants.

It would be impossible to manage a social housing organization without a wide range of operational risk indicators. This includes the monitoring of:

- building costs (e.g. raw-material prices);
- lead times for new-build houses;
- potential legal title issues (pollution liability, uncertainties over boundaries, tree protection orders, etc);
- new-build faults and repair costs for the total housing stock;
- void rates (the speed with which unoccupied houses can be rented);
- lead times for property repairs;
- customer complaints regarding property defects, customer service, anti-social behaviour, etc;
- health and safety incidents;
- gas and electrical safety checks;
- staff absence rates, to maintain operations;
- internal and external fraud (e.g. employee and tenant fraud);
- compliance with applicable laws and regulations (e.g. data protection, social housing regulation, etc).

2. Definitions

Operational risk indicators are measurable metrics that provide a proxy for operational risk exposure. A change in the value of a metric signals that a particular risk exposure may be changing, that it may be increasing or decreasing in probability or impact, or that a risk event may be about to occur very soon. In this regard an indicator may signal:

- a potential change in inherent/gross exposure (the underlying probability and or impact of risk events) to one or more categories of operational risk;
- control weaknesses and hence a change in residual exposure;
- a decline in the performance of the organization due to the impact of operational risk exposures;
- a decline in the performance of the operational risk management framework.

Here it is important to emphasize the proxy nature of most operational risk indicators. In statistics a proxy is used when direct evidence of a variable is unavailable or unobservable. In order for a proxy to be useful it must be closely correlated with the underlying variable; this means that it should move (either positively or negatively) in response to changes in the underlying variable and that these movements must be reliable and predictable.

The use of proxy variables is common in risk management, especially when probability distributions, such as probability density functions and cumulative distribution functions for a given distribution of impacts (see Chapter 8), cannot be constructed reliably in advance. In a world full of uncertainty, the construction of reliable probability distributions is rare. Either historical data is unavailable or is a poor predictor of the future, because of the changing risk environmental. This is especially the case in the context of operational risk, where data can be especially scarce and risk environments changeable. As a result, it is rare that organizations can construct accurate, forward-looking probability distributions.

In the absence of reliable, forward-looking, statistical data on the probability of potential impact outcomes from operational risk exposures, the only alternative is to make use of proxy risk indicators. If chosen correctly, these proxies can be a very effective substitute for direct statistical data. However, if poor-quality proxies are chosen, then an organization may formulate an inaccurate and misleading picture of its exposure to operational risk.

2.1 Risk indicators

A risk indicator acts as a proxy for risk exposure. This means that a change in the value of a risk indicator signals a change in probability and/or impact. In this regard risk indicators may relate to changes in the causes or effects of operational risk events. Table 9.1 contains some examples of causal and effect indicators:

Table 9.1   Example risk indicators for cause and effect

Causal Indicators	Effect Indicators
Number and type of causes identified in loss event or near-miss data collection	The direct financial cost of operational loss events (asset write downs, provisions for liability claims, etc)
Staff turnover as a % of staff	The indirect costs of operational loss events (e.g. lost market share, goodwill payments to customers, fines, etc)
Staff morale (collected from staff surveys)	Duration of staff absence due to health and safety incidents
Number of IT operating system or application patches not implemented	Customer satisfaction scores
Number of attempted IT hacking attacks	Number and duration of disruptions to operational processes and systems
Number of overdue internal audit actions	Number of negative press reports following a loss event
Number of manual interventions to correct automated process failures	Number of negative social media posts following a loss event

Usually, risk indicators signal a change in an organization's underlying exposure to risk, also known as inherent or gross risk (see Chapter 7 on risk and control self-assessments). This means that action may be required to enhance the control environment to maintain the current level of residual or net risk (exposure net of controls). If action is not taken, then an increase in inherent or gross risk may translate into an increase in residual risk.

2.2 Control indicators

Control effectiveness indicators, sometimes referred to as key control indicators (KCIs), are metrics that provide information on the extent to which a given operational risk control is meeting its intended objectives. Control effectiveness indicators provide an indication of the effectiveness of particular controls at a particular point in time. Examples of control effectiveness indicators include the results of formal control testing, along with loss and near-miss information that relates to the success or failure of controls in relation to specific operational risk events.

For further guidance on the assessment and monitoring of control effectiveness please refer to Chapter 7 on the use of risk and control self-assessment tools.

2.3 Performance indicators

Performance indicators, sometimes referred to as key performance indicators (KPIs), measure performance or the progress made towards the achievement of targets. This might include financial performance, or the performance of processes and systems, along with progress towards the achievement of financial targets, business plans and project plans.

Performance indicators are used widely in finance, accounting and general business management, but are equally applicable in the context of operational risk. Some financial, accounting or business management performance indicators may function as risk indicators (e.g. a high level of business growth can put pressure on governance systems and internal controls, increasing the potential for fraud, human error, etc. In addition, indicators that relate to the performance of organizational systems, processes and human resources may also signal a change in operational risk, including the performance of the systems, processes and tools that comprise the operational risk management framework.

Examples of operational risk-relevant performance indicators include:

- metrics on the efficiency of IT systems, including systems availability, security or recovery times;
- metrics on the efficiency of operational processes (e.g. machine breakdowns, product faults, etc);
- metrics on the reliability and performance of products and services (breakdowns, complaints, etc;
- metrics on service-centre performance (e.g. time taken to respond to or resolve a service request);
- metrics on the performance of outsource service providers;
- metrics on the performance of (operational) risk management processes and procedures;
- metrics on the efficiency of internal and external audit processes, such as whether all agreed items in the annual plan have been audited.

CASE STUDY 9.2   Using financial performance metrics as operational
risk indicators

Specific metrics may be used as risk, control or performance indicators in different
contexts. For example, a regional mutual bank (a UK building society) used asset growth,
a common performance indicator, as an indicator of its inherent exposure to operational
risk. The rationale for this was that a large increase in asset growth, beyond the 10 per
cent annual growth target, could signal an increase in operational risk exposures. The
building society had experience of rapid asset growth and knew that such growth put
significant strain on its governance systems and internal controls. For example, customer
services and branch staff were required to work significant overtime (opening new
accounts, processing transactions, etc), increasing the potential for process errors, and
breaches of financial crime regulations. In addition, prolonged levels of high workload
tended to increase sickness absence and damaged staff morale.

2.4 Key indicators

Indicators are not automatically key indicators in every context. An indicator becomes 'key' when it tracks an especially important risk exposure (a key risk), or it
does so especially well (a key indicator in the sense that it is a good proxy for the risk
in question).

What this means is that terms like KRIs, KCIs and KPIs are often overused. In the
context of operational risk, the term 'key' is best applied when it is used as a proxy
for a significant and typically organization-wide operational risk. These significant
operational risks are usually key because of the size of an organization's exposure.
For example, an operational risk, and hence its associated risk control and performance indicators, may be considered key because the level of exposure is high enough
to impact on the future of an organization, threatening its solvency or the achievement of its objectives. Equally, operational risk exposures may be considered key
because they exceed agreed appetite or tolerance thresholds.

Assigning risk, control or performance indicators to key risks will allow an organization and its management to monitor these risks and control them effectively.
Indicators might also be used to signal effective internal control (where they are
within stated thresholds or limits) and to provide assurance to the board that these
risks are being managed effectively.

In this context, the first step for an organization implementing KRIs for
operational risk should be to identify its key risks. The results of a group-wide or

executive-level risk and control self-assessment process could be used as the basis for this exercise (please refer to Chapter 7). An organization's key risks should be those that have the largest inherent and/or residual risk exposure scores – these being the risks that represent the greatest threat to the achievement of an organization's objectives.

CASE STUDY 9.3   Identifying key operational risks and indicators

A financial institution and a third-sector (not-for-profit) organization working to improve social housing in local communities each went through a risk and control assessment exercise to identify their key operational risks. In both cases they identified people risks as key (e.g. poor conduct, compliance breaches). The financial institution also identified IT systems risks as key, while the third-sector organization focused on health and safety.

Table 9.2 provides examples of the key risk, control and performance indicators that they identified to monitor these key operational risks.

Table 9.2   Example key risks and key indicators

Key Risks	Key Indicators
People Risk	Outcome of staff performance reviews (% satisfactory or above)
Sickness absence (deviation from the industry norm)	
IT Systems Failure	Systems availability
Number of external hacking attacks	
Health and Safety	Number of reported serious incidents under the UK Reporting of Industrial Diseases and Serious Incident Reporting (RIDDOR) rules
Number of overdue gas safety inspections	

3. Using operational risk indicators

Operational risk indicators have a range of uses. First and foremost, they are a business intelligence tool that provides information to enhance the efficiency and effectiveness of operational decisions. In this regard they can support operational risk monitoring and assessment, the implementation of an operational risk appetite framework and operational risk governance.

3.1 Risk monitoring

Operational risk indicators can be used by organizations to track changes in their exposure to operational risk, especially when they are forward-looking leading indicators (see section 4.3, this chapter). Leading indicators help signal the potential for future changes in probability and/or impact. As proxy variables, indicators do not reveal the actual/precise change in probability or impact, but they can be used to provide an early warning that a change is occurring or will occur in the near future. Such a signal should then prompt action to investigate the situation and implement further controls where necessary.

A further benefit of using indicators for the purpose of monitoring operational risks is that collecting and reporting data on indicators is usually less time-consuming and resource intensive than a full-blown risk and control self-assessment. This means that indicators can be used to track changes in inherent risk, control effectiveness and residual risk between each assessment update. For example, risk and control self-assessments might be updated quarterly, while indicators might be updated monthly or potentially even weekly, daily, hourly or real time (e.g. the monitoring of financial crime is often real time in larger banks).

3.2 Implementing risk appetite

As explained in Chapter 5, procedures should be put in place to ensure that an organization remains within its chosen appetite for operational risk, including its tolerances for specific operational risk exposures.

The monitoring of risk, control and performance indicators is a common method used in organizations to help ensure they remain within their appetite for operational risk. Tolerance thresholds and limits may be set for specific metrics, which are aligned with the chosen appetite. Then when these thresholds or limits are breached, or trending towards a breach, targeted action can be taken to address the situation and bring the organization's exposure to operational risk back within its appetite.

CASE STUDY 9.4   Using indicators to keep within appetite

A manufacturer operating a just-in-time production process has a low appetite for process interruptions. To help keep the risk of process interruptions within appetite it sets red and amber tolerance thresholds for a range of risk and control indicator metrics. Table 9.3 provides some examples of these metrics.

Table 9.3 Example risk tolerance metrics and thresholds

Metric	Amber Threshold	Red Threshold
Total duration of component delivery delays (daily)	1 hour	3 hours
Overdue machine maintenance (monthly)	2 working days	5 working days
Staffing shortfall (number of staff hours per week)	20 hours	50 hours

By monitoring whether these metrics stay within the agreed tolerance thresholds the manufacturer can be reasonably assured that it is within its appetite for process interruption risk. Where metrics breach an amber threshold the production line management are informed and must decide whether action is required to correct the situation. Where metrics breach the red threshold, immediate action is required on the part of production-line management to correct the situation, and senior management must be informed of the action taken.

3.3 Governance and assurance

Many governance codes, including the UK Governance Code, expect boards to monitor an organization's significant risk exposures and to keep these exposures within appropriate limits. Boards are also expected to assure themselves that the organizations they govern have appropriate risk management and internal control systems.

Operational risk, control and performance indicators can be used to help support these governance responsibilities. High-level, organization-wide indicator reports can be used to help them monitor significant operational risk exposures (the key risks) and to assure themselves that the associated controls are effective. Metrics on the performance of the operational risk management framework may also be used to help assure the board that this framework is effective.

3.4 Risk assessment and modelling

Risk and control indicators may be used to support risk and control self-assessments and statistical risk modelling where appropriate.

In relation to risk and control self-assessments a significant rise or fall in particular risk or control indicators should prompt a review of probability and/or impact scores. It may be that risk and control owners decide that these scores should remain unchanged. But this should be a conscious decision that follows an appropriate discussion of the situation.

In relation to risk modelling, risk and control indicators may be used as variables in statistical models. Alternatively, they may be used to help validate these models. Questions should be asked when there is a significant change in the predictions of a risk model, but there is no change in the related risk and control indicators or vice-versa. Such a situation may indicate that either the risk model is imperfect or that the wrong indicators have been identified.

4. The desirable features of operational risk indicators

The selection and use of too many operational risk indicators can be as detrimental as too few. This is because decision makers will struggle to take in all of the information (failing to see the wood for the trees) and because of the costs involved in collecting and reporting the information. Organizations are advised to establish very specific characteristics for the data they use as indicators, separating broad data from specific metrics used to indicate changes in exposure levels (which may include metrics on inherent/gross risk exposure, control effectiveness or risk management performance).

The characteristics that organizations should consider when selecting effective operational risk indicators are outlined below.

4.1 Relevant

Operational risk indicators must be good proxies, providing reliable and accurate information on an organization's operational risk exposures. This should include providing information on both current and future exposures.

Relevance can change over time, as new operational risk exposures emerge, and existing exposures are either mitigated or modified. Linking periodic reviews of the selected suite of operational risk indicators with the completion of risk and control self-assessments is an effective way to maintain relevance, as is drawing on the experience, knowledge and understanding of risk and control owners to help select the initial set of indicators and to suggest changes, as necessary. This should include both the addition of new indicators and the removal of existing ones to ensure that the total number monitored does not become excessive.

The following questions are useful to consider when assessing the relevance of existing operational risk indicators, or when considering adopting new ones:

- Does the metric help quantify or measure the risk?
- Does the metric help monitor the exposure?
- Does the metric help manage the exposure and its consequences?

4.2 Measurable

Indicators should be measurable in a consistent and reliable manner. This is to allow the construction of trends to facilitate comparisons over time. It also enables the use of targets, limits and thresholds.

This feature requires that indicators should be one of the following:

- numbers or counts (number of days, employees, etc);
- monetary values;
- percentages and ratios;
- time durations;
- a value from some pre-defined rating set (such as that used by a credit-rating agency).

Non-metric-based indicators that are described by text are prone to being subjective, can easily be misinterpreted and are subject to manipulation through the structure of the text employed. Hence they are not recommended, though they are in theory possible.

Measurable indicators (usually described as metrics) should reflect the following characteristics:

- They must be quantifiable as either a cardinal (absolute) or ordinal (relative) value. Cardinal values are 'real' numbers that imply that 2 is twice as large numerically as 1 and so on. Ordinal values simply provide an indication of scale (e.g. we can say that 2 is greater than 1, but not by how much greater). The probability and impact scores determined through risk matrices are ordinal values (see Chapter 7). Statistical risk models provide cardinal values (i.e. real probabilities and precise financial impacts) that can be used to construct probability distributions.
- Indicators must have values that are precise and not prone to excessive subjectivity (cardinal values are much more precise than ordinal ones).
- Values must be comparable over time.
- Indicators should be based on primary source data (e.g. data direct from the original source and not subject to interpretation or modification by a third party) and be meaningful without interpretation to some more subjective measure or benchmark (e.g. a subjective maturity framework).

Good indicators are those that quickly convey the required message, without the need for comparison or reference to other information. In this regard, percentages and ratios – presented against an appropriate benchmark – are typically far more useful than the actual underlying information.

4.3 Forward looking (leading)

The use of so-called 'lagging' indicators, which provide information on past events or issues, is not recommended, unless past trends can be relied upon to provide an indication of the future. Rarely is this the case in the modern world. Much better to use 'leading' or 'preventive' indicators that provide management with sufficient lead time to correct the situation before operational risk events happen.

Critical to this preventative feature of operational risk indicators is the capacity to capture the causes of the risks rather than counting the number of realized events. This is where loss data collection (both internal and external) can be invaluable, where data is collected on the causes of events. Forward-looking scenario analysis can also help identify causes not currently reflected in the loss data.

Table 9.4 compares some examples of leading and lagging indicators.

CASE STUDY 9.5   Leading indicators for tracking Covid-19

During the Covid-19 pandemic a wide range of infection statistics were monitored and reported by public health officials, some more leading than others. These statistics ranged from the number of new cases and the total number of cases, through to the number of hospitalizations and Covid-related deaths.

The number of virus-related deaths is very much a lagging indicator. Though it was possible to calculate the number of Covid-related deaths with a reasonable degree of accuracy, the past rate of deaths did not prove to be a good predictor of the future rate, especially as countermeasures were employed (e.g. lockdowns and vaccines) and as the virus mutated into new strains. However, the number of new cases proved to be a relatively good leading indicator of the near future progress of the virus, especially when converted into the reproduction number (known as the R_0), which indicated how quickly the virus was spreading in a given geographical area.

The R_0 is an epidemiological statistic that shows whether the current rate of infection of a virus is rising or falling, along with the speed of this rise or fall. A value above 1 indicates a rising rate of infections, the higher the number the faster the projected rise. A value below 1 means that the rate of infection is falling, the smaller the number the faster the projected fall. Using this data, it was then possible to predict the number of hospitalizations and deaths based on the trends in serious illness and mortality (e.g. using statistically robust estimates of the percentage of infected people likely to become seriously ill and die).

It should be emphasized that the accuracy of these R_0 calculations were not perfect. Rates of new infections were hard to assess in most countries, because of incomplete testing (not every newly infected person was tested, especially those who did not exhibit symptoms). As a result, the R_0 was usually presented as a range. For example, 0.72–0.81 or 1.1–1.4. The width of these ranges reflected the level of confidence in the estimate. The narrower this width the higher the degree of confidence.

As Covid-19 vaccines were rolled out, new leading metrics were added, notably the numbers of people partially (first dose) and fully (first and second dose) vaccinated. As vaccination rates rose the potential for future outbreaks diminished, as did the potential for hospitalization and death. Scientifically robust medical trials were used to provide evidence of the effectiveness of vaccines in preventing infections, hospitalizations and deaths.

Major operational risk events are often the result of a chain of causes and effects. For example, bad IT, leading to poor information, leading to a wrong decision, leading to poor customer service, leading to complaints, is an example of one such cause-and-effect chain. Therefore, a lagging indicator for one risk can be leading for another: for example, a lagging indicator of bad IT (such as IT breakdown) can be a leading indicator of customer dissatisfaction, since poor customer service can be caused by IT disruption. Similarly, consider the number of unresolved customer complaints – such complaints relate to issues that have already occurred (the lagging aspect), but which still need to be addressed (the current aspect).

Lagging and current indicators can also have a leading element to them that may need to be considered. For example, in the case of unresolved customer complaints an organization's failure to address these could give rise to a costly lawsuit at some point in the future and/or bad publicity, leading to reduced sales.

Table 9.4 Comparing leading and lagging indicators

Leading Indicators	Lagging Indicators
Pay gap and job satisfaction metrics to capture the causes of staff resignations	Staff turnover as a measure of staff morale
Metrics on product/service-quality control	Customer complaints (counting the number of unhappy customers having already told their friends and relatives how much they dislike your product or service)
Frequency of policy and procedure breaches	Losses from breaches
Frequency of machine/vehicle servicing	Cost of machine/vehicle breakdowns

Truly leading indicators are rare and are usually related to causal drivers within the business environment within which the organization operates – they tend to be measures of the state of people, process, technology and the market that affects the level of risk in a particular organization. A leading or preventive indicator can be something as simple as the number of limit breaches on market or credit risk exposures, or cash movements, or the average length of delays in executing particular activities. In themselves, such occurrences may not be loss events in their own right, but if their value starts to increase this may point to the potential for a higher frequency or severity of operational loss events.

In addition to causal indicators, indicators of exposure, stress or failure may provide more leading information on operational risk exposures for managers.

4.3.1 Exposure indicators

Exposure indicators relate to the nature of the business environment and to its critical dependencies. The business environment may be volatile or stable, growing or mature, regulated or free. Critical dependencies in the external environment include the solvency and conduct of service providers, suppliers and vendors, or large clients. They may also include external events that impact on essential systems or staff. Example events include the spread of a pandemic, regulatory change or trends in cyber crime.

Exposure indicators are typically one-off signals, alerting management when a change in exposure has occurred. This means that they do not necessarily fit well into traditional, routine, red–amber–green-style metric reports, but they do allow an alert to be raised whenever there is a change in a key stakeholder to the organization. This means that exposure indicators are normally reported on an exception basis.

4.3.2 Failure indicators

Failure indicators typically warn of failures in important operational risk controls or wider processes, procedures and systems. In this regard control indicators are a common source of failure indicator (see section 2.2, this chapter).

4.3.3 Stress indicators

Stress indicators reflect the stretch in business resources, systems and processes, whether human, financial or physical. Tiredness is a well-documented cause for accidents, mistakes and slips, whether in medical services or road safety. Many human resources departments capture the number of hours of overtime per staff member. In equipment, overloaded machinery, IT hardware or software are all likely to lead to downtime or crashes. Hence, metrics like equipment usage rates or production rates can be used as stress indicators, as can the number or duration of computing hang/freezing problems.

4.4 Easy to collect and monitor

Ease of monitoring means that the value of the data collected for a metric must exceed the costs of collection: this cost-benefit rule is as applicable to investments in operational risk metric reporting and monitoring (with the exception of mandatory reporting for regulatory purposes), as it is to any other type of business investment.

An indicator's cost of collection and ease of monitoring should be at the centre of the selection decision. One way to achieve this is through recycling: reusing what already exists. As explained above, organizations make use of a wide range of metrics to support their operations; these metrics offer a good starting point for the selection of operational risk indicators.

The use of automated risk indicator systems, often provided as part of IT packages for operational risk assessment and reporting, can further reduce the costs of collection and facilitate easy monitoring. However, they are only recommended for organizations with mature operational risk indicator frameworks. In most cases, organizations should start by selecting a small set of the most relevant indicators and collecting the data manually. This facilitates a good understanding of where the data is coming from, what it actually indicates, and how it can be used. Once an indicator or set of indicators have proven themselves useful, then consider technology solutions to reduce the manual workload, but in a manner that allows the easy replacement and addition of new indicators.

An important aspect relating to the collection process is quality assurance. The collection cycle needs to incorporate specific deadlines for submission and should be auditable in terms of data sources and collection channels. There should also be an independent quality control process to ensure that erroneous or misleading data is not sent to management.

4.5 Comparable

Operational risk indicators must provide data that is comparable with some form of benchmark. Comparability allows management to understand the relative 'scale' of the indicator. This helps them to determine when action is required to address the value of the indicator or the risks or controls that it relates to.

Relevant benchmarks are either over time or across comparable internal departments or business units and external organizations. An organization can track its own evolution through time, provided that the type of indicator and information collected is stable over a long period. Cross department/unit or external organizational comparisons are also very useful. They provide a wider context and are not prone to inconsistent historical trends. Some industries share data in less sensitive areas like staff sickness absence or health and safety incidents, for example. Where data is shared in this way it should be used as a benchmark. For example, along with the 'raw' metric an organization's position relative to the industry distribution could be provided (fourth to first quartile). Comparisons between internal departments and units could be made in the same way and used to help facilitate friendly competition to improve the value of indicators and, by extension, the related operational risk exposures.

CASE STUDY 9.6   Using staff turnover as a risk indicator

A consumer retail organization monitored new starters and leavers on a monthly basis. This provided raw data on the number of staff joining and leaving the organization.

The organization relied on a large number of staff with part-time contracts ranging from full-time equivalent (FTE) 0.1 to 0.9. As a result, the number of joiners and leavers each month was quite high. To make the metric more meaningful, the organization adjusted the raw number of leavers and joiners to reflect the range of contracts. As a result, staff turnover was reported as a percentage of the total number of FTE staff present in the organization. This was further broken down to reflect the FTE of specific departments and functions.

In time, to make the metric even more meaningful the staff turnover percentage for the organization was compared to industry benchmark data for the consumer retail sector. This involved reporting the quartile in which the organization's staff turnover was located. By making this enhancement the retailer was able to track its performance relative to industry norms. This helped it to understand how well it was doing in areas like the proportion of experienced staff to inexperienced staff, staff morale and the appropriateness of its salary scales.

4.6 Auditable

Auditable means that the data used to produce a metric is:

- comprehensive and accurate, and that this remains consistent over time;
- comes from a documented course;
- is constructed using a clear and consistent formula; and
- is reported in a clear and timely manner.

As part of effective operational risk governance, an independent validation of the indicator selection process (including the manner in which data is sourced, aggregated and delivered to management) should be undertaken reasonably early in the lifecycle of an organization's operational risk indicator programme. The organization's internal audit function should normally perform such a validation.

Periodically, further quality assurance checks should be made to ensure that indicators remain relevant, and that the data used is timely, accurate and complete. This may also be conducted by internal audit or the operational risk function.

The results of any risk indicator audits, along with any associated action plan, should be reported to the operational risk committee or equivalent, as well as the statutory audit committee.

5. Selecting indicators and setting thresholds and limits

As explained in section four of this chapter, indicators should be selected with care and used effectively. This section contains guidance on the processes that can be used to select a set of indicators and for setting appropriate thresholds and limits.

5.1 *Selecting indicators: top-down or bottom-up?*

There are two main approaches that organizations can use to select the operational risk indicators they wish to monitor: top-down or bottom-up. The top-down approach starts with senior management and/or directors who select the indicators that are to be monitored across the business, while the bottom-up approach allows business entity/area-level managers to select and monitor their own sets of indicators. In both cases, the aim is to cover the most significant information requirements that each level of the organization requires in order to achieve their objectives.

Neither approach is automatically better than the other; both can, or should, co-exist. A top-down approach can facilitate aggregation and senior management understanding, while a bottom-up approach ensures that local managers can select and monitor the operational risk indicators that are most relevant to their particular situation. In practice, many organizations employ a combination of the two and this is generally considered to be the best approach.

The selection process for top-down operational risk indicators could be conducted vertically (by business line) or horizontally (by department) depending on the organization structure of the company. Top-down indicators should meet the following criteria:

- reflect the operational risk profile of the division, business line, country or region or of the overall organization, depending upon the level at which selected;

- facilitate aggregation across relevant business entities, product or service areas, countries or business lines, resulting in a meaningful and understandable metric at the relevant level of management;

- apply to all parts of the organization structure below the level where they are being applied; and

- are usually imposed by management and must be reported on, without choice.

Typically, the selection process for bottom-up operational risk indicators should consider:

- the results of risk control self-assessments, ensuring that indicators are identified to facilitate the ongoing monitoring of identified risks and controls;

- the results of any regulatory examinations or audit findings to help facilitate the rectification of any control or monitoring deficiencies that may have been identified;

- being identified during the new product review process (mainly short term) to monitor and manage the operational risk during the implementation phase;

- the views of the appropriate risk owners (e.g. the relevant department managers or business line managers) or that of the local operational risk manager, both during and between formal risk assessments;

- any insights that may have been provided by recent loss events (for example in terms of the identification of significant new indicators); and

- changes in the economic environment, which might mean that certain indicators become more important (e.g. indicators of fraud risk may become more important in a recession, etc).

CASE STUDY 9.7   Combining bottom-up and top-down selection of operational risk indicators for organization-wide reporting

Some organizations combine bottom-up and top-down selection processes to build organization-wide operational risk indicator reports.

A small to medium-sized enterprise, working in the home-improvement sector, with 600 staff and around 20 departments, achieved this by surveying the management in each department to ask them about the operational risk indicators that were important to them. The operational risk manager organized the survey and spoke to the management in each department to collect their views. The operational risk manager then looked at the results to identify themes. One common theme was an interest in staff turnover, another was in IT systems availability. Where such metrics were identified as important by a significant number of managers these were included in the draft group-wide report.

The operational risk manager also looked at the outlier metrics, ones mentioned by only one or two departments, and considered whether some of these might be relevant also, based on current industry and regulatory trends. This led to the addition of two data protection metrics (the numbers of reported internal and external data protection incidents).

A draft list of recommended bottom-up metrics was presented to the board risk committee for review. The committee agreed with most of the recommendations but made some changes to the design of certain metrics and added two metrics on Brexit/Covid-related supply chain risk. One metric tracked the cost of supplies, the other tracked supply lead times, both of which were increasing and threatening the profitability of the business.

5.2 Deciding on the number of indicators

There is no right or wrong answer for how many operational risk indicators should be monitored or reported. Too few may not deliver a clear picture and too many may present an overly confusing picture.

The following factors should be considered when deciding on the appropriate number of indicators:

- number and nature of the identified key operational risks;
- availability of the data necessary for the key risk, control or performance indicators;
- the cost needed to extract the data for the key indicators; and
- the intended audience (local management, executive, board, etc).

In terms of the last point concerning the intended audience it is usually appropriate to collect a more detailed set of metrics for the local management of a specific business area/entity than for executive management or the board. This is because local management will probably require a detailed set of indicators in order to help them monitor and control the day-to-day activities of their area/entity effectively, while executive management/boards, whose time is limited, should normally only focus on the most relevant metrics that relate to the most significant risks that may be threatening their organization at the current time.

CASE STUDY 9.8   Board reporting of operational risk indicators

To arrive at an appropriate list of operational risk indicators to report to its board a bank completed an annual significant operational risk exercise. The purpose of the exercise was to identify the operational risks considered most likely to impact on the bank's strategic objectives. Executive management completed this exercise, with support from the operational risk function.

Usually, three or four significant operational risks were identified each year. These changed depending on the external risk environment (e.g. pandemics, Brexit, etc), significant new laws or regulation, such as data protection regulation and whether major internal change projects were scheduled (e.g. IT core systems replacement). For each of the significant operational risks two to four metrics were identified. The focus was on identifying the most relevant (best proxies) and leading metrics as possible.

Each quarter, the Board Risk Committee received a full report on all of the selected metrics. Any metrics that breached their amber or red threshold were subsequently escalated to the full board, with an accompanying action plan approved by the Board Risk Committee.

5.3 Deciding frequency

The frequency with which data is collected on an operational risk indicator will typically follow the cycle of the related operational activity: from real time (usually measured using automated systems) to monthly, quarterly or semi-annually.

It is important to note that the frequency of data capture is not the same as frequency of reporting. Data may be captured on a real-time basis, but only reported on an exception basis, for example. Alternatively, the operational risk function may collect data monthly, but report this to the operational risk committee on a quarterly basis.

Table 9.5 provides some examples of typical data collection frequencies.

Table 9.5   Example data collection frequencies for operational risk metrics

Metric	Frequency
Suspicious transactions	Continuous, real time
Environmental safety (e.g. harmful gas levels)	Continuous, real time
Equipment and IT systems availability	Daily
Account reconciliation errors	Daily
Operational loss amounts and number of near misses	Monthly
Staff turnover	Monthly
Progress against internal audit actions plans (e.g. number of late actions)	Quarterly or semi–annually
Electrical testing	Quarterly or semi-annually

5.4 Thresholds and limits

Implementing a set of operational risk indicators without any guidelines on how to interpret the data and what actions are required will not deliver much benefit to an organization. The organization needs to establish, for each relevant indicator being monitored, a set of threshold values or limits where, if the indicator's value breaches the threshold or limit, the organization knows it needs to act. Equally the establishment of thresholds and limits for specific indicators is an important part of an effective operational risk appetite framework.

However, the establishment of thresholds and limits in isolation of an informed understanding of the indicator and its values over at least a minimum period of time is equally likely to deliver little value. When organizations implement a set of operational risk indicators, while they should monitor and react to outcomes as they are reported they should collect data for six months at the very least, but preferably one year, before setting specific thresholds and limits. This will allow them to assess any data trends over that time and thus establish more meaningful thresholds and limits. If possible, draw upon any publicly available information or benchmarks to assist in establishing the starting points for an organization's thresholds and limits.

Thresholds may take several forms, including:

- A *cap* or upper boundary, where as soon as the indicator value exceeds the threshold value, the escalation process kicks in.

- A *floor* or lower boundary, where as long as the indicator value is above the threshold value, nothing happens, but when it drops below that level, the escalation process starts.

- A *collar* or combination of a cap and floor/upper and lower boundary, where essentially the indicator values are expected to remain within the pre-defined range.

Caps, floors and collars may be specified using a variety of numerical options. Table 9.6 summarizes those in common use.

Table 9.6 Common types of numerical thresholds

Numerical Option	Description
Absolute numerical values	A pre-specified cardinal (quantity) threshold. A common example is a specified cash amount, such as the maximum amount of loss from operational risk events over a given time period.

(continued)

Table 9.6   (Continued)

Numerical Option	Description
Percentage or ratio-based	A relative threshold that specified a minimum or maximum percentage value. Percentage base thresholds are commonly used for availability-based metrics (e.g. equipment or systems availability). They are also used for things like staff sickness absence (the number of lost workdays as a percentage of the total staff resource).
Discrete data	Discrete data thresholds are derived from observations that can only take certain numerical values, usually an ordinal count of some variable. Examples include specifying tolerance thresholds for the number of reported near misses or the number of customer complaints.
Variance	Thresholds linked to acceptable levels of variance from the norm. In statistics variance this refers to the expected standard deviation of a variable from its mean value. Often variance-based thresholds are combined with some other option, such as a percentage threshold. For example, a variance threshold of 10% might be set for fluctuations in staff turnover. This reflects the fact that a certain level of staff turnover is to be expected, potentially desirable, to attract new skills, etc, but that a significantly higher or lower level of turnover compared to the norm may not be considered tolerable.

Over a period of time, as operational risk indicator monitoring is embedded, indicator thresholds may be tightened to improve the efficiency and effectiveness of an organization's operational risk management activities (e.g. to enhance the level of control). This implies that the organization should periodically review not just the indicators it is using, but the thresholds applied to those indicators. However, if the thresholds are too narrow, they will result in false alerts and then, over time, people may ignore the alerts altogether. Too broad, on the other hand, and the organization may learn too late that a major operational risk issue has emerged, with potentially significant adverse consequences.

To establish the initial threshold values, decide first on whether a cap, floor or collar is required, then establish whether the threshold is an absolute number or value, a percentage, ratio or other derived value or some form of deviation or variance. Next, review historical data for the indicator in question and establish its

Table 9.7   RAG thresholds for operational risk metrics

- The value of this indicator is higher/lower than normal suggesting that the organization may be exposed to an elevated and potentially significant level of risk.
- Management attention is required to determine whether action needs to be taken soon.

- The value of the indicator is within normal parameters, suggesting that the organization is not exposed to significant risk.
- No action is required – the indicator and its associated risks are under adequate control.

ranges over time. Assess existing budgets or targets, relevant public information and the organization's risk appetite and apply this information to the historical ranges. Then, decide where the first level of slight discomfort within the data range lies and use this as the basis for establishing your first threshold. Monitor the next few data submissions against the threshold and adjust if necessary.

It is common to set limits and thresholds using a RAG (red–amber–green) approach. Indicators that are within their amber zone should normally be given greater priority than those that are green, with even greater priority being given to red indicators. Table 9.7 illustrates the normal significance and response criteria that are assigned to red, amber or green indicators. Note that for indicators that are assigned a single limit (indicating zero tolerance for values above or below this limit) there may be a case to omit the amber threshold and present such indicators as being either red or green.

Remember, as operational risk indicators are proxy variables, the aim is not to manage the indicator, but rather the associated operational risk exposures. A breach of an indicator is a signal of potential threats ahead. Getting the indicator back into the amber or green zone does not necessarily mean that these threats have been averted.

Limits and thresholds should reflect the implementation of the risk appetite statement cascaded down to the organization. Please refer to Chapter 5 for more information.

5.5 Triggers for escalation

Having set one or more thresholds, the final step is to determine the response required when a threshold has been breached. This is commonly referred to as a trigger condition, which determines what action is to be taken and by whom.

Where an organization has implemented an escalating series of thresholds (e.g. amber and red thresholds), it is likely that each threshold will result in some form of triggered notification to increasingly senior levels of management.

In the same manner as different boundary thresholds can be applied to different indicators, different trigger conditions can be established. The most common is a 'touch' trigger, where as soon as the boundary is reached, the trigger is initiated, and alerts generated as appropriate. In addition, 'repetitive touch' triggers may be used. Repetitive touch triggers are less sensitive because they are only triggered when a boundary is breached two or more times in a row. This means that when a repetitive touch boundary is first reached nothing happens, but if in the next (or subsequent) data submission period the boundary is still in breach, then the alert is triggered. Repetitive touch triggers are useful where occasional breaches of thresholds occur and an organization is confident that such breaches are not a reliable indication of an increase in risk exposure (e.g. occasional spikes in staff sickness absence due to a seasonal flu outbreak).

As with the associated thresholds and limits, triggers should be linked to an organization's operational risk appetite. Triggers should also be linked to the degree of sophistication required in the warning system and must consider the resource overhead (people, systems and cost) necessary to implement more sophisticated structures.

6. Managing and reporting operational risk indicators

Once an initial set of indicators are determined and thresholds and/or limits are determined, the focus shifts to review and reporting. All the initial effort will be wasted without time and resources devoted to the effective reporting of the selected indicators. Plus, selected operational risk indicators and their thresholds/limits should be reviewed on a regular basis to ensure that they remain relevant. At a minimum it is recommended that selected indicators and their thresholds/limits should be reviewed on an annual basis, although the appropriate frequency will vary depending on the nature, scale and complexity of an organization and the dynamism of its operating environment.

Emphasis should also be given to documentation that supports the implementation of operational risk indicator reporting. At a minimum, documents should be drafted on the following:

- procedures for adding or changing indicators and their associated thresholds;
- documentation on each selected metric, which notes the data source, any formulae used to calculate the metric, frequency of collection and the rationale for selecting the indicator and any assigned thresholds or limits;
- procedures for the reporting of risk indicators.

As part of effective operational risk governance, the operational risk function is normally responsible for the design, implementation and documentation of management processes for operational risk indicators.

6.1 Adding or changing indicators

Organizations should review their selected operational risk indicators whenever there are changes in their key operational risks (e.g. the addition or removal of operational risks that could impact on the achievement of an organization's objectives) or when the relevance of the chosen indicators changes.

A procedure for adding or changing operational risk indicators should be put in place that explains:

- The frequency with which the chosen indicators should be reviewed.
- Who has the authority to approve the addition, change or removal of particular risk indicators, bearing in mind that different individuals may be responsible for different areas of risk.
- Whether changes can be made on a top down and/or bottom-up basis.
- When removing a previously monitored indicator, what will happen to the data that has been collected (will it be retained or deleted?).
- When replacing an existing indicator with another, similar indicator, whether past data should be recalculated or amended and applied to the new indicator.
- The introduction of indicators relating to new product or new business activities, including how long such indicators should be monitored for post-implementation.
- The introduction of indicators following recommendations by department manager(s), regulators and/or auditors (both internal and external).

6.2 Changing thresholds and limits

Changes to thresholds and limits are a common occurrence, especially for new indicators where, initially, relatively little data is available (see section 5.4, this chapter).

A documented procedure is essential to control the setting and changing of limit/threshold levels. This procedure should explain who has authority to make changes and who may approve these changes.

From a bottom-up perspective, local management may be authorized to change thresholds and limits, with approval provided by the operational risk function. From a top-down basis, authority will normally rest with senior management, with approval by the board or board-delegated risk committee or equivalent.

6.3 *Taking action to resolve threshold or limit breaches*

When an amber or red threshold is exceeded action is required (see section 5.4). Actions should be documented and assigned to an owner (e.g. the risk or control owner). In addition, it is recommended that actions are Specific, Measurable, Actionable, Realistic and Timebound (SMART) and that progress is reviewed to ensure an on-time completion.

6.4 *Reporting*

There is little point collecting data on operational risk indicators if this is not reported to the appropriate level of management in a timely and usable fashion. However, organizations that have just begun to collect data on new operational risk indicators may decide to wait six months to a year before producing regular reports. This is to ensure that sufficient data is collected to facilitate trend analysis and the setting of thresholds or limits. However, this should not be used as an excuse to avoid or delay taking action, where there are concerns about something material. For example, a sudden (adverse) change in the available data might trigger an ad hoc exception report, with suitable health warnings about the lack of sufficient trend data.

Where pre-existing data is available there is no need to delay the commencement of routine risk reporting. However, such data should only be used if it meets the desirable criteria set out in section four, this chapter.

The effective reporting of operational risk indicators requires consideration of a number of additional factors:

- the report recipients (audience);
- frequency of reporting;
- data visualization.

These factors are expanded upon below.

6.4.1 Reporting to different audiences

Different audiences within an organization will require different reports on risk indicators. Figure 9.1 illustrates this according to the traditional management hierarchy.

Where possible, operational risk indicator reports should be developed in conjunction with the intended audience to ensure maximum comprehension and usability. However, central coordination can help to ensure that a consistent view of information is delivered so that reports can be compared across business lines and functions, and/or aggregated for senior management. In larger organizations documented procedures for indicator reporting may also be necessary to ensure consistency.

Figure 9.1 Levels of operational risk indicator reports (author's own)

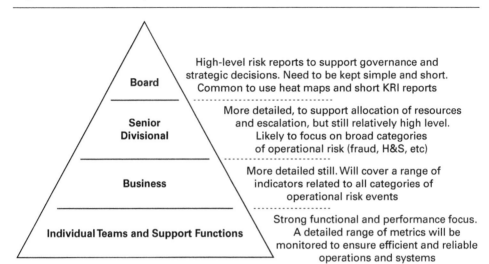

Some features of a sound indicator report/reporting process include:

- Short – care must be taken to avoid producing overly detailed reports with large numbers of indicators. Management will not have the time or attention required to process large amounts of information. One way to achieve this is through exception reporting, only reporting on indicators that have breached thresholds or limits, or which are trending adversely, indicating that a future breach is likely.

- Simple – reports should not be overly complex or contain jargon terms, large tables of data or complex mathematical formulae. Where possible, the simplest available graphs and charts should be used.

- Timeliness – reports should be produced in a timely manner so that they can be acted upon while the data they contain is still relevant.

- Accuracy – inaccurate metrics will provide a false picture of an organization's exposure to operational risk and may mean that it ends up overexposed or spends too much reducing certain risks. Processes should be in place to check the accuracy of reported metrics on an ongoing basis.

- Trending – reports should make clear the historical trends of the chosen indicators to provide some indication of their volatility and/or where they may be heading.

- Clear escalation procedures – so that the recipients of a report know when to escalate areas of concern to more senior management.

- Compliance – with any regulations that may exist, where appropriate.

Table 9.8   Frequencies for operational risk indicator reports

Interval	Benefits	Suitable For	Audience	Drawbacks
Daily	Potential risk or control issues identified immediately	Dealing with routine issues (e.g. running a call centre or IT function)	Local management	Too frequent to allow detailed analysis
Weekly	Track common issues on a regular basis	As above	Local management	May not capture the full extent of an ongoing issue or concern
Monthly	Aligns with monthly management committees	Monitoring operational performance	Local and senior management	May not be sufficiently timely
Quarterly	Aligns with quarterly reporting and many audit/risk committees	Monitoring threats to organization objectives	Senior management Board committees	Lacks sufficient detail Not timely
Yearly	Concurrent with year-end financial results and reports	Reviewing the high-level operational risk profile and impact on going concern	Senior management Board	Lacks sufficient detail Not timely

6.4.2 Frequency of reporting

There is no right answer to the frequency of reporting. It will depend on the nature of the risks, indicators and environment. Reporting should be linked to the timeliness of decision making and action formulation, and reports of different frequency will be required to suit specific audiences.

Table 9.8 outlines the common frequencies that are used for operational risk indicator reporting.

6.4.3 Data visualization

An indicator report should be presented in a user-friendly manner with appropriate visual aids, and use clear and simple language. The presentation can be in the form of:

- country or regional view reports;
- organization-wide reports;
- business-specific reports;
- special theme reports (i.e. focus on a specific control topic, e.g. fraud, information security, etc).

Figure 9.2 Example simple risk indicator report (author's own)

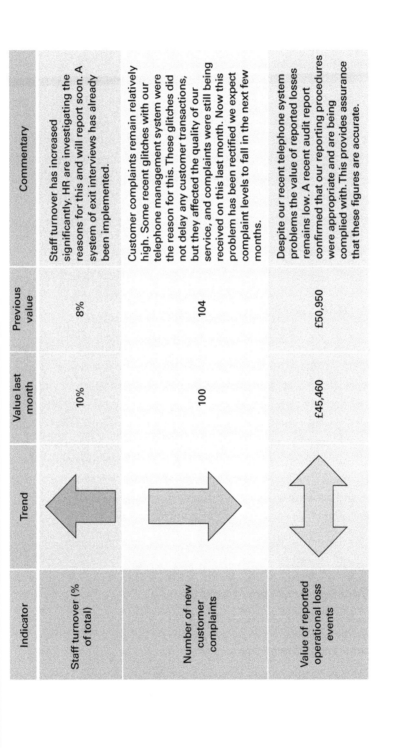

Indicator	Trend	Value last month	Previous value	Commentary
Staff turnover (% of total)	←	10%	8%	Staff turnover has increased significantly. HR are investigating the reasons for this and will report soon. A system of exit interviews has already been implemented.
Number of new customer complaints	→	100	104	Customer complaints remain relatively high. Some recent glitches with our telephone management system were the reason for this. These glitches did not delay any customer transactions, but they affected the quality of our service, and complaints were still being received on this last month. Now this problem has been rectified we expect complaint levels to fall in the next few months.
Value of reported operational loss events	↕	£45,460	£50,950	Despite our recent telephone system problems the value of reported losses remains low. A recent audit report confirmed that our reporting procedures were appropriate and are being complied with. This provides assurance that these figures are accurate.

Judgement on the part of the (operational) risk function on what to include or exclude from a report may be necessary to help report users to reach the right conclusions. However, users and auditors should be able to access data on all available indicators, on request, so that they can satisfy themselves that the most appropriate indicators have been presented.

The provision of suitably detailed narrative to support the figures is critical to ensure that information consumers are able to interpret the reports that they receive and use them to support decision making. In particular, brief and relevant commentary should be provided to explain abnormal items and data trends.

Many operational risk indicator reports are presented in a very simple format (see Figure 9.2). More sophisticated data visualizations are also possible and are used in some organizations. This can include heat maps, interactive geographical maps, such as the Kaspersky Cyberthreat Real Time Map (Kaspersky, 2021) or Covid-19 maps (John Hopkins University, 2021) and network diagrams that highlight relationships between different operational risk indicators.

7. Conclusion

This chapter has explored how to select, monitor and report on risk, control and performance indicators for key operational risks. It is hard to imagine a sound framework for the management of operational risk without the use of such indicators. Though the implementation of operational risk indicator monitoring and reporting can be time-consuming, the benefits are considerable. Management is effectively blind without access to the appropriate risk metrics. It is impossible to drive a car without access to metrics on factors like speed or temperature. Similarly, management require operational metrics to support effective decision making and to ensure that they steer organizations away from threats to their objectives and towards value-creating opportunities.

Reflective practice questions

1 Has your organization begun collecting and reporting data on operational risk, control and performance indicators?

2 How did you select these proxy operational risk indicators? Did you consider their relevance, along with the costs associated with data collection?

3   How leading are your operational risk indicators? Do they provide information about your future exposure to operational risk, or do they simply tell you what happened in the past?

4   Do you regularly review your chosen set of key operational risk indicators, adding and removing indicators when appropriate?

5   To whom are operational risk indicators reported? Are reports provided for management at all levels of your hierarchy?

6   How are operational risk indicator reports used? Are they primarily for compliance purposes (to signal compliance with regulations) or are reports used to support value-creating business decisions?

References

John Hopkins University (2021) Coronavirus Resource Centre, https://coronavirus.jhu.edu/map.html (archived at https://perma.cc/XC4C-CVA5)

Kaspersky (2021) Cyberthreat Real Time Map, https://cybermap.kaspersky.com/ (archived at https://perma.cc/J7VS-MJ3Y)

Scenario analysis and stress testing 10

LEARNING OUTCOMES

- Explain the role and benefits of scenario analysis, stress testing and reverse stress testing in an operational risk context.
- Be able to conduct effective scenario analysis, stress testing and reverse stress testing workshops.
- Know how to use the output from scenario analyses and stress tests to support operational risk assessment and management decision making.

1. Introduction

The accurate assessment of operational risk exposures is a major challenge for organizations. Often historical data on probability and impact is limited and, even when available, there is no guarantee that historical trends will repeat themselves.

Particularly problematic are low-probability, high-impact 'tail' events, where data is often non-existent. Likewise, dynamic organizational environments, where there are high levels of internal or external change (e.g. political, technological or social change), further reduce the value of tracking historical trends.

CASE STUDY 10.1   Global warming and extreme weather events

Research shows that climate change is causing an increase in severe weather events such as flooding, droughts and windstorms (e.g. Stott, 2016). In turn this is increasing the risk exposures of organizations to external weather events (Huber and Gulledge, 2011).

Though it is known that climate change has increased organizations' exposure to severe weather events it is impossible to attribute climate change to specific events or estimate precisely the degree to which the probability and impact of extreme weather events are increasing. As a result, it is difficult to assess the extent to which past and current trends of extreme weather events are a reliable predictor of the future.

Scenario analysis is one way to help address the uncertainties associated with assessing the probability and impact of severe weather events, including their economic impacts (Bouwer, 2013). Using scenario analysis, it is possible to estimate a range of possible economic outcomes, based on plausible assumptions about the future prevalence and intensity of specific types of severe weather events over the next few decades.

Scenario analysis, and the related tools of stress and reverse stress testing, have emerged as common responses to the problems of limited data and unreliable trends. When done effectively, these tools can shed light on uncertainty and help organizations to prepare for and proactively respond to operational risk events. This includes, but is not limited to:

- enabling management to test the resilience of their organization in relation to major (low-probability, high-impact) operational risk events and providing an opportunity to discuss, in advance, how to respond to them;
- providing a forward-looking perspective, by focusing managers' attention on future operational risk events that may differ from those in the past;
- offering a break from day-to-day operational risk management activities, helping managers to think creatively about future operational risk events and to share their knowledge and expertise in a less time-pressured environment;
- complementing other operational risk identification and assessment techniques, such as loss event analysis and risk and control self-assessment, by incorporating the data produced by these techniques and providing structured methods to fill in knowledge gaps;
- improving the control environment, where potential gaps or weaknesses in existing controls are identified as part of the analysis.

2. Demarcating scenario analysis, stress and reverse stress testing

Figure 10.1 illustrates the relationship between scenario analysis, stress testing and reverse stress testing.

Figure 10.1   Comparing scenario analysis, stress testing and reverse stress testing

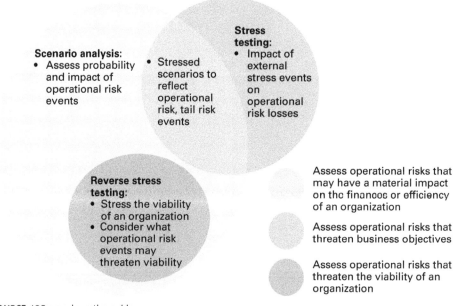

Scenario analysis:
- Assess probability and impact of operational risk events

- Stressed scenarios to reflect operational risk, tail risk events

Stress testing:
- Impact of external stress events on operational risk losses

Reverse stress testing:
- Stress the viability of an organization
- Consider what operational risk events may threaten viability

Assess operational risks that may have a material impact on the finances or efficiency of an organization

Assess operational risks that threaten business objectives

Assess operational risks that threaten the viability of an organization

SOURCE IOR sound practice guidance paper

Stress testing involves the assessment of specific stress events that might occur within the external operating environment of an organization, and that may impact on a range of risk types, including operational risk. Examples include an economic recession, a pandemic or political events such as Brexit. Stress events have the potential to seriously disrupt the strategy and operations of an organization, making them high impact, though usually the probability of occurrence is low.

Reverse stress testing involves analysing events that threaten the viability of an organization, causing insolvency or bankruptcy. The starting point of reverse testing is to identify the point of non-viability, usually in terms of determining the maximum financial loss that an organization can withstand and then considering the types of internal risk event that may cause losses that exceed this value. From an operational risk perspective this may include a major IT failure or fraud, for example.

Scenario analysis encompasses elements of stress and reverse stress testing but can be used in a wider range of applications. Scenarios need not be extreme stress events, for example, but more common situations that have a higher probability of occurrence, up to and including events that may be expected to occur once or more a year. In contrast the events considered as part of stress, and especially reverse stress testing, will occur much less often and have a significantly higher impact.

An alternative perspective on demarcating stress and scenario testing, commonly used in the disciplines of accounting and finance, is in terms of the number of variables analysed. From this perspective, stress testing involves analysing the impact of major changes in a limited number of variables (usually one or two), while scenario analysis is said to involve the analysis of changes in a wider range of variables. For example, a stress test might analyse the financial impact of a significant change in interest rates or the rate of inflation. In contrast, scenario analysis would consider the wider implications of an economic recession (increased unemployment, reduced credit ratings, etc).

While a variable-based distinction between scenario analysis and stress testing might apply in an accounting or finance context, it does not apply so well from an operational risk perspective. This is because operational risk events are multifaceted and necessarily involve changes in a range of variables. These changes may be relatively small or stressed to a significant degree. Hence a better way to distinguish between operational risk scenario analysis and stress testing is in terms of severity of impact, rather than the number of variables to be considered.

3. Conducting effective scenario analysis, stress testing and reverse stress testing

Like most risk identification and assessment tools, effective scenario analysis, stress testing and reverse stress testing is a process that involves a number of stages. These are as follows:

- identifying and agreeing the focus of analysis;
- determining the level of analysis;
- preparing for a workshop;
- conducting a workshop;
- validation of the outputs;
- governance of the process.

Each of these sub-elements is explored further below.

3.1 Identifying and agreeing the focus of analysis

Effective scenario analysis, stress testing and reverse stress testing can take significant time and resources. This means that the potential number of topics that can be analysed at any given time is limited. As a result, it is important to ensure that those selected are the most relevant.

For organizations that categorize their operational risks (see Chapter 3), one common approach is to select one topic for each of the level 1 or 2 operational risks that the organization is exposed to. However, this is a rather arbitrary approach, especially where some categories are considered more or less significant than others. Ultimately the number of topics per category of operational risk should vary depending on the nature, scale and complexity of an organization and the stability of its internal and external operational risk environments. There is no point selecting a topic for a non-significant risk category. Equally, the most significant risk categories may require the analysis of multiple topics.

CASE STUDY 10.2   Deciding the focus of analysis: comparing a financial
institution and a housing developer

Different types of organizations will often select different operational risk scenarios and stress events to focus on.

Financial institutions produce fewer tangible products, such as savings accounts, insurance contracts and advice. To produce these products, they rely on IT systems and a range of human and automated processes and procedures. In contrast, a housing developer produces something tangible (a house), using skilled manual labour, physical tools and equipment.

Both organizations are exposed to a wide range of operational risks, many of which overlap (health and safety, fraud, IT systems failure, etc). However, the significance of these exposures varies. Table 10.1 summarizes the types of operational risks that each might select for the purposes of scenario analysis and stress testing, using the Basel level 1 operational risk categories as the basis for this comparison.

Table 10.1   Example scenarios by Basel operational risk types for a financial institution and housing developer

Level-1 Event Type	Financial Institution	Housing Developer
Internal Fraud	Significant (multi-million) theft of client funds by an employee.	Executive or senior manager taking bribes for the awarding of supplier contracts.
External Fraud	Major hacking attack leading to theft of client assets or information.	Unlikely to be a significant risk. Hacking attack likely to be the most significant but limited sensitive data or cash assets.

(continued)

Table 10.1   (Continued)

Level-1 Event Type	Financial Institution	Housing Developer
Employment practices and workplace safety	Major diversity and discrimination case.	Major health and safety incident leading to loss of life and liability claim(s).
Clients, products and business practices	Major breach of conduct of business regulations, including financial crime regulations.	Housing development has major problem with defects or environmental quality (e.g. houses built on contaminated land).
Damage to physical assets	Loss of head office or a major IT processing site.	Flooding significantly damages a development site near completion.
Business disruption and system failures	Prolonged core systems failure.	Delays in the development of a site due to staff or material shortages (e.g. as a result of Covid-19 or Brexit).
Execution, delivery and process management	Incorrect financial reporting information sent to a regulator.	Major problem with the supply of building materials (e.g. wood, bricks or cement).

In choosing the topics to focus on, a consultative approach is recommended. The operational risk function should work with the wider management of the organization to select the topics considered most relevant. This includes working with senior management and business unit management where appropriate. It may also include working with the board for the analysis of the most significant organization-wide operational risks, especially in relation to topics for reverse stress testing.

From an operational risk perspective, relevant topics for analysis/testing will come from the external and internal environment of an organization. Table 10.2 summarizes some common environmental sources.

A key factor in the selection of topics to focus upon, reflecting all of the sources in Table 10.2, is the potential for a significant increase in operational risk exposure. Where operational loss event data, risk assessment and monitoring tools, or a scan of the external environment, reveals that a significant increase in the probability or impact of particular operational risks has occurred, or is likely to occur, then this should be a particular focus of attention and the risks in question should be worked into the topics for analysis/testing.

Table 10.2 External and internal environmental sources of topics

External Environment	Internal Environment
Operational risk events that have recently impacted similar organizations. Plus, operational risk events identified as being of particular significance over the coming year (e.g. as identified by professional organizations, regulators, or publications like the World Economic Forum Global Risk Report: WEF, 2021).	Operational risk-loss events and near misses that have occurred within the organization. Near misses can be especially useful in topic selection. Allowing the organization to investigate how impactful they would have been as they crystallized into losses.
Regulatory or legislative changes, such as the risks associated with new laws or regulations (e.g. data protection regulations).	Output of the risk and control assessment process, especially the most significant risks in terms of probability and impact or risk exposures that have increased significantly.
Social changes, such as changes in norms and behaviours (e.g. attitudes towards data privacy, the environment, etc).	Information on control weaknesses, including the output from internal audits, to help understand how control failures might contribute to a scenario or stress event.
Economic changes, such as a recession.	Trends in key risk or control indicators, especially those that indicate a large increase in potential risk exposure.
Political changes, such as the impact of a new government.	Changes in the financial or operational performance of the organization.
Technological change, such as the 'Internet of Things' and other IT innovations.	Strategic change, such as IT systems implementation, new products, etc.
Environmental events, such as pandemics or the effect of climate change.	Operational changes such as process improvements, changes in supply chains, outsourcing, etc.

CASE STUDY 10.3 Horizon scanning

A social housing organization in the UK has an annual board away-weekend. As part of this weekend a board member workshop is routinely scheduled on emerging operational risks that could impact on the strategic objectives of the organization.

The session is facilitated by the operational risk manager. They use the strategic environment tool PESTLE analysis. This tool provides a structured approach to exploring changes in the organization's internal and external operating environment that could provide sources of significant new or significantly increased exposures to operational risk.

PESTLE analysis looks for changes in the following environments:

- Political
- Economic
- Social
- Technological
- Legal
- Environmental

The results of the annual emerging operational risk PESTLE analysis are used to inform the scenario analysis and stress testing required by the Regulator of Social Housing. Emerging operational scenarios have included issues such as fire safety (changes to building regulations related to building cladding), data protection regulation, Brexit-related supply chain risks and the Covid-19 pandemic.

Another influence on the focus of attention on the above environmental sources is the degree of confidence that can be placed in current risk assessments and the accuracy and completeness of loss event and near-miss data. For example, where an organization is not confident about the accuracy of risk and control self-assessments, especially where it has insufficient data on actual events, and historic trends appear unstable, it should supplement these assessments with scenario analysis and stress/reverse stress testing to help fill in the gaps. This might include using scenarios to analyse the relationships between the causes of one or more risk events (causes that are likely to come from the environmental sources identified in Table 10.2) or stress testing the scale of the effects (e.g. the effects of IT failures of different durations).

Other factors that may increase the focus of attention on the sources outlined in Table 10.2 include:

- The pace of change – the faster an area is changing (e.g. technological innovation), the greater should be the level of focus.
- Concerns about future changes that might create major new emerging risks.
- The degree of internal strategic or operational change – the greater the level of change the greater the focus.
- The ability of an organization to manage potential sources of operational risk. For an example concerned about technological change and its ability to manage the associated risks an organization may choose cyber risk as an important topic for scenario analysis and stress testing.

Ultimately these factors are linked to two fundamental elements that should influence the choice of topics for analysis/testing: the *proximity* of an organization to potential operational risk scenarios/stress events and its *vulnerability* to these scenarios/stress events. The more urgent or pressing a source (e.g. imminent regulatory change) the higher its priority for inclusion. Equally the less able an organization feels in relation to controlling a source (e.g. rapid internal change) the higher the priority for inclusion.

In some sectors regulators may stipulate specific scenarios or stress/reverse stress tests for analysis. This is most common in financial services but can occur in other heavily regulated sectors such as social housing, as is the case in the UK. It is imperative that organizations fulfil their regulatory obligations and analyse any scenarios or stress/reverse stress tests set by their regulators.

3.2 Determining the level of analysis

At a minimum, scenario analysis and stress/reverse stress testing should be conducted at the organization-wide (i.e. group) level. Additionally, organizations may choose to conduct analyses/tests at the business unit or even department and functional level, though the latter two (department and function) are less common.

Stress and reverse stress testing is especially important at the organization-wide level. Stress and reverse stress tests may be used to help the organization (especially board/senior management) understand its financial sustainability. Though an organization may appear to have a strong balance sheet, it may be that future operational risk events (such as a pandemic) will weaken it severely. The sooner that board directors/senior managers can understand and prepare for these events the stronger will be their organization over the long term.

Organization-wide analyses/tests should be determined on a top-down basis, with the operational risk function working with senior management to agree the topics for analysis. Business unit or department/function analyses and tests may be agreed on a bottom-up basis. It is, however, recommended that the choice of topic is reviewed and signed off by the operational risk function – to ensure maximum relevance and to maintain consistency across the organization for reporting, where possible.

3.3 Preparing for a workshop

The best way to conduct scenario analysis, stress testing or reverse stress testing in an operational risk context is through a workshop. Given the multifaceted nature of operational risk (multiple causes, effects, etc) no one individual, department or function will have the knowledge and expertise required to complete an effective analysis/test.

However, workshops are resource intensive, and it is important to conduct them as efficiently as possible. This means that research will be required in advance of the workshop, to help save time on unnecessary details and to avoid any misunderstandings or loss of focus on the central topic for analysis/testing.

Table 10.3 summarizes the key tasks pre-workshop.

Table 10.3   Key tasks required before conducting a scenario or stress test workshop

External Environment	Internal Environment
Operational risk events that have recently impacted similar organizations. Plus, operational risk events identified as being of particular significance over the coming year (e.g. as identified by professional organizations, regulators, or publications like the World Economic Forum Global Risk Report, WEF, 2021)	Operational risk loss events and near misses that have occurred within the organization. Near misses can be especially useful in topic selection. Allowing the organization to investigate how impactful they would have been as they crystallized into losses.
Regulatory or legislative changes, such as the risks associated with new laws or regulations (e.g. data protection regulations)	Output of the risk and control assessment process, especially the most significant risks in terms of probability and impact or risk exposures that have increased significantly.
Social changes, such as changes in norms and behaviours (e.g. attitudes towards data privacy, the environment, etc)	Information on control weaknesses, including the output from internal audits, to help understand how control failures might contribute to a scenario or stress event.
Economic changes, such as a recession	Trends in key risk or control indicators, especially those that indicate a large increase in potential risk exposure.
Political changes, such as the impact of a new government	Changes in the financial or operational performance of the organization.
Technological change, such as the 'Internet of Things' and other IT innovations	Strategic change, such as IT systems implementation, new products, etc.
Environmental events, such as pandemics or the effect of climate change	Operational changes such as process improvements, changes in supply chains, outsourcing, etc.

3.4 Conducting a workshop

Workshops should take place in a suitable environment, one that is quiet and away from the participants' 'day job'. This will allow participants to focus on the workshop.

Workshops should typically last for two or three hours. Longer durations will lead to fatigue. A short break should be scheduled every one or two hours.

As indicated above, workshops should be facilitated and follow an agenda that is agreed in advance. This will ensure that the workshop stays focused and finishes on time.

A number of additional factors are discussed below that must be considered when conducing a scenario or stress test workshop. This includes:

- inviting the right participants;
- knowing the output that is required from the workshop;
- ensuring that probability and impact are assessed;
- deciding whether the workshop will be conducted using a structured analysis tool such as the Structured What If Technique (SWIFT).

3.4.1 The participants

Key to the successful outcome of any sort of workshop is inviting the right participants. These participants must have relevant skills and experience and the necessary confidence to speak up. Also important is inviting people from a diverse range of backgrounds, to help avoid problems like group-think, where a desire for conformity results in incorrect outcomes (Janis, 1971).

The selection of participants will depend on the focus of the workshop (e.g. the type of risk and focus, etc). As a rule, the following should attend:

- the relevant risk owner(s);
- the senior manager(s) with responsibility for the topic of focus, where they are not the risk owner;
- other subject-matter experts, covering key control areas like IT systems and security, customer relations, marketing, human resources, finance, etc;
- an independent observer, such as an internal auditor or representative from the risk function.

Around six to eight attendees are optimal, with 12 as a maximum. As workshops increase in size, facilitation becomes harder and there will be insufficient time to ensure that all voices are heard.

The role of the independent observer is to look for potential bias. The observer should only speak if they are concerned that a risk exposure or control effectiveness assessment is being over or underestimated.

Even if vocal, senior managers have an important role to play in scenario/stress workshops. Experience shows that if this task is delegated to more junior members of the team, the quality of the workshop output is often reduced and consequently there is a lack of senior management buy-in. Executive and the senior management teams are often the ones with ultimate accountability line when certain types of severe scenarios materialize, so they should be engaged in the process.

CASE STUDY 10.4   Managing the participant mix in a scenario workshop

A retail bank organized a scenario analysis workshop to explore the risk of a major IT systems disruption. Attendees were invited from the following departments:

- branches and customer services;
- finance;
- internal audit;
- IT applications and networks;
- IT infrastructure;
- IT security;
- operational risk;
- treasury.

The discussion focused on the likely duration of a core systems failure and the number of systems that could fail. Many attendees were confident that the duration of a failure would be short (up to 24 hours), and that failure would be limited to a single system, as most operated independently.

An attendee from the IT infrastructure department spoke up. She pointed out that the bank's core systems were all reliant on a single IBM-PC disc operating system (DOS), that has been in place since the 1980s. Though it had proved extremely reliable, a failure of the DOS system would impact on all core systems. The IT infrastructure attendee went on to explain that only two people in the organization had the necessary skills to work on the DOS system and that one of them was retiring in a month's time.

Following a discussion, it was agreed that the potential duration and scope of a severe IT systems failure scenario should be increased to reflect the essential nature of the DOS system and the limited resources available to maintain and repair it.

3.4.2 Key output variables from scenario and stress test workshops

Though open discussion is important in a scenario or stress test workshop, this must be focused on producing usable management information, to support operational risk assessment, monitoring and control. Table 10.4 summarizes the key variables that should be discussed during a workshop.

The outcomes of the discussion on these variables should be recorded on a template of some form; Table 10.4 can be used as the basis for such a template. Alternatively, many operational risk assessment and reporting systems offer scenario analysis and stress testing modules. In addition, it is recommended that minutes are taken during each workshop to ensure that items discussed before reaching any conclusions are recorded.

These minutes will help those not in attendance to understand why particular outcomes were agreed. Ideally a member of the operational risk function should take the minutes, as they have the necessary technical expertise to understand the points that should be recorded.

To help the participants arrive at plausible outputs for the variables in Table 10.4, workshops can be conducted in one of two main ways:

1 Unstructured – the workshop relies on open discussion of the selected scenarios or stress events. Participants are free to highlight the issues of most concern to them.

2 Structured – discussion is directed using a specific analysis technique, such as fault and event trees or the Delphi technique.

Table 10.4 Key output variables from a scenario or stress test workshop

Variable	Explanation
Scenario Description	A brief description of the narrative (storyline) of the scenario or stress event in question. What has happened and in what context (e.g. a major fraud that occurs during a recession, business disruption during a pandemic, etc).
Causes	The events that lead up to the scenario/stress event, including people, process and systems failures or external events.
Effects	The effects of the scenario/stress event, notably whether a financial or reputational impact is expected, as well as potential impacts on people (e.g. health and safety or employee morale).
Controls	An assessment of how well controls might cope during the scenario, especially a stressed scenario. Participants should discuss whether controls will remain effective and what if any controls might fail.
Mitigating Actions During the Scenario or Stress Event	Management actions that could be taken during the scenario or stress event to help mitigate its effects and reduce any financial impact.
Assessing Probability and Impact	Where possible estimates of probability and financial impact should be recorded. Further guidance on this is provided below.
Current Actions	Actions that should be taken following the workshop to help reduce the probability or impact of the scenario or stress event in question. Typically, this will include enhancing existing controls or adding new controls.
	In extremes a decision might be taken to reduce or cease a particular activity to help prevent the occurrence of a scenario or stress event. However, this is only recommended where the benefits of doing so outweigh the costs associated with ceasing the activity.

A structured approach is not necessarily superior. This is because it may limit participant creativity and divert their attention from important aspects of a scenario or stress event that are especially relevant to an organization. Equally an unstructured approach does not mean the absence of an agenda, just that the discussion of specific agenda items are not structured using formal analysis techniques.

Chapter 7 – on risk and control self-assessment – explored a range of risk analysis techniques that could also be used to structure scenario and stress test workshops. These include the Structured What If Technique (SWIFT), Root Cause Analysis and the Delphi Technique (see Table 7.8).

3.4.3 Assessing probability and impact

Assessing probability and impact during a scenario or stress testing workshop can be challenging. The lack of objective information means that assessments of probability and impact will often involve a significant element of subjectivity. Nevertheless, it is possible, in a well-organized workshop, to arrive at meaningful estimates.

Chapter 7 – on risk and control self-assessments – provides general guidance on the assessment of probability and impact. The guidance in Chapter 7 should provide the foundation for any assessment during a scenario analysis or stress test workshop.

3.4.4 Probability

A key difference in the context of scenario analysis and stress testing relates to the comparative rareness of these events. Hence, the probability scales used for routine risk and control self-assessment may prove to be insufficient. In addition, accurate probability assessments for scenarios, and especially stressed events, can be hard, if not impossible, because of a lack of objective data.

If formal percentage or decimal point probabilities are used it is recommended that these are presented in terms of ranges, for example 1–10 per cent, 11–20 per cent, or 0.01–0.1, 0.11–0.2, etc. This is because of the difficulties in assigning precise probabilities to rare events, due to the lack of reliable data. However, the use of statistical probabilities is not recommended in the context of scenario analysis and stress testing, because non-risk professionals tend to struggle with formal statistical representations of probability, especially when these probabilities are very small (Tversky and Fox, 1995). Hence for scenarios and stress events, it is better to use duration ranges or qualitative terms. For example:

- 1 in 10-year or 'routine' event – that is expected to occur several times during a working lifetime. It is likely that an organization will have prior experience of these within the working lifetime of the workshop participants.

- 1 in 40-year or 'stressed' event – that will only occur once, if at all, during a working lifetime. It is less likely that workshop participants will have personal experience of such an event, but they may have observed them affecting other organizations.

- 1 in 80-year or 'tail' event – that may occur once during an individual's whole lifetime. There may not be any examples of such events, except possibly in historical records, although such historical examples would have to be extensively reworked to bring them up to date. Alternatively, there may be examples of such events that have affected other, similar organizations in recent years.

Workshop participants should be provided with definitions like the three above during a workshop, to help them discuss and agree the estimated probability of occurrence.

Different versions of a scenario or stress event will have different probabilities. There is no need to try to define every possible version of a scenario. The point is to examine scenarios and stress events that are representative of hypothetical, yet foreseeable and plausible, operational risk events. In short, the focus should be on events that could occur, and which management should discuss openly and prepare for.

Alternatively, some organizations take one central scenario for a particular risk category (e.g. damage to physical assets) and then work on different versions for two to three probability levels. For example, a routine version of the scenario (e.g. repairable damage to an area of a building), followed by a stressed (repairable damage to the whole building) and tail event (destruction of the building). This is more time-consuming but can help highlight a wider range of possible future events.

3.4.5 Impact

Scenarios, especially when worked into stress or reverse stress events, are by definition high impact. In the case of reverse stress events, impact is effectively determined in advance, since by definition such events threaten the financial sustainability (solvency) of an organization.

Impact need not be quantified for scenarios and stress events. Instead, events might simply be labelled routine/expected, stressed/unexpected or extreme/tail, as indicated above.

Where an organization does wish to quantify impact, it is recommended to start with a discussion of the effects and to then think about the quantum of these effects, typically in financial terms, but reputational impacts may also be considered (e.g. impact on customer goodwill).

Table 10.5 summarizes some financial and reputational effect factors that could be estimated quantitatively during a scenario or stress test workshop.

Where financial quanta are estimated it is recommended that they are presented in terms of a range. Precise estimates of impact are impossible, given the hypothetical nature of scenarios and stress events, and imply a false sense of accuracy and objectivity. The use of a financial impact range reinforces the fact that these impacts are estimates and could be exceeded.

Additional guidance on the estimation of impact in relation to more severe stress and reverse stress test events is provided in section five below.

Table 10.5   Examples of quantifiable impacts

Financial	Reputation
Cost of replacing or repairing assets	Loss of customers/market share (number of customers or % loss of market share)
Fines or liability claims	Negative press (extent and duration)
Clean-up costs	Impact on staff morale (e.g. staff retention)
Third-party costs, e.g. legal costs	Credit-rating downgrade
Loss of revenue due to business interruption	Regulatory censure (number of times organization is named and shamed and duration of regulatory attention)
Bad debts and other non-recoverable assets	
Loss of investment income	

3.5 Validating workshop outputs

To help combat subjective bias it is recommended that the output from scenario analysis and stress testing workshops are validated in a systematic fashion. Unlike risk and control self-assessments, a comparison of the output from similar scenario workshops is rarely possible, as each scenario will be unique. However, there are other approaches that could be used. For example:

- Comparison with the available data on external events, through the use of public data or an external loss database. Though an organization may not have experienced a stressed or extreme tail scenario it may be that other, similar organizations have. Often, for more extreme operational risk events, expenditure on an external loss database is not required. Such events are often reported in the public press, meaning that an internet search can reveal much valuable information, including data on the financial impacts of such events.

- Where an organization has access to an external loss database it may be possible to determine the probability of occurrence for more extreme (very low probability, very high impact) events, providing that sufficient data is available to build a reliable probability distribution. Alternatively, specialist statistical techniques are available to help construct probability distributions for tail events, such as Extreme Value Theory (see De Haan, Ferreira and Ferreira, 2006; Gourier, Farkas and Abbate, 2009).

- For business unit or department/function-level scenarios, intra-organization comparisons may be possible, providing similar loss events have occurred elsewhere in the organization. This is most likely to be effective in larger organizations.

- Where the operational risk function participates on practitioner forums with representatives from the operational risk functions of other organizations, they might agree to share information on operational risk scenarios and stress events to help them compare results. Information can be checked for commercial sensitivity before sharing. The more operational risk managers can learn from the experiences of operational risk managers in other organizations, the better.

- Some operational risk software vendors and consultant organizations offer standardized lists of completed scenarios for organizations in certain sectors. While these standardized scenarios do not reflect the nature, scale and complexity of an organization they may help in providing a simple benchmark against which to compare results. Organizations could use these lists to aid both scenario selection and to compare results. Where an organization's choices and results differ significantly from the standardized scenarios they should investigate the reasons why.

To support the validation of workshop outputs an organization's scenario analysis and stress testing approach should be subject to periodic review by the internal audit function. This should include reviewing the conduct of workshops, how scenarios and stress events are selected, and how probability and impact are estimated. Ideally this should include comparing an organization's approach with available good practice guidance, such as this chapter.

3.6 Governing the process

The operational risk function should be responsible for the design and implementation of an organization's scenario analysis and stress test processes for operational risk events. The function should ensure that these processes are effective, and periodically review their design and implementation. This may be complemented by periodic internal audits of these processes.

Where an organization has a board-delegated risk committee with responsibility for operational risk, it may decide to give this committee the authority to review and sign off the design and implementation of these processes. This is especially important where scenario analysis and/or stress/reverse stress testing is a regulatory requirement. Where scenario analysis and/or stress/reverse stress testing is a requirement, but there is no board-delegated risk committee with responsibility for operational risk, the audit committee should sign off design and implementation to ensure that the processes are compliant. Internal audit reports on scenario analysis and stress testing processes should also be reported to the audit committee, as with any other internal audit report.

It is rare that boards will be asked to sign off operational risk scenario analysis or stress/reverse stress testing processes. However, it is common for them to receive reports on the outputs of operational risk scenario analyses and stress/reverse stress tests to support their governance responsibilities.

Beyond the immediate confines of operational risk, boards may be asked to review the agreed topics for scenarios and stress tests and suggest any additional ones they feel are necessary, which might include scenarios/tests that have an element of operational risk exposure. In some sectors this may be a regulatory requirement, as is the requirement for boards to receive information on the most significant, organizational-wide scenario analyses and stress tests. For example, within financial services it is common for scenario analysis and stress testing to be used as part of the Pillar II supervisory review and evaluation process (SREP) that forms part of the banking and insurance capital adequacy regulations. This process covers exposures to a range of risk types, including operational risk.

In terms of reverse stress tests, where conducted, these should always be reported to boards. Reverse stress tests provide important information on the long-term viability of organizations and their ability to remain a going concern.

Finally, some organizations may be required to report the results of their scenario analysis and stress/reverse stress testing processes to regulators. This is the case for systemically important financial institutions and in non-financial sectors such as social housing in the UK.

4. Making effective use of the workshop outputs

Given the resources required to complete scenario analysis and stress testing workshops, it is important to make full use of the outputs. This will include using these outputs for governance and compliance purposes and to support strategic and operational decision making.

4.1 Reporting the outputs

As explained above, boards should receive reports on completed operational risk scenario analyses, stress tests and reverse stress tests, especially where these relate to events and effects that could impact on the strategy, business plan and financial viability of an organization.

Senior management and, where relevant, the operational risk committee or similar should also receive reports on the output, including the actions being taken to mitigate the probability and impact of the operational risk events analysed as part of this process.

Reports should not contain any unnecessary detail. Boards and senior management have limited time and must allocate this to a wide range of tasks. The focus of these reports should be on the potential impacts of events (financial or reputational) and the implications for the organization's financial position and business plan.

Where appropriate, information might also be provided on the actions taken to mitigate identified control weaknesses. This is especially relevant for senior management and the operational risk committee or equivalent.

4.2 Using scenarios to support risk assessments

The results of operational risk scenario analysis and stress testing can be used to inform risk and control self-assessments. This is especially the case for assessments of inherent (gross) risk. This is because inherent risk assessments reflect a hypothetical level of exposure, assuming the absence/ineffectiveness of key controls. Management can find it hard to determine reliable assessments of inherent risk, given its hypothetical nature. Scenario analysis and stress testing provide a structured means to achieve such assessments.

CASE STUDY 10.5   Using scenario workshop outputs to support inherent risk assessments

An international charity that provides relief for communities hit by natural disasters organizes regular scenario workshops to discuss potential disasters and the ability of the charity to respond to them. During these workshops participants discuss the effectiveness of key controls (e.g. emergency response procedures, contingency finance, communication networks, health and safety of first responders, etc) and the consequences of failures in these controls.

Participants also discuss the inherent risk of potential disaster scenarios, considering factors such as political turmoil, population movements and climate change. The idea is to consider plausible future scenarios, the potential frequency of occurrence and impact on local populations.

The outputs from the workshops are used to estimate the inherent risk of natural disasters over the coming one to five years, plus the ability of the charity to respond to them in a safe and effective manner. For example, the output from the workshops are used to help assess the charity's inherent exposure to health and safety risks related to its employees and the people that they help during disasters.

For more on the conduct of risk assessments please refer to Chapter 7 on risk and control self-assessment.

4.3 Risk and capital modelling

A few organizations, especially in the financial services sector, construct statistical models to estimate probability and impact distributions for operational risk events. The aim is to understand the fullest possible range of outcomes and to assign probabilities to each of these outcomes.

A key input into this modelling is internal and external loss data. However, such data is historical and is often incomplete. Hence scenario analysis, stress and reverse stress testing is often used to supplement internal and external loss data.

Where organizations attempt to build statistical models for operational risk it is strongly recommended that they incorporate into these models the outputs from their scenario analysis and stress/reverse stress testing processes. These outputs can provide valuable information on the 'tail' of the probability and impact distributions that they construct. Risk models are only effective if they represent the full range of outcomes for a given risk event.

5. Further guidance on stress testing and reverse stress testing

5.1 Stress testing

Within an operational risk context, stress testing involves the assessment of a major stress event across a range of risk factors. Such events may include crises and natural/human-made disasters. Examples include:

- environmental disasters (e.g. floods, storms, volcanos, etc);
- pandemics – Covid-19 is an example;
- a significant economic recession;
- political disruption, such as trade wars;
- the failure of an important counterparty (e.g. supplier, outsource service provider or customer);
- major cyber attack;
- adverse social media campaign;
- terrorist attack.

The idea is to stress (increase the hypothetical severity of) an organization's operational risk exposures and to investigate how its controls may be impacted by such events. Key questions include:

- Will controls remain effective? What if any controls might fail?

- What would be the financial and reputational impacts of such events? How might control failures/ineffectiveness escalate these impacts?
- Can action be taken to mitigate these financial and reputational impacts during the event?
- Might additional controls be required to help reduce the probability and/or impact of stress events?
- Should existing controls be reinforced to ensure they are effective during stress events?
- Do other factors, such as the timing of an event, influence the scale of the stress event?
- Could multiple stress events occur simultaneously? What would the impact of this be?

In relation to the timing of an event, sensitivity analysis can be used to examine whether timing is a factor. For example, an organization that experiences a stress event during a seasonally busy period (e.g. Christmas) may suffer a higher level of loss at that time, relative to a less busy period. Sensitivities might also be performed to take account of differences in the business cycle or other economic variables such as changes in inflation or interest rates.

CASE STUDY 10.6   The impact of timing

A university used sensitivity analysis to examine the differing impacts that could be experienced due to a failure in its student registration and examination systems.

The analysis revealed that the timing of such a failure could have a significant impact on the financial and reputational impacts of a failure. The most vulnerable months were May and June, when student final results were being compiled for progression or graduation, and September, when the majority of students were registered onto degree programmes. Here the impact of even a one-day failure would be significant.

In contrast the impact of even a prolonged (one week) failure over the summer (July and August) was negligible, while the impacts during other months were modest, providing the systems could be restored within a week.

In relation to multiple stress tests, it is recommended that individual tests are combined to examine the cumulative financial impact on an organization. This might include combining potentially correlated stress events (e.g. a cyber attack followed by an adverse social media campaign) that could occur together (e.g. a new wave of Covid-19 coupled with a no-deal Brexit).

In addition, organizations might investigate how many of the identified stress events they could withstand at the current time. It is unlikely that any organization could withstand every identified stress event, were they to occur simultaneously. But it is useful to understand the number that could be survived at a given point in time. Such analysis should be reported to the board and senior management to help them better understand the future financial viability of the organization.

5.2 Reverse stress testing

The purpose of reverse stress testing is to understand when an organization becomes non-viable. This may include the viability of the organization's business plan, as well as its financial viability (solvency).

The starting point for reverse stress testing is usually the financial accounts of an organization. Meaning its:

1 statement of income and expenditure (annual profit and loss account);

2 statement of financial performance (balance sheet);

3 cash flow statement.

In terms of the statement of income and expenditure, an organization might start with its previous year's profit or surplus, or, for a more forward-looking approach, the predicted profit or surplus for the current year, and consider the impact of this being reduced to zero. Alternatively, an organization with long-term debt might determine the point at which any interest cover debt covenants are breached. These covenants typically require a debtor to maintain a specific level of net income, often accounted for as: earnings before interest tax, depreciation and amortization (EBITDA), over and above its required interest payments. Such covenants exist to protect creditors from insolvent debtors. They allow the creditor to cancel a loan, or to renegotiate the interest payment, if a debtor's EBITDA falls below an agreed threshold.

In terms of the statement of financial performance an organization could determine the point of non-viability where it ceases to be a going concern (e.g. where all capital is lost, and the value of its liabilities exceed those of its assets). Finally, in terms of the cash flow statement an organization might determine the point at which it can no longer meet its liabilities as they fall due.

Having determined these points a common next stage is to consider the stress events or combination of stress events that could cause such severe financial impacts. From an operational risk context, this might include:

- events that eliminate the capital base of an organization, such as a major environmental disaster that results in crippling clean-up and litigation costs;

- events that destroy the infrastructure of the organization and therefore its ability to generate income (e.g. major systems failure, loss of key buildings, prolonged supply chain failure, etc);

- sudden loss of liquidity, such as a major debt covenant breach or loss of investment-grade credit rating;

- major loss of reputation, leading to the loss of many customers, employees, suppliers, etc;

- serious regulatory or legal sanctions (e.g. forced closure).

It is unlikely that every potential extreme scenario will be, or can be, considered. This is not the point of reverse stress testing. Primarily the aim is to help the board and senior management understand when the organization becomes non-viable, so that they can ensure that the organization has sufficient funds (capital and liquidity). However, it is also prudent for them and their organization to understand the types of events that may cause non-viability. From an operational risk perspective there are many such events and boards/senior management will better understand the value of operational risk if such events are identified.

6. Conclusion

This chapter has explored how to design and use scenarios and stress tests to support the management of operational risk. Scenario analysis, stress testing and reverse stress testing are important components within an organization's operational risk management framework. Operational risk events are often the most serious of all for organizations, eclipsing pure market, credit or business risk events in terms of their magnitude. Equally the probability and impact of these more extreme operational risk events can be very difficult to assess, without the use of effective scenario analysis or stress testing approaches. The Covid-19 pandemic is a recent example of how severe and unpredictable such events can be (see Chapter 11), as was the global financial crisis of 2007–08 (Ashby, Clark and Thirlwell, 2011).

It is imperative that organizations prepare for the unexpected, including so-called 'tail' events that may threaten their viability. Though it may be impossible to anticipate every possible extreme operational risk event, that is not the point. The point is to help management, especially the board and senior management, to understand the types of operational risk event that may threaten the viability of their organization, and to ensure that their strategic and operational decisions do not significantly increase their exposure to such events or render the organization excessively vulnerable to their impacts.

Reflective practice questions

1 Do you understand the differences between scenario analysis, stress testing and reverse stress testing in an operational risk context?

2 Does your organization use scenario analysis and stress testing to support the assessment of its operational risk exposures?

3 How do you complete these analyses and tests? Do you organize workshops to gather the views of a range of relevant experts?

4 What measures have you taken to validate scenario analysis and stress test outputs? Do you make use of public information on events that have affected other organizations and consider whether such events could occur in your organization?

5 Who decides on the operational risk scenarios and stress events that are analysed? Are executive management involved in this process to provide a strategic perspective and does the board receive information explaining why particular scenarios and stress events were chosen?

6 How do you make use of the outputs from scenario analyses and stress tests? Are these outputs used to support strategic and operational decision making, as well as to satisfy any regulatory requirements?

References

Note: Some of the sources included in this chapter have been listed previously. Only new sources are listed below.

Ashby, S, Clark, D and Thirlwell, J (2011) Waking the sleeping giant: Maximizing the Potential of Operational Risk Management for Banks, *Journal of Financial Transformation*, 33, 127–36

Bouwer, L M (2013) Projections of future extreme weather losses under changes in climate and exposure, *Risk Analysis*, 33 (5), 915–30

De Haan, L, Ferreira, A and Ferreira, A (2006) *Extreme Value Theory: An introduction*, vol 21, Springer, New York

Gourier, E, Farkas, W and Abbate, D (2009) Operational risk quantification using extreme value theory and copulas: From theory to practice, *The Journal of Operational Risk*, 4 (3), 3

Huber, D G and Gulledge, J (2011) Extreme weather and climate change: Understanding the link, managing the risk, Arlington: Pew Center on Global Climate Change, www.c2es.org/site/assets/uploads/2011/12/white-paper-extreme-weather-climate-change-understanding-link-managing-risk.pdf (archived at https://perma.cc/MZ8K-UCTF)

Janis, I L (1971) Groupthink, *Psychology Today*, 5 (6), 43–6

Stott, P (2016) How climate change affects extreme weather events, *Science*, 352 (6293), 1517–18

WEF (2021) The Global Risks Report, World Economic Forum, www.weforum.org/reports/the-global-risks-report-2021 (archived at https://perma.cc/PG9J-9KHA)

Organizational resilience   11

LEARNING OUTCOMES

- Explain the role of organizational resilience in an operational risk context and why it is essential to the survival and success of 21st-century organizations.
- Know the operational risk management capabilities that are essential for effective organizational resilience.
- Understand how organizations can implement effective capabilities for resilience that help them to mitigate the threats and maximize the opportunities that can come from major operational risk events.

1. Introduction

When managing operational risk in complex and dynamic operational environments organizations are faced with two alternatives: anticipation or resilience (Comfort et al, 2001).

Anticipation is a risk management strategy rooted in the assumption that it is possible to look into the future and estimate what may or may not occur. Many of the chapters in this book, so far, have been based on this strategy, resting on the assumption that the nature, probability and impact of operational risk events can be estimated. For example, operational categorizations rely on the assumption that 99.9 per cent of operational risk events share the same basic characteristics of those that have occurred before. Equally, risk assessment and monitoring tools – such as risk and control self-assessments, loss event databases, risk indicators and scenario analysis – assume that history is often repeated, allowing us to use past events and trends to estimate what operational risk events may occur over the coming months and years.

In contrast, the notion of resilience rests on the assumption that the past is not always a good predictor of the future and that organizations must prepare for unexpected surprises. That such surprises occur in the 21st century should be clear to us all. Events such as the global financial crisis of 2007–08 and the Covid-19 pandemic possess elements that may be considered unprecedented, if not by their causes then certainly in terms of their effects on organizations (see section 2.1. below). Hence resilience as a strategy is less about prediction and more about preparing for and adapting to an uncertain and ever-changing future – a future that cannot always be inferred by events that have gone before.

This chapter will outline the sound practice of organizational resilience in organizations in the face of increasingly uncertain and severe operational risk events. In so doing, lessons from recent operational risk events such as the global financial crisis and the Covid-19 pandemic will be explored. The aim is to help organizations prepare for and adapt to operational risk events that have not occurred before, along with events that, though familiar, have implications for organizations that far exceed those that have occurred in the past.

2. Understanding organizational resilience: key concepts

The term 'resilience' has been described as a 'conceptual umbrella' (Masten and Obradović, 2006, p 14) that is assigned different meanings depending on the context (Bhamra, Dani and Burnard, 2011; Linnenluecke, 2017). In this section a number of key concepts are explored to help operational risk professionals understand what organizational resilience is in the context of operational risk, and why resilience matters.

2.1 Organizational versus operational resilience

The Institute of Operational Risk (IOR) and Institute of Risk Management (IRM) recently issued a Sound Practice Guidance Paper on operational resilience (IOR, 2021). The IOR's guidance paper distinguished between organizational and operational resilience.

In line with guidance from the International Organization for Standardization (ISO 2236:2017) the IOR guidance paper defined organizational resilience as: *the ability of an organization to absorb and adapt in a changing environment.* Operational resilience was identified as a sub-set of organizational resilience and defined as: *the ability of an organization to deliver critical operations through disruption.*

The Sound Practice Guidance Paper explained that effective organizational resilience requires strategic, cultural and operational elements and subsequently focused on the operational elements only. Hence the paper provides guidance on how to mitigate disruption and maintain the continuity of operations in the face of change.

This chapter builds on the recent definitions and guidance issued by the IOR. Specifically, the focus will be on how to build capabilities for effective organizational resilience in response to change that takes the form of major operational risk events.

2.2 Resilience and change

Fundamentally, organizational resilience is about responding to change, usually sudden and unplanned (i.e. non-routine and surprising) change that disrupts the operations of an organization. This change is described in the literature on resilience as 'challenging conditions' and may occur within or outside an organization (Vogus and Sutcliffe, 2007). Examples include internal, self-made, crises, external economic or political shocks, the progressive build-up of operational stresses and strains (e.g. overloaded production processes), competitive disruption and natural events such as pandemics. Many of these challenging conditions have their roots in a common cause of operational risk – external events – though others are linked to people, processes and systems issues, such as overloaded production processes, a major fire or pollution event and staffing shortages.

With any sudden or unplanned change comes opportunities and threats, often linked to the ability of an organization to acknowledge and respond to this change. These opportunities and threats are not always known in advance, and even where they are known their scale and probability of occurrence may be hard to estimate.

Hence, effective organizational resilience can help organizations to manage these challenging conditions. This is achieved through the mitigation of any associated threats and the exploitation of potential opportunities. Operational risk management plays a central role in these mitigation and exploitation efforts, partly through its traditional anticipation-oriented activities, but also through a range of operational risk-related resilience capabilities.

2.3 Change and black swans

Sudden and unplanned change in the form of challenging conditions can manifest in many different shapes and sizes, some more predictable than others. For example, a major fire, as occurred at the Aisin Seiki factory in 1997 (see Chapter 8, Case Study 8.3) is not an unusual occurrence, even though such a fire can represent a major challenge for the organization concerned. Hence, when thinking about resilience it is important to distinguish between sudden and unplanned changes that are relatively predictable, versus those that are not.

One concept that has been used to highlight the unpredictability of sudden and unplanned change events is the concept of a 'black swan' (Taleb, 2007). Black swan events are unpredictable, and their effects exceed what might normally be expected from similar prior events. Hence, black swan events possess unique and potentially very severe consequences.

The unpredictable nature of black swan events mean that traditional, anticipation-based operational risk management tools, like risk and control self-assessments, will be ineffective. Tools like scenario analysis will also be of limited use, as it is unlikely that previously unknown events will be reflected in such analysis. Hence, to deal with the effects of black swan events organizations must focus on building their robustness to the negative aspects of black swan events (threats) and their ability to exploit the positive aspects (opportunities).

Though some organizations may be surprised by what is to them a black swan event, Taleb notes that other organizations may not be so surprised, based on their capabilities for organizational resilience. Hence, black swan surprises are specific to organizations. This means that black swans can be made more predictable by effective organizational resilience.

CASE STUDY 11.1   The global financial crisis as a black swan event for banks

The global financial crisis of 2007–08 was a major operational risk event that surprised many banks and regulators, but not all (Ashby, 2010; Ashby, Peters and Devlin, 2014). For those banks and regulators surprised by the crisis it was a black swan event. Banks such as Lehman Brothers, Bear Stearns, Halifax Bank of Scotland and Northern Rock were totally unprepared for the crisis and either failed, as in the case of Lehman Brothers, or received government-funded bailouts.

One bank that was not so surprised by the crisis was the Hong Kong and Shanghai Banking Corporation (HSBC). In early 2007 it warned that a crisis in the US mortgage market was emerging, observing that the mortgage arrears rate in one of its US subsidiaries was rising. Many market observers and bank executives dismissed this warning. In contrast, HSBC took steps to mitigate its exposure to US mortgages and the associated financial securitization products, such as collateralized debt obligations, which were hard hit during the crisis.

One reason HSBC might have been better able to see the global financial crisis coming in 2007, was its experience of the Asian financial crisis in 1997 (Kynaston and Roberts, 2015). HSBC was one of only a few Western banks to operate extensively in Asia, meaning that it learnt lessons other banks did not. This meant that for HSBC the global financial crisis of 2007 was not a shocking black swan, but an anticipatable event, given its experience of the Asian financial crisis.

2.4 Transboundary crises

During the 21st century a new form of crisis has been observed, the transboundary crisis (Boin, 2019). Transboundary crises usually emerge from the occurrence of known operational risks such as volcanic eruptions (the Eyjafjallajökull volcano in 2010), tsunamis (the Fukushima Daiichi nuclear disaster in 2011), human/political unrest (the so-called European migrant crisis of 2015) or pandemics, as in the case of Covid-19. However, there is nothing familiar about the effects of these events. Often these effects and their resulting operational and financial impacts are exponentially greater than the prior norm, pumped up by 21st-century factors such as complex supply chains, computerization, social media and the rise of both liberal and illiberal politics.

Figure 11.1 summarizes the key features of transboundary crises, as explained in Boin (2019).

Like the concept of a black swan, research into transboundary crises provides a useful lens from which to understand the operational risk management challenges associated with effective organizational resilience. Organizations must prepare for seemingly familiar operational risks to escalate, with little warning, into new, much more disruptive events. This requires organizations to accept that historical data on prior operational risk events can be woefully insufficient and potentially misleading. Organizations must also be prepared to adapt their anticipated responses to operational risk events where they escalate into transboundary crises, and take account of unforeseen problems or opportunities, along with new information and priorities. Exclusively relying on tried and tested anticipation-based operational risk management techniques, or adopting a wait-and-see approach in such circumstances, is rarely sufficient.

Figure 11.1   The characteristics of transboundary crises (author's own)

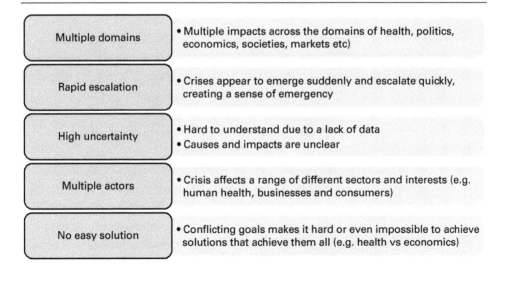

Multiple domains	• Multiple impacts across the domains of health, politics, economics, societies, markets etc)
Rapid escalation	• Crises appear to emerge suddenly and escalate quickly, creating a sense of emergency
High uncertainty	• Hard to understand due to a lack of data • Causes and impacts are unclear
Multiple actors	• Crisis affects a range of different sectors and interests (e.g. human health, businesses and consumers)
No easy solution	• Conflicting goals makes it hard or even impossible to achieve solutions that achieve them all (e.g. health vs economics)

Though transboundary crises can be a source of major operational disruption for organizations, like any change their effects are not necessarily bad. With change, whether small, large or unprecedented, comes the potential for opportunity – especially if an organization is able to adapt to the new normal that follows. This means that the successful management of transboundary crises can not only help to mitigate impacts that may threaten the survival of an organization, but also help it to grow stronger and better prepared for the transboundary crises of the future.

CASE STUDY 11.2   The Covid-19 pandemic as a transboundary crisis

No one predicted the year that was 2020. Though the World Economic Forum Global Risk Report (WEF, 2020) had identified infectious diseases as an emerging global risk, the probability and impact of this risk was rated well below the then more immediate concerns of environmental issues (e.g. global warming) and cyber attacks. Many organizations and governments were unprepared for the pandemic and were forced to make difficult social and economic decisions to help combat the spread of the virus (e.g. the temporary closure of business premises and household lockdowns). Never have lives and livelihoods been disrupted so significantly, for so long, and on a global scale. As early as April 2020, the IMF predicted an economic impact larger than the Great Depression of the 1930s (Goparth, 2020), predictions that only worsened as time, national lockdowns and international travel restrictions continued (Williams, 2020).

Pandemics are an inevitable consequence of human life. For thousands of years humans have moved around the globe, helping to spread disease. Historical pandemics include the so-called 'Spanish flu' after the First World War (the virus had nothing to do with Spain, it was called that because Spain was one of the few countries to permit news reporting on the spread). That virus infected 500 million people worldwide (one-third of the global population) and may have killed more than 50 million people (CDC, 2021). More recently SARS (Severe Acute Respiratory Syndrome) in 2002–04, MERS (Middle East Respiratory Syndrome) in 2012 and Ebola in 2013–16, caused global concern. All of these more recent pandemics impacted on the operations of organizations, prompting many to include pandemics for the first time in their business continuity planning activities. However, none of these early 2000s pandemics impacted on operations to the extent that Covid-19 did. In all cases the outbreaks were contained, and people's social/business lives soon returned to normal.

Hence, before Covid-19, it was known that pandemics could, hypothetically, disrupt the operations of organizations should large numbers of workers (or those they care for) become unwell or find that they are unable to travel into work. What was new about Covid-19 was the rapid escalation, scale and duration of the government responses to rising infection rates. All of a sudden, in March 2020 borders and businesses were closed and people in many countries were locked down in their homes, except for a small number of essential activities. Worse, these restrictions remained in place for weeks, often months. Subsequently, restrictions were repeatedly eased and reimposed in many countries as new transmission waves and virus strains spread. The net result was that human social and economic activity was curtailed for an extended period, causing ongoing operational disruption.

The Covid-19 pandemic illustrates how a medical problem can spread into politics, economics and business. It also shows that this can happen very suddenly with little or no notice, and progress into a major health and economic crisis. That said, although the pandemic created many threats for organizations it also brought opportunities, and not just for the medical and hygiene sectors. In particular there were significant opportunities for organizations willing to increase their use of the internet, both to support initiatives like home working and to develop new delivery channels for products and services.

2.5 The stages of organizational resilience

Effective organizational resilience requires consideration of three stages in the anatomy of sudden and unplanned change events (challenging conditions), including black swans and transboundary crises (see Ponomarov and Holcomb, 2009):

- readiness and preparedness (pre-event);
- response and adaption (during an event);
- recovery or adjustment (after the event).

These three stages are relevant for any type of operational risk event, including more-routine and less-disruptive events. But the last two stages take on greater significance in the context of organizational resilience. This is because of the difficulties associated with anticipating sudden and unplanned change events.

Taking first the response and adaption phase, the emphasis here is on recognizing sudden and unplanned change and ensuring that organizations respond to this, both by attempting to mitigate the associated threats and maximizing potential opportunities. Recognizing the presence of sudden and unplanned change can be difficult, especially if the risk culture of an organization (see Chapter 4) does not promote awareness of operational risk, or there is a blame culture. There are numerous examples of organizations that deny the significance of an event and/or are slow to respond – the VW emissions and BP Deepwater Horizon cases illustrate that (see Case Studies 1.4 (Chapter 1) and 8.5 (Chapter 8) respectively). Equally, other organizations are much quicker to respond, as in the case of Toyota and the Aisin Seiki fire (Case Study 8.3, Chapter 8). Here, speed of response is key. The sooner an organization recognizes that sudden and unplanned change has occurred and taken steps to mitigate and/or exploit this change, the better. This is true both for sudden and unplanned change that is the fault of an organization (e.g. due to some type of management failure), as when it is due to external factors such as a pandemic.

Moving to the third phase the focus is on getting the organization back to routine operations, although not necessarily the same routine as before. Here it is helpful to consider first-order versus second-order change (Meyer, 1982). First-order change is concerned with overcoming the change event and returning operations back to the way they were before the event (the old normal). Second-order change embraces what has occurred and involves the adoption of new practices (e.g. new operational processes and working arrangements). Sometimes second-order change is discussed in terms of embracing the 'new' normal that can follow a major change event.

CASE STUDY 11.3   Embracing the new normal post-Covid-19

The scale and significance of the Covid-19 pandemic has resulted in significant social change. One major change for organizations is expected to be a permanent shift towards a distributed working model that permits a blend of onsite, remote and hybrid working. Plus, greater flexibility in relation to when and how work is completed, leading to a move away from the traditional 9–5 working day (Martin, 2021).

Organizations may choose to resist this change and return to the old normal of onsite working during fixed office hours. However, this resistance could affect their productivity and result in staff seeking new employment. Alternatively, they can embrace the new normal and work to exploit the benefits it can bring in relation to productivity and staff satisfaction (Ipsen et al, 2021).

Finally, in terms of readiness and preparedness, there are two elements to consider. Firstly, the standard notion of anticipation. Not all sudden and unplanned change events are black swans or transboundary crises. This means that organizations should, where possible, look to anticipate events that might disrupt their operations in the future. Secondly, it is important to remember that even when sudden and un-planned changes cannot be anticipated it is often possible to put in place planned responses, pre-event, to help an organization adapt to events when they occur. This will be explored further in section three below.

3. Building capabilities for organizational resilience

This section will explore the types of capabilities that organizations should develop to ensure effective organizational resilience in the face of major operational risk events. These capabilities may be used both to mitigate the threats and exploit the opportunities that come with sudden and unplanned change events. They are also designed to help manage the three stages in the anatomy of such events – the before, during and after.

3.1 A capability-based framework

Figure 11.2 illustrates a four-factor capability-based framework that can be used to implement effective organizational resilience. The basis for this framework is threefold:

1 Organizational resilience requires a harmonious blend of people, processes and systems. This requires both formal and informal elements, similar to those discussed in Chapter 2 on embedding operational risk management. The formal side includes tools like operational risk assessment and reporting; the informal side is more people-focused and includes things like risk culture.

2 Organizations must prepare for and respond to sudden and unplanned change events through pre-planning, in-event adaption and post-event learning without necessarily knowing in advance what will occur (Vogus and Sutcliffe, 2007).

3 The 12 capabilities are illustrative and not intended to be exhaustive. As with many aspects of operational risk management, there is no one best approach to the design or combination of resilience capabilities. How one organization blends specific capabilities will differ from another. That said, there should always be a combination of planning and adaption with formal and informal elements.

Section 3.6 below puts these capabilities together using a case study of the Texan supermarket chain H-E-B. This case shows how, with the right capabilities, organizations can thrive in the most challenging of conditions.

3.2 Planned and formal capabilities for organizational resilience

The primary aim of planned and formal capabilities is to create an adequate level of physical or financial 'slack' in the operations of an organization. This should include using tools like scenario analysis to help create 'deterministic' slack, as well as

Figure 11.2   Capability framework for operational risk (author's own)

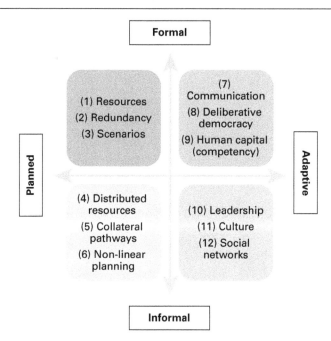

preparing for unimagined situations through the creation of 'non-deterministic' slack. Deterministic slack has a specific application, such as an accounting provision or a backup internet connection. Non-deterministic slack can be applied to a wider range of situations. Maintaining a general cash reserve or surplus capital requirements are examples of non-deterministic slack, as are 'fog' computing systems found in 'smart' buildings and next-generation mobile communication infrastructures (Moura and Hutchison, 2020). Three specific examples of planned and formal capabilities are outlined below:

1 All organizations require resources to operate, and most will maintain some degree of surplus resource. This is especially the case in industries like financial services. Resilient organizations should ensure that they have sufficient financial (cash or credit) and physical resources for both normal and abnormal operating environments. This could range from contingency finance arrangements to stockpiling vital components and equipment, such as personal protective equipment (PPE) or virus testing kits.

2 Redundancy is an extension of maintaining 'excess' resources and involves the development and maintenance of sites, systems or equipment that are not necessary in normal operations. Examples include maintaining mothballed office space or manufacturing capacity, access to a dedicated or shared continuity site, backup generators or multiple internet connections.

3 As explained in Chapter 10, scenario analysis and the related tools of stress testing and reverse stress testing can be used to imagine future operational risk events, especially more severe events. The results from this work can subsequently be used to support other planned measures, such as resource planning, or to test adaptive tools like information cascades. Remember that effective scenario analysis need not involve imagining specific (deterministic) situations. Techniques such as reverse stress testing allow organizations to analyse the point at which their operations, business plans or finances become non-viable without having to determine specific scenarios in advance.

CASE STUDY 11.4   Using slack to build organizational resilience

The Swiss Government maintains one of the largest stockpiles of essential goods in the world (Bryce et al, 2020). This includes maintaining 3–6 months' supply of essential foodstuffs, medicines and equipment, including personal protective equipment (PPE). In 2016 the Swiss Government increased these supplies due to concerns over the stability of increasingly complex and international supply chains.

The stockpiles are maintained to cover any form of essential supply disruption, including political conflict (e.g. trade wars and sanctions); accidents, such as the March 2021 Suez canal blockage; and pandemics such as Covid-19. Given this range of applications, these stockpiles may be considered non-deterministic slack.

3.3 Planned and informal capabilities for organizational resilience

Planned and informal capabilities are used to improve the flexibility of resilience planning. The aim is to widen the range of events that can be managed using a degree of pre-event planning, coupled with some during-event alterations to these plans.

Planned flexibility is not fully adaptive in the strict sense of the word. Usually, the objectives of such hybrid before- and during-event organizational resilience activities are determined in advance (e.g. to return operations to the previous steady state, rather than some 'new normal'). However, flexibility is created in terms of the range of response. Hence, though the destination may be fixed, planned and informal, capabilities allow different routes to be taken along the way, allowing an organization to circumvent potential blockages to its organizational resilience activities. Three specific examples of planned and informal capabilities are outlined below:

1 The notion of distributed resources first emerged in manufacturing processes, such as chemical processing and electrical distribution systems (Arghandeh et al,

2014). The aim is to develop localized event monitoring and resource management systems that allow for the widest range of response (see Case Study 11.5). Another form of distribution is distributed governance (Barasa, Mbau and Gilson, 2018), where staff are empowered to develop bottom-up solutions to problems, rather than relying on a slower and less flexible top-down response. Effective distributed governance requires clear statements (policies and procedures) on the circumstances and situations where decisions may be taken outside the conventional hierarchy and what should be escalated. Training may also be required to help staff understand these policies and procedures.

2 Collateral pathways involve using different routes to achieve a goal (Barasa, Mbau and Gilson, 2018). The aim is to find an alternative route or course of action when an established system, process or procedure is unavailable. Authorized workarounds may be planned in advance, or staff may be empowered to implement unforeseen workarounds if required. The use of distributed resources and non-linear planning can improve the ability of an organization to find collateral pathways.

3 Non-linear planning (Barasa, Mbau and Gilson, 2018) incorporates feedback loops when using pre-planned responses during an event. This allows response plans to be refined through iteration and trial and error. The idea is to act quickly and then to reflect on the outcome, adjusting the response as necessary.

CASE STUDY 11.5   Using distributed resources to maintain electricity supplies

Modern organizations and households are increasingly reliant on stable electricity supplies. However, the increased prevalence of extreme weather events (e.g. storms, extreme cold and heatwaves) makes maintaining these supplies a major challenge (Arghandeh et al, 2014).

Distributed resource techniques are used to help reduce the number of outages and speed up repair times. The approach relies on a combination of technical resource and human initiative. The technical side includes internet-based distributed control systems (smart grids) that facilitate the monitoring of energy supplies throughout a network, coupled with localized recovery resources (e.g. large diesel generators) and teams of human engineers empowered to resolve problems.

One of the cornerstones of distributed control in electricity supply is vulnerability analysis. The aim is to understand the consequences of disturbances and determine the speed with which services must be restored. This allows jobs to be better prioritized, for example by targeting the most vulnerable locations first (e.g. a hospital) or identifying interdependencies between faults, where one fault must be repaired before another can be resolved, and so on.

Often distributed resources are combined with the use of collateral pathways. For example, power supplies can sometimes be rerouted around the problem area (e.g. a faulty pylon); in addition, multicustomer microgrids can be created that permit electricity customers to be dynamically 'islanded', meaning they can be temporarily isolated from the main grid to sustain supplies, so long as local electricity generation or storage resources are sufficient.

3.4 Adaptive and formal capabilities for organizational resilience

Adaptive and formal capabilities are tangible mechanisms that support the development of what has been termed conceptual slack (Sutcliffe and Vogus, 2003). Conceptual slack comes from diversity, having a team of people managing the organization who possess multiple, diverse, human perspectives and experiences – basically people with different skills, life experiences, professional knowledge and perspectives on risk. The rationale behind this is that such diversity can stimulate more open-minded debate, allowing for creative solutions to be found to an unfolding crisis. In this regard, conceptual slack facilitates flexibility and allows organizations to accept and adjust to the changing world around them. It may even help them to find solutions to problems that might otherwise have appeared insurmountable:

1   Timely, accurate and complete information is essential, both in terms of detecting and responding to challenging conditions. Formal communication structures must be created in advance to help manage information flows (e.g. escalation processes, reporting systems, committees, information cascades, etc), but how the information is used should not be specified in advance. It is for the relevant decision makers to decide, during the response and adaption (during) phase of an event, to decide how to respond to the information they receive.

2   Deliberated democracy can be used to promote fair and reasonable discussion over simple majority voting. The aim is not to 'win' a debate, but rather to share information and ideas and to build trust, motivation, consensus and commitment (Harris, Chu, and Ziervogel, 2018). Tools such as the Delphi Technique (see Chapter 7) can be used to provide structure to a debate.

3   Human capital is an important element of adaptive resilience (Lengnick-Hall, Beck and Lengnick-Hall, 2011). Organizations that are comprised of skilled and experienced (i.e. competent) staff should be better able to adapt to change and develop to new ways of working. The adaptive resilience of human capital can be enhanced through the recruitment of people with diverse skills, professional backgrounds and experience. Training and education can also be used to enhance skills diversity and to promote mechanisms such as deliberated democracy.

CASE STUDY 11.6 Human capital and diversity in the boardroom

Research by Ashby, Bryce and Ring (2018) into the management of risk at the level of the board revealed that the risk environments faced by organizations are becoming increasingly uncertain. Traditional, anticipation-based risk management techniques still have value, but increasingly boards are having to respond to unanticipated events.

Interviews with board directors revealed that boardroom diversity was an essential element in effective resilience. Specifically, diversity in terms of the skills, knowledge, experience, education and training of board members – the aim being to combine different **S**kills, **K**nowledge, **E**xperience, **E**ducation and **T**raining (SKEET) to create what the report termed 'Risk Intelligence' or RI-SKEET.

'If you have an organization, for example, that's been a board composed of people who've come up through the ranks, and understand the culture of the organization and understand what really makes it tick and how things, how politics work, and how communication really works in practice, and you have non-execs who all come from the same industry, then you have a board that is very good at understanding what I would describe as internal risk... If they lack true exec and non-exec members who have come from outside of the organization and ideally outside the industry, then they will lack that external perspective and there will be a lens around the boardroom table that is missing' (Ashby, Bryce and Ring, 2018, p17).

3.5 Adaptive and informal capabilities for organizational resilience

The final group of capabilities are linked to the behavioural process of 'mindful organizing' (Vogus and Sutcliffe, 2007, p3420). The aim is to create a group mind, whereby the people that comprise an organization are able to cooperate and coordinate their actions, thinking as one but benefiting from the synergies that come with diverse perspectives, skills and experiences (see above). Mindful organizing involves people developing, refining and updating a collective, shared understanding of how to achieve effective organizational resilience, one that can help them respond to, recover from and potentially exploit sudden and unplanned change:

1 The capabilities and styles of leadership can affect organizational resilience in several ways. One element is leadership style (e.g. autocratic versus democratic and facilitative), which may reinforce or weaken more planned capabilities like deliberated democracy or distributed control. Another relates to the ability of a leader to create and maintain a shared vision to help support motivation and

collaboration. Leaders may also help promote 'emotional ambivalence', a reinforcing component for mindful organizing (Vogus et al, 2014), which helps people to think creatively. Emotional ambivalence combines contradicting feelings of doubt and hope and helps to balance feelings of confidence and caution (both of which are necessary emotions when faced with sudden and unplanned change).

2 Organizational culture (and risk culture) influences the response to sudden and unplanned change. Cultural factors might include the collective ability of staff to view change as an opportunity rather than a threat, or how groups react to change events (e.g. denial versus acceptance). Willingness to think creatively is another potential factor, as is 'pro-social' motivation (Vogus et al, 2014), which encourages people to think of others and work together towards a common good. This links culture to the final capability: social networks.

3 Social networks play a major role in strengthening (or weakening) organizational resilience (Tisch and Galbreath, 2018). The more fragmented the network the less resilient an organization is likely to be. One key problem is that a socially fragmented social network can slow down communication and may cause people to question the information being reported because they do not know and trust those communicating it. In contrast, a socially integrated group of people, supported by an appropriate organizational culture, can respond quickly and adaptably to sudden change. Here communication will be faster, more open and trusted, because the people concerned know each other.

CASE STUDY 11.7   Roads to ruin or resilience?

In 2011 the Association of Insurance and Risk Managers in Industry and Commerce (AIRMIC), published a major report on the causes of major operational risk events: 'Roads to Ruin' (Atkins et al, 2011). This report used multiple cases of public-sector and corporate disasters and crises to reach its conclusions. Subsequently AIRMIC published a more positive report looking at how real-world organizations build effective organizational resilience: 'Roads to Resilience' (Goffin et al, 2014).

Each report highlights the importance of leadership, culture and communication, both as escalation factors at the onset of major operational risk events and as important mitigating controls. In terms of adaptive and informal capabilities for organizational resilience the Roads to Resilience report identified two key factors:

● Relationships and networks – to ensure that information flows freely vertically (up and down) and horizontally (across) a network. Here the report warns of 'risk blindness', especially at board level, where some boards focus too much on the exploitation of strategic opportunities and can ignore significant downside threats, until it is too late.

- Rapid response – where organizations must be willing and able to act when faced with sudden and unexpected change.

To support the findings of the Roads to Resilience report a number of case studies are discussed to highlight the elements of effective resilience. One such case is the InterContinental Hotels Group (IHG), which places significant importance on risk culture. To help achieve this IHG uses a four-stage maturity framework to review risk management activities in its hotels. The aim is to move its hotels from reactive risk management (stage 1), through compliant (2), embedded (3) and finally rooting risk management as a core value that is second nature for staff (4).

IHG recognizes that it is working in an uncertain environment where staff must regularly deal with the unexpected, not least because every guest has different expectations regarding the service they wish to receive.

3.6 Putting the capabilities together: a case study of Texas retailer H-E-B

H-E-B is a privately owned supermarket chain based in San Antonio Texas. The chain has around 340 stores across Texas and northeast Mexico. H-E-B was ranked number 12 on Forbes' list of 'America's Largest Private Companies'. The supermarket was praised for its response to the early phases of the Covid-19 pandemic. While other retailers floundered, H-E-B was able to maintain supply chains and cope with sudden changes in consumer demand, while at the same time, keeping their staff and customers as safe as possible from infection (Solomon and Forbes, 2020).

H-E-B's success illustrates the value of combining planning and adaption with the formal and informal. Many years ago, H-E-B learnt that the hindsight of past incidents provides a window of foresight for those prepared to look into what their organizational resilience (or lack of) could be (Meyer, 1982). H-E-B maintains a permanent state of emergency preparedness, led by a team of full-time specialist staff. This includes keeping emergency supplies (water, fuel, medicines, hygiene products, etc) in almost every warehouse (a planned and formal capability), allowing the supermarket to react quickly to a range of crises, whether extreme weather or a pandemic. In addition, H-E-B have been developing and refining their emergency preparedness plans for over 15 years. The H1N1 swine flu virus in 2009 provided them with a 'window into the future' by which to learn key insights about ensuring product supply chains and employees were resilient to the challenges Covid-19 would eventually bring to their organization. As early as the second week in January 2020 the chain's personnel were establishing what worked and what didn't across the supply chains of all the major countries affected by the pandemic and making sure their local communities were resourced correctly (a planned and informal capability).

In addition to effective pre-planning, H-E-B adapted its activities in the light of new information. The adaptive and formal capability of communication played a central role. From January, H-E-B maintained regular, often daily, contact with its suppliers around the world, to ensure that their supply chains could adapt. At the same time H-E-B investigated how the initial spread of the pandemic in China was affecting retailers there and adjusted its approach accordingly (e.g. by enhancing hand sanitation and social-distancing procedures). The aim was to learn quickly, so that H-E-B could get ahead of the pandemic before it spread to the United States.

In terms of the adaptive and informal element of resilience, the H-E-B case illustrates the value of effective leadership and culture. Staff health was prioritized by H-E-B's leadership, in terms of protecting staff from the virus and through the maintenance of good working conditions. Store hours were reduced (slightly) to give staff more time to put product on the shelves. Plus, head-office staff were encouraged to work in stores and warehouses to help ease the pressure (hundreds volunteered to do so) and front-line staff were paid an additional US \$2 per hour hazard pay. The sick-leave policy was also enhanced for staff forced to self-isolate and stocks of essential household items (toilet roll, cleaning products, dried/tinned goods, etc) were maintained for staff unable to access stores during working hours. Medical advice and support was provided to staff. These measures, plus a culture that emphasized having fun at work, helped to maintain staff morale and provide them with the stable platform they needed to continue to take care of the chain's customers.

One final adaptive and informal capability exhibited by H-E-B was an emphasis on community (social networks within and beyond the organization). H-E-B recognized the essential nature of the services it provides and the importance of being a beacon of stability within the localities that it serves. Its customers have learnt that they can rely on the supermarket to provide the goods and services they need. Equally important is the workplace community, where staff feel supported by their employer and proud to work for a respected local retailer. Plus, community is maintained with suppliers through regular communication and long-term/fair supply contracts.

By maintaining a strong sense of community H-E-B was further able to reinforce its communication networks and ability to adapt to change. Staff, suppliers and customers all provided valuable information that the supermarket was able to use to refine and change its planning, as necessary. Few financial organizations can lay claim to a similar strong sense of community. Though with stakeholder engagement and communication as effective as H-E-B's, there is no reason why they could not create equally strong communities within their employee and customer bases.

4. Conclusion

Organizational resilience is a journey, not a destination. Major operational risk events such as the Covid-19 pandemic provide organizations with valuable opportunities to learn and enhance organizational resilience, providing an organization is willing to learn and adapt to sudden and unplanned change.

In terms of the future and the next black swans or transboundary crises, the only certainty is that organizations that are able to adapt and exploit uncertainty will thrive. In this context, organizational resilience is less a mechanism to help organizations return to 'normal' and more a diverse set of formal, informal, planned and adaptive capabilities that help organizations to mitigate the threats and maximize the opportunities that can come with sudden and unplanned change.

This chapter is not designed to cover every aspect of effective organizational resilience, but what it has attempted to do is highlight the key concepts and capabilities that organizations must consider when dealing with an increasingly changeable and uncertain future. In this context the traditional objective of anticipating operational risk exposures – and developing strategies to mitigate their probability and impact – still has a role. However, it is essential that operational risk professionals, as well as all others in an organization's management hierarchy, recognize that the future cannot be predicted accurately. Instead, they must embrace uncertainty and prepare for the unexpected. In addition, they must accept that even the best-made plans can sometimes fail. Hence planning must be complemented by mechanisms that support flexible, dynamic, adaptive responses to sudden and unexpected change.

Reflective practice questions

1 Do you understand the significance of black swans and transboundary crises for operational risk management? What discussions have you had in your organization about the potential for such events?

2 Does the scope of the operational risk function include business continuity management (BCM)? Are operational risk professionals routinely involved in BCM activities?

3 How vulnerable are the operations of your organization to disruption? Have you considered the implications of concepts like just-in-time manufacturing and lean production on the effects of disruption? What steps have you taken to establish financial contingency funds, as well as resource stockpiles of key equipment and supplies?

4 How flexible are your business continuity and disaster recovery plans? Are they able to adapt to new, unplanned for, situations?

5 What steps have your organization taken to build risk intelligence in your organization? Do managers and directors have a diverse range of skills, knowledge, experience, education and training?

6 How does your risk culture support organizational resilience? What steps have you taken to influence your risk culture to enhance resilience?

References

Arghandeh, R, Brown, M, Del Rosso, A, Ghatikar, G, Stewart, E, Vojdani, A and von Meier, A (2014) The local team: Leveraging distributed resources to improve resilience, *IEEE Power and Energy Magazine*, 12 (5), 76–83

Ashby, S (2010) The 2007–2009 Financial Crisis: Learning the risk management lessons, *Financial Services Research Forum*, Nottingham

Ashby, S, Bryce, C and Ring, P (2018) Risk and the strategic role of leadership, Professional Insights Series, Association of Certified Chartered Accountants, www.accaglobal.com/sg/en/professional-insights/risk/risk-and-the-strategic-role-of-leadership.html (archived at https://perma.cc/36Y6-4ET7)

Ashby, S, Peters, L D and Devlin, J (2014) When an irresistible force meets an immovable object: The interplay of agency and structure in the UK financial crisis, *Journal of Business Research*, 67 (1), 2671–83

Atkins, D, Fitzsimmons, A, Parsons, C and Punter, A (2011) Roads to ruin: A study of major risk events, their origins, impact and implication, AIRMIC, London, www.airmic.com/technical/library/roads-ruin-study-major-risk-events-their-origins-impact-and-implications (archived at https://perma.cc/9G4C-JNQP)

Barasa, E, Mbau, R and Gilson, L (2018) What is resilience and how can it be nurtured? A systematic review of empirical literature on organizational resilience, *International Journal of Health Policy and Management*, 7 (6), 491

Bhamra, R, Dani, S and Burnard, K (2011) Resilience: The concept, a literature review and future directions, *International Journal of Production Research*, 49 (18), 5375–93

Boin, A (2019) The transboundary crisis: Why we are unprepared and the road ahead, *Journal of Contingencies and Crisis Management*, 27 (1), 94–9

Bryce, C, Ring, P, Ashby, S and Wardman, J K (2020) Resilience in the face of uncertainty: Early lessons from the Covid-19 pandemic, *Journal of Risk Research*, 23 (7–8), 880–7

CDC (2021) 1918 pandemic (H1N1 virus), Centre for Disease Control and Prevention, www.cdc.gov/flu/pandemic-resources/1918-pandemic-h1n1.html (archived at https://perma.cc/85JQ-N9VS)

Comfort, L K, Sungu, Y, Johnson, D and Dunn, M (2001) Complex systems in crisis: Anticipation and resilience in dynamic environments, *Journal of Contingencies and Crisis Management*, 9 (3), 144–58

Goffin, K, Hopkin, P, Szwejczewsk, K and Kutsch Dipl Kauf, E (2014) Roads to resilience: Building dynamic approaches to risk to achieve success, AIRMIC, London, www.airmic.com/technical/library/roads-resilience-building-dynamic-approaches-risk-achieve-future-success (archived at https://perma.cc/3X43-QBRC)

Goparth, G (2020) The great lockdown: Worst economic downturn since the Great Depression [blog] IMF, 14 April 2020, https://blogs.imf.org/2020/04/14/the-great-lockdown-worst-economic-downturn-since-the-great-depression/ (archived at https://perma.cc/DV9T-XCEG)

Harris, L M, Chu, E K and Ziervogel, G (2018) Negotiated resilience, *Resilience*, 6 (3), 196–214

IOR (2021) Operational resilience, Institute of Operational Risk/Institute of Risk Management, https://www.ior-institute.org/sound-practice-guidance/operational-resilience (archived at https://perma.cc/GJ6E-PMXL)

Ipsen, C, van Veldhoven, M, Kirchner, K and Hansen, J P (2021) Six key advantages and disadvantages of working from home in Europe during Covid-19, *International Journal of Environmental Research and Public Health*, 18 (4), 1826

Kynaston, D and Roberts, R (2015) *The Lion Wakes: A modern history of HSBC*, Profile Books, London

Lengnick-Hall, C A, Beck, T E and Lengnick-Hall, M L (2011) Developing a capacity for organizational resilience through strategic human resource management, *Human Resource Management Review*, 21 (3), 243–55

Linnenluecke, M K (2017) Resilience in business and management research: A review of influential publications and a research agenda, *International Journal of Management Reviews*, 19 (1), 4–30

Martin, K (2021) Office, home or hybrid? Business must embrace the evolution of work, Financial Times, www.ft.com/content/55f6b382-dcbf-487a-8aca (archived at https://perma.cc/2URE-TYQH)

Masten, A S and Obradović, J (2006) Competence and resilience in development, *Annals of the New York Academy of Sciences*, 1094 (1), 13–27

Meyer, A D (1982) Adapting to environmental jolts, *Administrative Science Quarterly*, 27, 515–37

Moura, J and Hutchison, D (2020) Fog computing systems: State of the art, research issues and future trends, with a focus on resilience, *Journal of Network and Computer Applications*, 102784

Ponomarov, S Y and Holcomb, M C (2009) Understanding the concept of supply chain resilience, *The International Journal of Logistics Management*, 20 (1), 124–43

Solomon, D and Forbes, P (2020) Inside the story of how H-E-B planned for the pandemic, Texas Monthly, 26 March, www.texasmonthly.com/food/heb-prepared-coronavirus-pandemic/ (archived at https://perma.cc/YB9D-QPCV)

Sutcliffe, K M and Vogus, T J (2003) Organizing for resilience, in *Positive Organizational Scholarship: Foundations of a new discipline*, ed K Cameron, J Dutton and R Quinn, Berrett-Koehler, San Francisco, p 110

Taleb, N N (2007) *The black swan: The impact of the highly improbable*, Random House, New York

Tisch, D and Galbreath, J (2018) Building organizational resilience through sensemaking: The case of climate change and extreme weather events, *Business Strategy and the Environment*, 27 (8), 1197–208

Vogus, T J, Rothman, N B, Sutcliffe, K M and Weick, K E (2014) The affective foundations of high reliability organizing, *Journal of Organizational Behavior*, 35 (4), 592–6

Vogus, T J and Sutcliffe, K M (2007) Organizational Resilience: Towards a theory and research agenda, in *2007 IEEE International Conference on Systems, Man and Cybernetics*, IEEE, 3418–22

WEF (2020) The Global Risks Report, World Economic Forum, www.weforum.org/reports/the-global-risks-report-2020 (archived at https://perma.cc/3KW5-8W4G)

Williams, A (2020) IMF slashes economic outlook and warns of public debt burden, Financial Times, 24 June, www.ft.com/content/f29bf66c-d3fa-462e-9026-b1bba49ec2cd (archived at https://perma.cc/G6UD-729Q)

Regulating operational risk 12

1. Introduction

The operational risk management practices and decisions of organizations are subject to various regulations. Common areas of regulatory focus include financial crime, health and safety, environmental protection and legal liability requirements, such as compulsory insurance for employee and public liability.

Certain industries, such as financial services, are subject to significant additional operational risk management regulation aimed at protecting the overall financial system and preventing financial or legal misconduct (protecting consumers from being mis-sold financial products that do not meet their needs). Much of this regulation is now global, as financial markets and institutions become more interconnected.

In addition, there are a range of professional standards that relate to the management of operational risk. These standards explain what good operational risk management practice looks like. Some of these standards are linked to specific areas of regulation and have a degree of legal force behind them. Others are stand-alone, but organizations can still experience pressure from stakeholder groups (e.g. shareholders, creditors, customers and rating agencies) to comply.

Operational risk management professionals must understand the regulations and standards that relate to operational risk. This is to ensure that the operational risk management practices and decisions made within their organization are compliant with these regulations and standards. Plus, along with internal audit and compliance colleagues, operational risk management professionals may be involved in providing assurance, to senior management and the board, that the design and implementation of the organization's operational risk management is compliant with all relevant regulations and standards.

This chapter outlines some of the key regulations and standards that relate to operational risk and their implications for operational risk management practices. It must be emphasized that the objective is not to provide an exhaustive list of regulations and standards: there are too many and they change on a regular basis. Instead, the focus will be on some key ones that form the foundation for wider regulations and standards.

In terms of local (region or industry specific) regulations and standards, again there are too many. Hence the focus will be on internationally significant regulations and standards. That said, where appropriate certain local standards and regulations will be explored to illustrate the types of operational risk management activities and decisions that are expected.

2. The rationale for operational risk regulation

As explained in Chapter 6, all organizations have stakeholders. These include their employees, clients/customers, third parties and suppliers. Plus, in some cases, shareholders and creditors. Each type of stakeholder 'invests' something in the organization. This may include their time, skills, money or something less tangible such as their health and wellbeing. In return, stakeholders expect things like salaries, safe and reliable products and services, or interest payments to meet the cost of these investments. They also expect the organization to be managed in such a way that these returns are delivered in a consistent manner without any unpleasant surprises. For example, employees will expect the organization to remain in business to ensure that their salary is paid. They will also expect to be kept safe when at work. Customers expect to receive goods and services that are safe and reliable, and expect product guarantees to be honoured. Creditors will be concerned that the organization remains solvent to ensure that loan capital is paid back with the agreed rate of interest.

Most organizations work hard to satisfy the expectations of their shareholders, but problems arise when different stakeholder groups exhibit different preferences. One way to understand this is to remember that certain stakeholder groups may have different priorities. For example, shareholders look to maximize their dividends and the share price. Creditors want the security of knowing that their loan will be repaid with the agreed level of interest, and consumers will prioritize safe, reliable products and services. Equally, employees may be less concerned about the financial and physical welfare of an organization's customers than their own welfare, and vice-versa. Case Study 6.2, in Chapter 6, provides an example of an operational risk-related conflict between stakeholders. In this case, evidence was presented that shareholders tend to prioritize profit over employee safety. This is because the benefits of a safe working environment do not directly flow to shareholders.

Where risk-exposure-related conflicts exist between stakeholder groups, the practice of operational risk management takes on an additional objective: to further protect and create value by managing these conflicts and increasing the overall level of stakeholder satisfaction. Effective operational risk management is needed to help balance the conflicting interests of different stakeholder groups, weighing up different priorities and assessing the costs and benefits of different risk management decisions and risk exposure levels.

In a perfect world, organizations would implement this additional objective without the need for any legal coercion; after all, satisfied stakeholders should reward the organization in some manner, for example through greater loyalty, lower cost of credit or a higher share price. However, the world is far from perfect and, left to their own devices, not all organizations manage the operational risk-related conflicts that exist between stakeholders in an effective manner, as illustrated by Case Study 6.2.

The reason the world is not perfect in this context is because of market failures, failures that prevent stakeholders from exerting effective incentives on organizations to manage operational risk in accordance with their wishes. Stakeholders need efficient markets to ensure that their risk preferences are reflected in the risk management decisions made by organizations. For example, customers must know the health and safety, or quality risks associated with the use of a particular product if they are to decide whether to purchase it at a given price or even to choose to pay a higher price for a safer product. Equally, a prospective employee's decision to work for a company may be affected by the associated health and safety risks. They may demand higher wages for a higher-risk job or decide that the job is too risky at any price. From a financial perspective, employees and creditors must be able to assess the risk of bankruptcy before deciding how much to charge for their time and skills (in the case of employees), or loan interest (in the case of creditors).

A key factor that is needed to ensure market efficiency is *information*. Stakeholders must know the types and degrees of operational risk to which they will be exposed in order to generate market incentives for effective operational risk management. This can be hard to achieve in practice. Customers are unlikely to know how safe or reliable a product is before they purchase it, whereas the organization manufacturing the product will have a much better understanding of the product's safety and reliability. This is known as the asymmetric information problem.

Self-interested opportunism can arise in the presence of asymmetric risk management information between stakeholder groups. In the previous product safety and reliability example, it may be that an organization exploits a customer's lack of prior information by making a product less safe or reliable than it could be, thus saving the organization money but exposing the customer to an unacceptable level of risk.

A second market failure that can help to justify risk management regulation is the public goods problem. Public goods are products, services or other benefits that are enjoyed on a non-exclusive basis by all the members of a society. From an operational risk management perspective, key public goods are the environment and the protection of shared systems – such as the global financial system – from systemic operational risk events, like the global financial crisis of 2007–08 (McConnell and Blacker, 2013). The problem with these public goods is that individuals or organizations may make operational risk management decisions that benefit them, but which do not protect the wider environment or financial system. In the case of the environment, an organization may not invest as much in preventing pollution as required by society to preserve public health and wellbeing. This is because the organization may only consider the costs and benefits to itself from managing pollution risks, not those to society as a whole. The same can also be the case in financial organizations, which, left to their own devices, may not do enough to protect the financial system as a whole from operational risk.

Finally, consider the need for international regulations and standards. These are required because operational risk exposures often cross national boundaries. The removal of trade barriers, easier travel and tools like the internet mean that organizations are now more multinational in terms of their operations and markets. The impact of major operational risks on public goods like the environment or the financial system can have far-reaching effects. Diverse risks may be connected: for example, major environmental pollution events and weather events may affect financial markets across the world. In addition, the impact of operational risk events on financial markets and institutions can affect the supply of credit and cause global economic problems, as has occurred during the Covid-19 pandemic.

3. Solvency regulation

Solvency regulation for operational risk applies to financial institutions, including banks, insurers and investment firms. The purpose of this regulation is twofold:

- to prevent the bankruptcy of financial institutions in order to protect their clients and customers from losing their deposits, investments or insurance contracts;
- to maintain the stability of the global financial system.

The stability of the global financial system is important for both financial and non-financial organizations. For non-financial organizations, a stable global financial system is necessary to ensure that they continue to have access to capital resources to help finance their activities. Financial system instability can trigger worldwide economic problems, restricting access to consumer and government credit, threatening

the safety of saving deposits and disrupting payment systems. Ultimately, these problems can cause major economic recessions and even economic collapse of businesses
and nations alike.

There are few, if any, financial markets that are not interconnected in some way.
Money markets are by their nature international, and stock markets like the London
Stock Exchange attract investors and other stakeholders from around the globe.
Most other financial markets, such as commodities, bonds and derivatives, are also
inherently international. The net result of these interconnected markets is that financial problems in one country or even in a single, large financial institution can have
global implications. This is known as systemic risk and financial market contagion.

It is tempting to think that systemic risks are primarily market-, credit- or liquid-
ity-related. Certainly, systemic events impact on financial markets and the availability of cash and credit; however, often their root causes are operational in nature, such
as an external event, like a pandemic, or a failure in risk governance or risk culture.

CASE STUDY 12.1   Systemic operational risk events

Research by McConnell and Blacker (2013) reveals that systemic operational risk events
exist and can have a major impact on financial markets. Focusing on the global financial
crisis of 2007–08 the paper shows how people and process risks existed and increased
before the crisis. This includes factors like weaknesses in credit approval processes,
flawed sales incentives and ineffective operational risk governance.

Earlier research, looking at insurance company failures across Europe, reached a
similar conclusion (Ashby, Sharma and McDonnell, 2003). This research demonstrated
that operational risk factors such as an inappropriate risk culture, weak risk governance
and flawed underwriting processes are the most common underlying causes of insurance
company failures.

3.1 The Basel Accord for banks

The Basel Committee was established in 1974. Its purpose was to enhance financial stability by improving the quality of banking regulation and supervision
worldwide. As economies and financial markets grew and became increasingly interconnected, it was recognized that banking regulation could not remain country-
specific. Rarely in the modern world do the effects of a bank failure or systemic
risk event only affect the country of origin, if indeed such failures could be said to
be country-specific. Financial contagion can spread far and wide, and this includes
operational risk-related contagion, as highlighted in Case Study 12.1.

Figure 12.1   Basel Accord pillars, applied to operational risk (author's own)

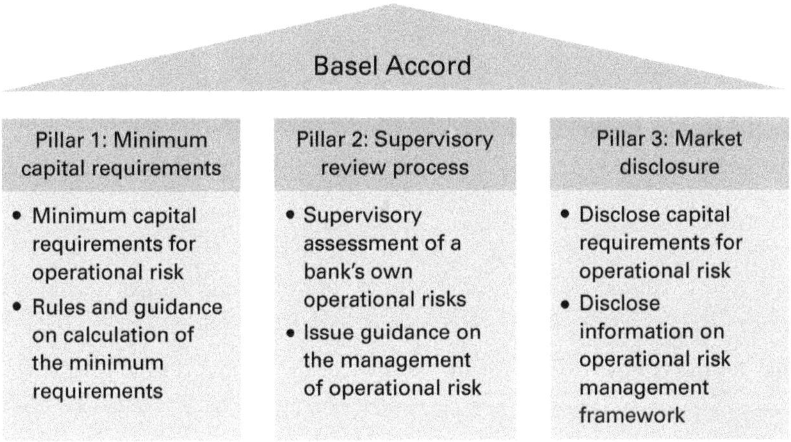

Basel Accord

Pillar 1: Minimum capital requirements	Pillar 2: Supervisory review process	Pillar 3: Market disclosure
• Minimum capital requirements for operational risk • Rules and guidance on calculation of the minimum requirements	• Supervisory assessment of a bank's own operational risks • Issue guidance on the management of operational risk	• Disclose capital requirements for operational risk • Disclose information on operational risk management framework

Originally the Basel Committee focused on market and credit risk, but in the late 1990s, during the negotiations for the second global Basel Accord, known as Basel II, the committee added operational risk to its remit. Subsequently the original Basel II regulation was reviewed and enhanced as part of the most recent Basel III accord, which followed the global financial crisis. For a history of the Basel Committee see Basel Committee (2021b).

The content of the Basel Accord is not legally binding on banks and other deposit-taking financial institutions. However, governments around the world sign commitments to implement them in their jurisdictions. This means that most deposit-taking financial institutions are subject to the operational risk-related regulations contained within the prior Basel II or current Basel III Accord.

Like all the other risk types covered by the Basel Accord, the Basel regulations on operational risk are built around three pillars, as illustrated in Figure 12.1.

As illustrated in Figure 12.1 there are two levels of regulation:

- rules that specify the minimum capital requirements, management standards and public disclosures for operational risk;
- guidance that provides further detail on the effective management of operational risk.

Banks and other deposit-taking financial institutions are expected to comply with all of the rules contained within the Basel Accord. Non-compliance would, in most cases, lead to supervisory intervention by the relevant local supervisory authority. In contrast, they have more discretion over compliance with the guidance issued by the Basel Committee, but local supervisory authorities do have powers to encourage compliance where appropriate. This includes supplementary capital requirements for operational risk under the Pillar 2 supervisory review process or taking legal enforcement action in their jurisdiction.

Though all of the rules on operational risk are contained within the official Basel III Accord, supplementary guidance is issued on a periodic basis on topics of supervisory interest. The Basel Committee website contains the full list of papers (www. bis.org/bcbs/publications.htm). Recent topics relating to operational risk include:

- prudential treatment of crypto-asset exposures;
- principles for operational resilience;
- principles for the sound management of operational risk;
- cyber resilience: range of practices;
- sound practices: implications for fintech developments for banks and bank supervisors;
- principles for effective risk data aggregation and reporting.

The latest and future, 2023, version of the Basel III Accord is available online via the Basel Committee website (Basel Committee, 2021a). In terms of operational risk, the rules contain, currently:

- three options for calculating the minimum capital requirement (Basic Indicator, Standardized and Advanced Measurement Approaches);
- minimum standards for using the Standardized and Advanced Measurement Approaches.

The three approaches to calculating the minimum capital requirements are soon to be revised (from 1 January 2023). As part of these revisions the Advanced Measurement Approach will be removed, and the method used to calculate the current Standardized Approach will be changed. In addition, new rules will be added on the identification, collection and treatment of operational losses.

The Basic Indicator Approach (BIA) will remain unchanged. The BIA calculation relies on calculating the average annual gross income over the last three years and holding 15 per cent of this three-year average as the minimum capital requirement. Hence the volume of business conducted by a bank is taken as a proxy measure for its overall exposure to operational risk. The higher the income the greater the minimum capital requirement.

The new Standardized Approach uses a more sophisticated financial statement-based proxy for operational risk exposure, known as the Business Indicator (BI). The amount of capital required to support this BI measure is then customized according to specific coefficients determined by a local supervisor, known as the Business Indicator Component (BIC) and an Internal Loss Multiplier (ILM) that reflects the historical operational losses of a bank. Hence the new Standardized Approach provides a more customized measure of operational risk capital and should incentivize banks to reduce their exposure to operational loss events.

For more information on the rationale for the changes to the minimum capital requirements for operational risk, see Basel Committee (2016).

3.2 Prudential requirements for insurers

The nearest insurance equivalent to the Basel Committee is the International Association of Insurance Supervisors (IAIS). Its reach and influence is less, but it does have a set of 'Insurance Core Principles' for insurance supervisors and internationally active insurance groups (IAIS, 2019). These principles cover certain aspects of the management of operational risk (e.g. the need for qualitative assessments, where data is unavailable), but do not provide the detailed rules and guidance contained within the Basel Accord.

The IAIS also publishes papers on operational risk-related topics from time to time. This includes papers on cyber risk, governance, and bribery and corruption. For the latest list see: www.iaisweb.org/page/supervisory-material/issues-papers.

Also influential are the European Union's Solvency II regulations, enforced via the Solvency II Directive and the European Insurance and Occupational Pensions Authority (EIOPA). The regulatory and supervisory approach taken by the Solvency II Directive and EIOPA is similar to that outlined under the Basel Accord.

4. Conduct regulation

Many industry sectors, including not-for-profit and charitable organizations, are subject to rules and guidance relating to the conduct of its employees and agents. The purpose of these rules and guidance are to prevent 'bad' (i.e. unethical or damaging) behaviours and to promote 'good' conduct in relation to the management of organizations.

Much of this conduct regulation covers topics related to common categories of operational risk (e.g. fraud, health and safety, improper business practices, etc) and therefore influences the management of operational risk.

CASE STUDY 12.2 Payment protection insurance mis-selling

A major example of bad conduct relates to the historic mis-selling of payment protection insurance in the UK.

Payment protection insurance (PPI), also known as credit protection insurance and loan repayment insurance, is a form of insurance that provides funds to help repay a loan if a borrower dies, is ill or injured or loses their job.

PPI is a form of insurance that can be sold as a stand-alone policy or as an add-on to a mortgage, personal loan or some other form of debt such as an overdraft or credit card. In the UK, the growth in popularity of PPI as an add-on product took place in the 1990s. Billions of pounds in premium income was generated.

Stand-alone PPI policies were not generally mis-sold, but many add-on policies have been found to have been mis-sold. Mis-selling occurred because the contractual provisions of the policy made it very difficult to claim or because information was hidden from customers, such as the full cost of cover or claim limits. In some cases, customers were not aware that they had purchased PPI.

Concerns about PPI mis-selling began in the 1990s, but it was not until 2005, when a super-complaint was brought by the Citizens Advice Bureau, that financial institutions were required to make changes to how they sold PPI and provide compensation to all affected customers.

It is estimated that up to 64 million policies could have been mis-sold, requiring refunds of around £33 billion (Financial Conduct Authority, 2020). The scandal led to significant changes in selling practices to avoid similar problems in the future. It also forced financial institutions to hold back large sums of money in provisions for these claims.

4.1 Financial institutions

Regulation relating to the conduct of financial institutions is primarily jurisdiction-specific. Sometimes the local central bank is responsible for regulation and supervision. Alternatively, a stand-alone regulatory authority is used, such as the Financial Conduct Authority in the UK.

Regulations tend to reflect the political priorities of countries or regions; however, a common focus is the desire to protect retail consumers (households) from harm. Most people do not understand financial products very well, making them prone to risks such as fraud or mis-selling, as in the UK PPI mis-selling scandal (see Case Study 12.2).

It is essential that operational risk professionals working in the financial services sector keep up to date with all applicable conduct regulation. Those working for internationally active financial institutions should also remember that regulations can differ across jurisdictions. Colleagues from the compliance and internal audit functions are important partners in this. They also have a role to play in ensuring that the design and implementation of a financial institution's operational risk management framework supports compliance with these regulations.

CASE STUDY 12.3   The UK Financial Conduct Authority

The Financial Conduct Authority (FCA) regulates the conduct of UK financial institutions. The FCA has three objectives (www.fca.org.uk/about):

1 protect consumers;

2 enhance market integrity;

3 promote competition.

In terms of protecting consumers the FCA ensures that they receive products that meet their needs and that financial institutions place the welfare of consumers before their own profits. To achieve this the FCA operates a licensing scheme for both financial institutions and their directors and officers. Both must meet appropriate 'fit and proper' standards before they are allowed to operate. In addition, the FCA works to educate consumers about conduct risks, including informing them about investment scams.

Market integrity is enhanced through a variety of mechanisms, including rules relating to the handling and safe return of client funds, holding senior management accountable for the actions of their organization and the monitoring of financial crime prevention activities.

Competition is promoted through the monitoring of markets to ensure fair competition and the enforcement of competition law where necessary. This includes preventing price fixing (collusion between financial institutions) and ensuring that fees and charges are transparent.

The FCA's approach to the regulation and supervision of financial services organizations is rooted in a number of Principles of Good Regulation (www.fca.org.uk/about/principles-good-regulation). These principles include:

• customer responsibility, for their actions;

• senior management responsibility (holding management accountable);

• openness and disclosure, publishing information on regulated persons;

• transparency, providing information to consumers and financial institutions on the decisions taken by the FCA.

In addition, financial services organizations are expected to:

• act with integrity and in the interests of customers at all times;

• conduct their business activities with due skill, care and diligence;

• communicate openly, providing accurate and complete information on products and services.

4.2 Corporate governance

Effective corporate governance is an important element in today's business environment. Weak corporate governance can lead to corruption, costly scandals, organizational failure and even systemic breakdowns that damage the interests of all stakeholder groups. International regulations and standards on corporate governance help to promote sustainable economic growth on a global level, ensuring that stakeholders are treated fairly and that organizations have cost-effective access to global capital markets. Without good governance access to global capital would be limited.

One of the most influential international standards on corporate governance is the G20/Organization for Economic Co-operation and Development (OECD, 2015) Principles of Corporate Governance. These principles are often referenced by countries developing local governance codes or guidelines and have been adopted by international agencies such as the World Bank and Financial Stability Board (FSB). The principles exist to provide a worldwide benchmark for good corporate governance practice and supervisory assessments of this practice. The principles cover issues such as the design of effective corporate governance arrangements, ensuring the fair treatment of shareholders and other stakeholder groups, and the disclosure of corporate governance and associated risk management information on key risk exposures.

From an operational risk management perspective, the key OECD governance principles are as follows:

- Ensuring that shareholders with a controlling interest do not force excessive risk taking to generate short-term returns because their limited liability may help to insulate them from the costs of this risk taking.
- Prevention of unethical or illegal practices through the use of whistleblowing controls.
- Public disclosure to ensure that stakeholders have information on all reasonably foreseeable material risks.
- The board is considered responsible for overseeing an organization's internal control and risk management systems. This includes board-level reviews of risk management policies and procedures and, where relevant, the creation of audit committees and risk committees to facilitate this work.

In terms of jurisdiction-specific corporate governance rules there are two main approaches: the 'comply or explain' and the 'comply and sign' approaches.

Under the comply or explain approach organizations subject to the principles and guidance contained within a governance code are not required to follow its contents in a strict rule-based way. An organization may decide not to comply or to amend specific principles to better suit its situation. When organizations decide not to comply or to amend a principle, they are expected to explain publicly why they have made such a decision. This requirement to explain ensures that stakeholders are kept informed of the organization's governance arrangements and the reasons why these arrangements may not follow precisely the principles contained within the code.

The advantages of this 'comply or explain' approach are that organizations are provided with clear principles in relation to their corporate governance practices but at the same time they are allowed a degree of flexibility in how they may apply them in their specific situation. This flexibility is appropriate, given the wide variety of contexts that organizations operate within and the diversity of their activities and operating environments.

A comply and sign approach is more prescriptive. Organizations must comply to the letter of the rule, with no exceptions. In addition, accountable individuals (usually the board of directors) are required to personally sign off the effectiveness of an organization's governance arrangements. If the organization is then found not to have effective governance they can face fines or even imprisonment.

The comply and sign approach ensures maximum compliance. But it is much less flexible than a comply or explain approach. A comply and sign approach can work well where there is agreed best practice or where organizations are very similar in terms of their nature, scale and complexity.

CASE STUDY 12.4   US comply and sign corporate governance regulation

Where organizations are listed on a US stock exchange or where they have a subsidiary that is listed they are required to comply with US corporate governance regulations.

The Sarbanes-Oxley (SOX) Act was signed into US federal law in 2002 (H.R. 3763). The act was a response to a number of high-profile governance scandals, such as the failure of Enron. Mostly the act relates to the production and disclosure of company accounts. A key requirement is section 302, which requires company accounts to be free of any untrue statements and material omissions. Further, to ensure this is the case the signatories of the accounts must satisfy themselves that appropriate internal controls are in place to present any accidental or deliberate (fraudulent) misstatements.

The signatories of a company's accounts (usually the CEO, CFO and Chair, where appropriate), are held personally liable for this action. Hence they may be subject to personal prosecution (criminal or civil) if material errors are discovered.

For more on effective governance from an operational risk perspective see Chapter 6.

4.3 Health and safety

The protection of human rights is a major focus for international law and regulation. This includes protecting people from work-related sickness, disease and injury, and from harmful actions of organizations located near to their homes.

Overall responsibility for international health and safety regulation rests with the International Labour Organization (ILO). The ILO produces a wide range of labour standards (www.ilo.org/global/standards/lang--en/index.htm). It also works to address areas of international concern, such as forced labour and child labour.

Most organizations in most countries are subject to health and safety regulation. Health and safety regulation exists to protect stakeholders from death, injury and ill health (whether physical or mental health). The key stakeholder groups that are protected are employees, customers and third parties. Third parties may include households who may live near an organization and who may be affected by its activities, such as noise, air or ground pollution.

Health and safety regulation exists because the market-based incentives for appropriate levels of health and safety risk management are generally thought to be insufficient. Workers or customers could, for example, incentivize health and safety activities by demanding higher wages or paying a lower price if they believe their health or safety to be at risk. However, market-based incentives can be ineffective because of asymmetric information and public good problems (see above).

Health and safety regulations generally cover the following operational risk management activities:

- The identification and assessment of health and safety hazards, including determining who might be affected (employees, customers and so on) and how they might be affected (injury or ill health).

- Taking appropriate measures to control health and safety hazards to protect stakeholders from harm.

- Recording health and safety incidents and reporting major incidents to the relevant regulatory authority.

- Liability insurance requirements, to ensure that compensation is paid to injured parties where necessary. In many countries this includes compulsory public liability and employer liability insurance.

- Implementing effective policies and procedures for all of the above.

CASE STUDY 12.5   Health and safety regulation in the UK

The UK regulatory authority is the Health and Safety Executive (HSE). The HSE is an independent health and safety regulator that draws its powers from the Health and Safety at Work Act 1974. The act gave the HSE its powers to create regulations, inspect health and safety practices in organizations and take enforcement action, such as issuing fines, where necessary.

The 1974 act places expectations on employees and employers, but prime responsibility for providing a safe working environment rests with the employer, which means an organization's management and directors. Employers are expected to ensure 'as far as reasonably practical' that employees are protected from hazards that may endanger their health and safety. This includes providing appropriate levels of protection against hazards such as fire, 'slips, trips and falls', dangerous equipment, excessively long working hours or undue workplace stress. In return, employees are expected to cooperate with the health and safety activities of their employers and to act responsibly to ensure that they do not endanger themselves or others.

The act covers non-employees who may be at a place of work, including contractors, suppliers, customers and third parties.

The HSE is responsible for enforcing three further pieces of UK legislation:

- Control of Substances Hazardous to Health (COSHH) Regulations 2002;
- Reporting of Injuries, Diseases and Dangerous Occurrences Regulations (RIDDOR) 2013;
- Employers Liability (Compulsory Insurance) Act 1969.

The COSHH regulations apply to substances that are deemed to be especially hazardous, such as acids, fumes, dusts and vapours, plus more modern developments such as nanotechnology and germs that are used in laboratories. Hazards such as asbestos and radiation are dealt with separately. Many organizations are affected by the COSHH regulations. For example, dangerous cleaning products like bleach are covered by the regulations, as is dust generated within agricultural processes and baking. Areas such as hairdressing and beauty are also covered by the regulations because of the chemical products, like peroxide, that may be used.

The RIDDOR regulations apply to all organizations in the UK. Here, organizations are required to report to the HSE any significant injuries, diseases or dangerous occurrences. Reportable incidents include the death or serious injury of any person on an organization's premises, occupational diseases (such as asbestosis) and dangerous occurrences such as a gas leak or building collapse.

The Employers Liability (Compulsory Insurance) Act 1969 requires most organizations to maintain employers' liability insurance. This helps the employer to pay compensation if an employee is injured or becomes ill because of the work they do. The purpose of this insurance is to ensure that an employee will receive the funds that they are due if they make a successful liability claim against their employer for a health- or safety-related incident. If, for example, an organization was to declare bankruptcy after a claim is awarded, then the employee might not receive the award. Compulsory insurance ensures that all legitimate claims are paid.

The premises of many organizations are subject to periodic inspections by trained HSE inspectors. The inspector will review health and safety management practices and examine how they are implemented. Areas of non-compliance with HSE regulations will be identified and an organization will be issued enforcement notices that allow it a set time period to achieve compliance. The frequency of inspections is usually risk-based: the premises of an organization that operates in a high-risk sector or one that reports high numbers of RIDDOR incidents will be inspected more frequently.

In addition to its regulatory, inspection and enforcement powers, the HSE issues a wide range of guidance documents, designed to help an organization to improve its health and safety management practices. This guidance is topic- and sector-based, focusing on high-risk sectors like nuclear power, chemical processing, farming, fishing and diving. Guidance on topics relevant to all sectors include dealing with workplace stress, manual handling, preventing industrial diseases, fire safety and preventing slips, trips and falls.

4.4 Environmental risks

Environmental risks such as ground, water and air pollution, along with global warming, do not respect national borders and are therefore a key part of the global risk environment. National regulation and standards in an area of significant global concern require careful coordination to ensure that weaknesses in one national regulatory regime are not exploited to the detriment of stakeholders in other nations.

Organizations that may cause pollution risk events, or who contribute in other ways to environmental concerns, may be subject to international laws and regulations on environmental risk management. These laws and regulations cover, among other things, the following areas:

- air quality;
- water quality;
- waste management;
- contaminant clean-up;
- chemical safety.

International law and associated environmental regulation is complex. It consists of legally binding treaties and subsidiary protocols, such as the Kyoto Protocol on climate change. For most organizations, these laws and protocols are incorporated into national regulation or in the case of the European Union (EU), EU Directives. This means that, except in complex multinational enterprises, it may not be necessary for organizations to understand in detail these international laws and regulations.

CASE STUDY 12.6   The Kyoto Protocol

The Kyoto Protocol is an international treaty that extended an earlier UN convention on climate change in the 1990s. The purpose of the protocol is to limit global warming by controlling human-made carbon dioxide emissions. Higher limits on emissions are applied to countries that have been industrialized for the longest, on the grounds that they have contributed the most towards global warming.

The protocol is now in its second round of carbon dioxide emission limit commitments. The first round took place from 2008 to 2012 and the second round commenced in 2012.

Most of the world's countries have signed up to their second-round commitments for limiting carbon dioxide. A few countries such as Russia and Japan have not taken on new commitments in the second round of the protocol, though they did meet their first-round commitments. The United States renewed its second-round commitments when President Biden took office.

5. International standards for risk management that relate to operational risk

5.1 ISO 31000:2018

The ISO provides a wide range of standards to help improve management practices. The ISO 31000 family of standards, first published in 2009 and revised in 2018, provides guidelines for managing risk in all types of organizations, regardless of their size, activities or industry sector. This includes the management of operational risk.

ISO 31000:2018 covers the essential aspects of risk management practices in organizations. It provides a set of principles, a management framework, and a process that can be used to evaluate and further improve the organization's risk management arrangements. This supports the achievement of an organization's objectives and the creation and preservation of value to its stakeholders.

The standard is used by regulators, external and internal auditors, risk management professionals and company secretaries/governance professionals to help improve the management of risk against an international benchmark for good practice.

In addition to the core standard, the ISO also provides a number of additional documents in this family, such as:

- ISO Guide 73:2009 (risk management vocabulary), which provides a collection of terms and definitions in relation to the management of risk;

- IEC 31010:2009 (risk management – risk assessment techniques), which looks at the use of a range of risk assessment techniques and concepts;

- BS ISO 31000:2018 (risk management – guidance), to assist the implementation of ISO 31000;

- PD ISO IWA 31:2020 (guidelines on using ISO 31000 in management systems).

The 2018 update of ISO 31000 did not change the core philosophy of the original 2009 standard, but is shorter and more concise, with the intention to make the various concepts easier to understand. It also places greater emphasis on top management leadership in the creation and preservation of organizational value through risk management. There is a greater focus on the integrated nature of risk management, whereby organizations should review and regularly update their risk management practices, taking account of new and changing risks such as cyber and terrorism risks.

Soon an additional member of the ISO 31000 family of standards is expected: ISO 31050 (guidance for managing emerging risks to enhance resilience). Work on this guide began in 2018, just before the Covid-19 pandemic, but no doubt the guide, when published, will reflect the lessons learnt.

5.2 COSO enterprise risk management

The Committee of Sponsoring Organizations of the Treadway Commission (COSO) is a joint initiative of five private-sector organizations in the United States: American Accounting Association; American Institute of Certified Public Accountants; Financial Executives International; Investment Management Association; and the Institute of Internal Auditors.

COSO was created to provide thought leadership on risk management, internal control and fraud deterrence to help improve organizational performance and governance. COSO may be a US-based organization, but its influence is global. Many organizations and regulatory agencies around the world base their governance and risk management practices on the guidance provided by COSO.

The initial focus of COSO was on financial reporting and supporting US corporate governance regulation but its remit has grown since its creation in 1985. In 2004 COSO launched its initial guidance on what was termed 'enterprise risk management'. This guidance was designed to support organizational stakeholders by improving risk management practices, ensuring that organizations achieve their strategic objectives and balancing the needs of different stakeholder groups into the long term.

Since 2004, COSO has provided a number of thought leadership papers on different aspects and applications of risk management practice, including board oversight, cyber risk management and risk assessment. In 2017, COSO released a major update to its enterprise risk management framework (COSO, 2017), which highlights the importance of considering risk in both the strategy-setting process and in driving the performance of an organization. As such, it takes important steps towards ensuring risk is managed as an integrated part of managing an organization.

5.3 COBIT framework for IT governance

The guideline Control Objectives for Information and Related Technologies (COBIT), published by the Information Systems Audit and Control Association (ISACA), provides a good-practice framework for the control of IT-related risks. COBIT is currently in its sixth iteration (COBIT, 2019).

The COBIT framework is business-oriented and links IT goals to business goals, providing example metrics and benchmark maturity models to help an organization assess and enhance the effectiveness of its IT risk management activities. The COBIT framework incorporates the following elements:

- six core governance principles;
- generic process descriptions for the governance of IT risks;
- control objectives;
- management guidelines;
- process maturity models.

The six core governance principles are as follows:

- *Providing stakeholder value*: by delivering a financial return or protecting them from risk.
- *Holistic approach*: one that covers the whole of the organization – all departments, activities and functions.
- *Dynamic governance system*: that adapts and improves, as required.

- *Governance distinct from management*: this ensures that those responsible for overseeing the operating of an organization's IT risk management activities are not involved in the day-to-day running of the organization. This should, in theory, mean that they maintain a degree of impartiality, allowing them to challenge management practices where necessary.

- *Tailored to enterprise needs*: there is no one best approach to good governance; organizations must implement an approach that helps them to achieve their objectives and deliver stakeholder value.

- *End-to-end governance system*: effective IT risk management must cover the entire operational processes and supply chains of an organization.

5.4 ISO 38500:2015

ISO 38500:2015 relates to the governance of IT for organizations. The standard provides governing principles for the acceptable use of information technology for organizations.

The standard covers the current and future use of IT, including the work of an organization's IT function and third-party service providers. A core part of the standard is the collection, holding and use of data, including customer and employee data. As a result, the standard is relevant from an operational risk management perspective since it relates to areas of operational risk exposure, such as compliance with data protection regulations and the potential for the theft or loss of sensitive data.

CASE STUDY 12.7   European General Data Protection Regulation (GDPR)

The GDPR regulation of the European Union (Regulation (EU) 2016/679 (General Data Protection Regulation)) covers all aspects of the collection, storage and use of data in organizations (see: https://gdpr.eu/). From a personal perspective the regulation provides important protections for EU citizens, ensuring that they have control over any data that is stored on them, including a requirement to keep the data within the EU and a right to have this data erased, when it is no longer necessary. From an organizational perspective the regulations are a significant source of operational risk. Failure to comply with the regulations can result in enforcement action, including large fines.

6. The compliance role of the operational risk function

Operational risk and compliance management are linked in two ways:

1 There are many laws and regulations that relate to the management of operational risks.

2 Whenever an organization breaches a law or regulation it runs the risk of enforcement action, including fines, compensation payments and the possible imprisonment of directors and officers. Such compliance risks fall within the remit of operational risk.

Many organizations have a compliance function that is separate from the operational risk function, although sometimes the two are combined. Where separate functions exist, it is essential that the two functions work together closely. Each will require the support of the other. The operational risk function will have the necessary expertise on the management of operational risks, while the compliance function will know how to implement appropriate processes and procedures to ensure that all applicable laws and regulations are complied with. This might include designing compliance monitoring activities, reviews and audits, for example.

CASE STUDY 12.8   Monitoring financial crime

Many countries have laws and regulations that are designed to prevent criminals from using the proceeds of their illegal activities. This can include regulations around the purchase and sale of high-value assets (cars and houses), and the opening and operation of bank accounts and bank loans.

Organizations that are found to be in breach of these regulations can face significant fines and other criminal sanctions. As a result, the associated exposure to compliance risk can be very high.

Compliance monitoring can be frequent and in-depth in relation to proceeds of crime regulations. Every single transaction (such as bank account transactions) may need to be monitored on a real-time basis to check for suspicious activity. Any such activities are then escalated to the compliance function or the Money Laundering Reporting Officer (MLRO) where required. The decisions made by staff members may also be assessed in detail. For example, regular checks may be made to ensure that a customer's identity is confirmed using multiple sources of verification. This can include recording and analysing phone conversations to provide additional assurance that staff members are using the necessary controls in a consistent and effective manner.

Larger organizations, especially those in highly regulated sectors such as financial services, may implement management frameworks that combine governance, risk management and compliance management activities, known as GRC frameworks (Rasmussen, 2009).

Governance, risk management and compliance management are inter-related sub-elements of an organization's wider management framework. Where these elements are not coordinated or integrated in an effective manner, the problem of silo-based management may occur. With a silo approach tasks may be repeated, reducing efficiency. For example, an organization might have separate arrangements for compliance risk assessments than for other types of risk assessment. Another problem is that reporting may not be integrated, meaning that separate but very similar reports are produced for governance, risk and compliance-related issues.

From an operational risk perspective, much of the output from an organization's operational risk management framework has applications to governance and compliance. This includes:

- how responsibilities for the management of operational risk are allocated;
- the organization's overall appetite for operational risk and tolerance for specific categories of operational risk;
- risk assessment and monitoring reports, including information on an organization's risk culture, operational loss events, near misses and other risk, control and performance metrics;
- actions taken to address operational risk exposures, particularly where these exposures are subject to regulation (e.g. financial crime, data protection, health and safety, and environmental exposures).

7. Conclusion

Operational risk exposures do not impact organizations in isolation. Many different stakeholder groups are impacted, including shareholders, creditors, employees, customers and third parties.

Regulations and standards exist to help ensure that organizations manage their operational risk exposures in a manner that meets the expectations of these stakeholders. Organizations that fail to comply with these regulations and standards face not only the disapproval of these stakeholders, but also sanctions from the regulatory and supervisory agencies appointed to protect these stakeholders from exploitation and potential financial or physical harm.

It is important that operational risk professionals are familiar with the key laws and regulations that relate to operational risk exposures. This includes international regulations, along with local laws and regulations. Equally it is important that they understand the international standards that relate to the management of operational risks, since these standards can help them to comply with these laws and regulations and further meet the diverse needs of their organization's stakeholders.

This chapter provides the operational risk professional with a starting point from which to continue their study into the various laws, regulations and standards that relate to operational risk. Sometimes this can feel like a never-ending task, as new laws, regulations and standards are issued on a regular basis. However, the operational risk professional is not alone in this task. They should work closely with compliance colleagues, as well as other colleagues with responsibility for risk governance, such as the company secretary, general counsel, chief financial officer, chief risk officer or chief legal officer.

Reflective practice questions

1 Does your organization consider the expectations of all relevant stakeholder groups when deciding how to manage specific operational risks (e.g. health and safety risks)?

2 Taking account of your industry sector and jurisdiction, do you know the laws and regulations that relate to the management of operational risk in your organization?

3 In a large, internationally active organization how do you ensure that all applicable laws and regulations in relation to operational risk are complied with? Is this the responsibility of the group operational risk function or operational risk managers in jurisdiction-specific business units?

4 How often do you talk to compliance colleagues? Do you and these colleagues work together to ensure compliance with operational risk-related laws and regulations?

5 Are you familiar with international standards on risk management and governance? Do you know what these standards have to say about the management of operational risk?

References

Note: Some of the sources included in this chapter have been listed previously. Only new sources are listed below.

Ashby, S, Sharma, P and McDonnell, W (2003) Lessons about risk: Analysing the causal chain of insurance company failure, *Insurance Research and Practice*, 18 (2), 4–15

Basel Committee (2016) Standardised measurement approach for operational risk, Consultation Document No 355, www.bis.org/bcbs/publ/d355.htm (archived at https://perma.cc/FUH7-EVNJ)

Basel Committee (2021a) Basel Framework, https://www.bis.org/basel_framework/index.htm (archived at https://perma.cc/T3KH-2M6M)

Basel Committee (2021b) History of the Basel Committee, www.bis.org/bcbs/history.htm (archived at https://perma.cc/T4RH-JC29)

COBIT (2019) Control Objectives for Information and Related Technologies, ISACA, www.isaca.org/resources/cobit (archived at https://perma.cc/2VT9-2MH8)

Financial Conduct Authority (2020) Payment protection insurance explained, www.fca.org.uk/ppi/ppi-explained (archived at https://perma.cc/WK84-AJYC)

H.R. 3763 (2002) Sarbanes-Oxley Act, US Congress, www.congress.gov/bill/107th-congress/house-bill/3763 (archived at https://perma.cc/4B37-7AJG)

IAIS (2019) Insurance core principles and common framework for the supervision of internationally active insurance groups, International Association of Insurance Supervisors, www.iaisweb.org/page/supervisory-material/insurance-core-principles-and-comframe//file/91154/iais-icps-and-comframe-adopted-in-november-2019 (archived at https://perma.cc/5XX6-6WH2)

McConnell, P and Blacker, K (2013) Systemic operational risk: Does it exist and, if so, how do we regulate it?, *The Journal of Operational Risk*, 8 (1), 59

Rasmussen, M (2009) An enterprise GRC framework: Defining a common governance, risk, and compliance architecture enables all parts of the organization to respond to these challenges together, *Internal Auditor*, 66 (5), 61–4

INDEX

The index is filed in alphabetical, word-by-word order. Acronyms are filed as presented. Numbers are filed as spelt out, with the exception of Basel Accords and ISO Standards, which are filed in chronological order. Page locators in italics denote information within tables and figures; those in roman numerals denote information within the preface.

www.ingramcontent.com/pod-product-compliance
Lightning Source LLC
Jackson TN
JSHW071954131224
75386JS00047B/1774

* 9 7 8 1 3 9 8 6 0 5 0 2 2 *